对外经济贸易大学中国奢侈品研究中心
对外经济贸易大学中国消费经济研究院

中国奢侈品消费者行为报告2015

——新常态下的中国奢侈品市场发展

洪俊杰 张梦霞 著

图书在版编目（CIP）数据

中国奢侈品消费者行为报告. 2015：新常态下的中国奢侈品市场发展/洪俊杰，张梦霞著. —北京：经济管理出版社，2016.4
ISBN 978-7-5096-4289-4

Ⅰ. ①中… Ⅱ. ①洪… ②张… Ⅲ. ①消费品—消费者行为论—研究报告—中国—2015
Ⅳ. ①F723.5

中国版本图书馆 CIP 数据核字（2016）第 051887 号

组稿编辑：张 艳
责任编辑：丁慧敏 高 娅
责任印制：黄章平
责任校对：赵天宇

出版发行：经济管理出版社
（北京市海淀区北蜂窝 8 号中雅大厦 A 座 11 层 100038）
网 址：www. E-mp. com. cn
电 话：(010) 51915602
印 刷：北京易丰印捷科技股份有限公司
经 销：新华书店
开 本：880mm×1230mm/16
印 张：21
字 数：273 千字
版 次：2016 年 4 月第 1 版 2016 年 4 月第 1 次印刷
书 号：ISBN 978-7-5096-4289-4
定 价：298.00 元

编写说明及致谢

《中国奢侈品消费者行为报告 2015》（以下简称《报告》）的主要目的是揭示 2015 年中国奢侈品消费市场的现状、特点和未来走势。首先，基于 2014 年中国奢侈品市场状况，在奢侈品消费市场发展的宏观经济分析的基础上，分析了奢侈品行业发展情况以及中国消费者奢侈品消费行为特征。其次，选择中国六个主要城市即北京、上海、深圳、广州、成都、苏州进行抽样调查，获得有效样本 3347 个，采用社会科学统计分析方法进行数据分析，深入探索了中国奢侈品消费者购买决策因素的一般性和特殊性，并基于人口统计特征变量的作用，对奢侈品目标消费者行为进行差异性研究。再次，基于中国传统文化价值观导向变量划分中国奢侈品消费族群，探索奢侈品消费族群差异形成的文化价值观归因。此外，我们将 2015 年和 2014 年的奢侈品消费者的行为指标进行了对比研究，总结其趋势性变化。接着，为了探索“新常态下的奢侈品市场发展”和“奢侈品行业与互联网科技的关系”，我们设计并实施焦点小组访谈和深度专家访谈等调研，并在此基础上进行定性研究。最后，报告给出基于整体调研结论的中国奢侈品消费市场未来走势的判断和预测。

在对外经济贸易大学中国消费经济研究院的支持下，对外经济贸易大学中国奢侈品消费行为研究团队承担了 2015 年报告的研究工

作。《报告》的作者是对外经济贸易大学洪俊杰教授、张梦霞教授。特别鸣谢往期《报告》的作者、对外经济贸易大学赵忠秀教授和朱明侠教授等前期为《报告》做出的基础性贡献。首都经济贸易大学工商管理学院陈静同学主要参加了调研数据的整理与统计分析工作，对外经济贸易大学国际经贸学院常辉、刘胜男、邵芊涵、陈姝霖同学主要参加了资料的收集与整理工作，邵芊涵同学和她的翻译小组负责《报告》的英文翻译工作，作者对上述研究员的辛勤劳动表示衷心感谢。与此同时，作者非常感谢张志伦先生在问卷调查中给予的积极帮助以及王菲、付瑜、谢春晨、郭颖、夏阳、张腾飞、王琼和 Gordan Yang 对《报告》的帮助。最后，非常感谢对外经济贸易大学中国奢侈品研究中心潘晓等同事的大力支持。

《报告》的主要读者是关注和研究中国奢侈品消费市场和中国消费者奢侈品购买行为的国际顶级奢侈品行业的高级经理人或投资人，奢侈品牌研究领域的专家、学者，以及关注该领域发展态势的各界人士。

《报告》的独特贡献和价值在于，研究团队是一支长期致力于奢侈品领域研究的专家学者队伍，课题立项通过严格审批，实施专项调研，采用科学抽样技术和统计分析，严格遵守科研规范，保持中立立场，从而保证了数据、结论和预测的客观性、真实性和科学性，以期最大限度地反映奢侈品市场的本质和客观规律。当然，《报告》一定会存在不足之处，作者期待各界同仁、读者给予批评指正，力争使中国奢侈品消费者行为年度报告越做越好。

对外经济贸易大学中国奢侈品研究中心
对外经济贸易大学中国消费经济研究院
2015 年 12 月

Acknowledgement

The main purpose of the *China's Luxury Goods Consumer Behavior Report 2015* (referred to as Report) is to reveal the current status, characteristics and development trend of luxury goods consumer behavior in China. First, on the basis of the Chinese luxury goods market in 2014 and macroeconomic analysis on the development of luxuries market, we analyze the industry development state of luxuries market and the characteristics of consumer behavior. Second, selecting 6 major Chinese cities—Beijing, Shanghai, Shenzhen, Guangzhou, Chengdu, Suzhou and collecting 3347 valid samples in total, we adopt statistical analysis to further study the universality and specificity of main factors affecting China's luxuries consumer decision. We conduct an otherness study on the consuming behavior of target consumers based on the function of demographic characteristic variables. Third, we use the cultural value variables to classify the luxuries consumers and explore the formation of cultural values and attribution on differences in various consumer groups. Moreover, we do a comparison study on indicators of luxury goods consumers' behaviors of the year of 2014 and 2015. Then, we design and carry on qualitative research like interviews of focus groups and depth expert interviews to ex-

plore the development of luxuries market in the New Normal and the relationship between luxuries industry and internet technology. Finally, on the basis of the above research, we predict the trend of the Chinese luxuries market in the future.

Under the support of Institute of Chinese Consumer Economics of UIBE, the team of luxury goods research center undertakes this study of 2015' report. The editors of this report are Professor Wang Junjie and Professor Zhang Mengxia from UIBE. Special thanks to Professor Zhao Zhongxiu and Professor Zhu Mingxia who are past editors and have made basic contribution to the report. Chen Jing from the Capital University of Economics and Business mainly participates in the works of collating data and statistical analysis. Chang Hui, Liu Shengnan, Shao Qianhan and Chen Shulin take part in the works of collecting data and arranging information. Shao Qianhan and her team are responsible for the translation of this report. We would like to extend our deepest appreciation to all the member for their hard work. In addition, editors give their sincere thanks to Mr. Zhang Zhilun who helps us in the process of investigation and also give thanks to the help of Wang Fei, Fu Yu, Xie Chunchen, Guo Ying, Xia Yang, Zhang Tengfei, Wang Qiong and Gordan Yang. Finally, we express our sincere thanks to workers in luxury goods research center of UIBE.

The main readers of this report are senior managers or investors, experts of luxuries industry and people from all walks of life who are research and focus on Chinese luxury market and shopping action of Chinese luxuries consuming.

The research team is organized by experts and scholars who are study luxury goods for long time. The specific contribution and value of

this report lie in objectivity, veracity and scientificity of data, results and prediction because of strict examination, scientific sampling technique and statistical analysis, severe research norms and neutral standpoint, which reflect the essences and objective law of luxuries market to the largest extend. Meanwhile, we look forward to readers' suggestions and comments.

The China Research Center for Luxury Goods and Services
The China Research Institute of Consumer Economics
University of International Business and Economics
December, 2015

前 言

2014 年是全球奢侈品业动荡、新奇、复杂和充满不确定性的一年。中国内地奢侈品市场在结束了 2008~2012 年持续两位数的市场高速增长后，增长速度开始减缓，2013 年增长速度下降至 2%，2014 年再下降 1 个百分点。我们看到，在全球范围内一些像香奈儿、古驰等一线奢侈品品牌的经典产品开始大幅降价销售。面对品牌实体店销售的普遍缩水，众多奢侈品品牌商已经或正在或将要试水电子商务，采用实体销售与电子商务相结合的全渠道分销模式。互联网和林林总总且层出不穷的新媒体为整合营销沟通提供了前所未有的信息传播与互动平台，在一些奢侈品大品牌那里出现了一种叫作首席数据官的崭新高管职位，LVMH 集团 2015 年 9 月已经宣布在公司内部设置该职位，标志着公司数字业务的全面开启。此外，奢侈品电商平台 NET-A-PORTER 和 YOOX 的合并标志着奢侈品业从竞争走向竞合的新趋势，互联网正在改变着传统奢侈品业的运营模式。在这样一个新常态环境背景下，本书面对全球奢侈品业的困境、挑战和新形势，追踪中国奢侈品消费者行为现状和变化特征，探讨奢侈品业的发展态势和机遇，力争为中国高端品牌走向世界和全球奢侈品业的健康发展提供市场依据，做出科学预测。

我们认为，行业的发展基于企业的发展，企业的发展以消费者

需求为基石，认识消费者行为源于对其决策行为的深刻理解。

《报告》发现，新常态下的中国奢侈品市场充满了机遇与挑战，突出表现在以下方面。

第一，奢侈品牌市场调整期仍将持续，调整性过渡将是一个连续的、相对较长的过程，度过目前这个阶段，奢侈品市场将会复苏并进入健康发展的新阶段。

第二，经典和创新并进是奢侈品市场可持续盈利的保障。我们发现，中国奢侈品消费市场是一个三元市场结构：保守型市场、先锋型市场和观望型市场，保守型市场仍然是主流市场。我们预测，未来中国奢侈品消费市场的态势是：高端定制市场蓬勃发展，小众定制市场稳步发展，规模定制市场中长期有望稳步回升。

第三，奢侈品行业的全渠道模式不断完善，且中国奢侈品消费者的优选渠道顺序依次是专卖店、出境游购物、名品折购店、代购、海淘和境内网购。奢侈品的全渠道零售模式逐渐显现，目前中国乃至全球的奢侈品业在全渠道模式方面的实践仍然处于探索阶段，这是奢侈品品牌商面临的新的市场机遇和挑战，或新的市场增长点。

第四，奢侈品理性消费行为下的个性化消费趋势明显。我们发现，中国奢侈品消费者正在逐渐从简单的模仿和炫耀行为向个性化和自我认同的消费行为转变。

第五，中国奢侈品消费者行为有文化价值观导向下的潜在市场集群特征，尤其是来自儒家文化价值观和道家文化价值观的影响显著，显然该结论是认识中国奢侈品消费者有别于西方消费者奢侈品消费行为的最根本的驱动因素。

总之，未来的奢侈品市场的整体发展是大趋势，科技创新驱动的奢侈品市场发展将是未来该市场发展的方向。奢侈品消费不同于奢侈浪费，奢侈品牌消费更要注重其品质与文化内涵，消费者购买奢侈品牌产品体现的是人类对美好生活的追求。以往发生在中国市

场的奢侈品牌价格歧视现象需要得到调整，奢侈品牌商需要考虑中国市场战略与全球市场战略的一致性和平衡性。面对中国经济的新常态，奢侈品牌商要在适应中国市场大环境和中国消费者奢侈品消费需求特点的前提下谋求可持续发展。

Preface

For global luxury industries, 2014 is a year of unrest, newness, complexity and uncertainty. The continuous rapid growth of over 9% of luxury market in Chinese mainland from 2008 to 2012 has gone and the growth speed has slowed down. The growth speed of 2013 was reduced to 2%, while that of 2014 was 1%. We can see that the classic products of Chanel, Gucci and other global top luxury brands have been sold with big price cuts. Many luxury brands are trying to adopt e-commerce in face of the decrease in sales of physical stores and they are going to adopt the full channel distribution model with physical sales combined with e-commerce. Internet and numerous new media provide the unprecedented information communication and interactive platform for integrated marketing communication. The new supervisory position of Chief Data Officer appears in some large luxury brands and the LVMH Group announced that it set this position in September of 2015. The appearance of Chief Data Officer marks the beginning of digital service of companies. Besides, the merger of two e-commerce platforms, NET-A-PORTER and YOOX, marks the new trend from competition to competition and cooperation; internet is changing the operating model of traditional luxury industries. Un-

der the "New Normal" situation, this investigation traces the status and change features of Chinese luxury consumers' behaviors in face of the dilemma, challenge and new situation for global luxury industries to investigate the development trend and opportunities of the luxury industries so as to provide market basis as well as scientific prediction for the development of Chinese high-end brands on the world stage and healthy development of the global luxury industries.

We think that the development of the industry is based on the development of the enterprise, while the development of the enterprise is based on the customers' demand. The understanding of the customers' behavior is the result of the deep understanding of their decision behavior. The main purpose of *Chinese Luxury Consumer Behavior Report 2015* (Report for short) is to reveal the current situation, features and future trend of Chinese luxury consumer market in 2015. Firstly, the development condition of the luxury industry as well as Chinese luxury consumers' behavior is analyzed based on the Chinese luxury market situation in 2014 and macro-economic analysis with the development of luxury consumer market. Secondly, sample investigation is conducted for six main cities in China, namely, Beijing, Shanghai, Shenzhen, Guangzhou, Chengdu and Suzhou and 3347 effective samples are obtained. The data is analyzed in use of social science statistic analysis method to further investigate the generality and particularity of purchase decision-making factors for Chinese luxury consumers. The difference study is conducted for luxury target consumers' behavior based on the effect of demographic characteristics as well. Thirdly, the Chinese luxury consumer groups are divided based on Chinese traditional cultural value orientation to explore the cultural value reasons for difference of luxury consumer groups. What's more, the

comparative study is conducted for the luxury consumers' behavior indexes of 2014 and 2015 to summarize the change of the trend. Fourthly, in order to explore "luxury market development under the new normal" as well as "the relationship between luxury industry and internet technology", the focus group interview, deep expert interview and other forms are designed and implemented and the qualitative research is conducted based on these interviews. At last, the judgment and prediction for the future trend of Chinese luxury consumer market based on conclusions concluded by the research are made in this report.

The report research shows that China's luxury goods market in the "New Normal" faces a great deal of opportunities as well as challenges, which can be seen in the following aspects. Firstly, the luxury goods market in China will still stay in the adjustment period, a relative long and continuous process before it recoveries and steps into a new and normal development process. Secondly, classic elements and innovation are not the guarantees for sustainable profits of the market. We find out that the market in China is composed of conservative, active and hesitating customers, most part of which is the first type. We predicted that the market will see the flourish growth in high-end tailored needs, steady growth in niche tailored demands and steady recoveries of mass customization during medium and long-term. Thirdly, the omni-channel mode of luxury goods industry is improving. The channels that Chinese luxury goods customers prefer are-listing by preference-boutiques, outbound tourism shopping, outlet stores, procurement through friends, overseas online shopping and domestic online shopping. The mode is gradually emerging in China but still at its infant period. So is that in other countries. This is the opportunity as well as challenge facing by the luxury goods brands or their new growth pole. Fourthly, the personalized consumption is increasingly popular among rational consumers of luxury goods. We observe that Chinese luxury goods consumers are transiting their behaviors from simple imitation or flaunt to self-identify. Lastly, consumption clusters are emerging in China luxury goods market under the influence of culture values, especially the Confucian and Taoist cultural values. The finding explains the fundamental difference between Chinese and Western luxury goods customers' behaviors.

Generally speaking, the luxury goods market requires a comprehensive development which should be drove by technical innovation. Furthermore, the luxury goods consumption doesn't mean the luxury goods waste for the former pays more attention on the quality and cultural connotation and represents customers' pursuit for better life. Luxury goods brands should take the same strategies in China as in the world in a balanced manner instead of price discrimination strategies in China. Facing the "New Normal", luxury goods brands, in pursuit of sustainable growth, need to adapt to the China's market and learn the features of China's luxury goods consumption.

目 录

Contents

图表目录

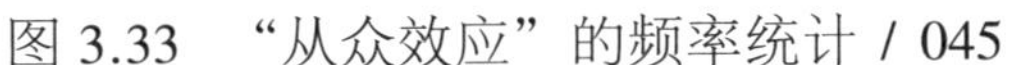

List of Figures and Tables

第1章　中国奢侈品消费市场现状分析

1.1　2014年中国奢侈品市场

2008~2012年五年里中国内地奢侈品市场始终保持着较快的发展速度，其中前四年年平均增速均在两位数以上，自2012年增长速度开始减缓，增长率降至7%。2013年增长速度进一步放缓，整体同比增长率仅为2%。到2014年，中国内地奢侈品市场首次出现下跌，较2013年下跌了1%，即市场规模为1150亿元。此外，2014年全球奢侈品市场总容量为2240亿欧元（约合15190亿元人民币），中国消费者在全球范围内的奢侈品消费达3800亿元，这意味着中国人买走了全球约25%的奢侈品，表明中国消费者仍旧是全球奢侈品的最大买家之一。2014年，中国市场上的国际奢侈品牌中的腕表、箱包、男士服装、珠宝、鞋履、女士服装、配饰以及化妆品、香水和个人护理用品八大类奢侈品中，腕表和男士服装下跌最为明显，箱包增速为零，而女士服装和鞋履却增长强劲，成为销售最好的奢侈品类。2014年中国消费者的出境购物规模占到总消费额的55%，除此之外海外代购规模约为650亿元，约占15%，涉及的商品主要是化妆品，次之是皮革箱包、

腕表和珠宝（贝恩，2009~2014 年）。[①]

近年来，我国经济进入新常态的变化给奢侈品行业的销售带来了一定的影响。意大利奢侈品巨头普拉达（Prada）公布的业绩显示，2015 年 4 月大中华区的销售净额为 7.741 亿欧元，同比减少 6.3%。法国奢侈品牌路易·威登（LV）表示，在 2014 财年，路易·威登在美国和欧洲市场上的销售表现强劲，但来自中国消费者的需求却保持疲软。全球业绩较好的法国奢侈品集团爱马仕（Hermes）2014 年净利润达 11.4 亿美元，较上年上涨 8.7%；但其腕表业务出现了负增长，销售额由前一年仅 1%的增长恶化至 10.6%的负增长。

我们认为，中国奢侈品消费市场自 2013 年开始步入“调整期”，市场的增速放缓是可以预见的。不论是厂商的调整，还是消费者的观望，中国奢侈品市场进入成熟阶段必须要经历来自市场的“阵痛”。再加上中国的新兴消费群体逐渐成熟以及购买渠道多样化，使得他们对时尚和奢侈品表现出需求理性化和选择个性化，这给奢侈品牌企业带来了机遇和挑战。

1.2 中国奢侈品消费市场发展的宏观经济基础

奢侈品市场只是消费品市场的一部分，国内消费品市场的快速发展必将带动奢侈品行业的迅速成长。而国内的消费品市场之所以能够保持快速增长，首先得益于我国国民经济持续平稳、快速的增长，其次得益于城乡居民尤其是城镇居民收入快速增长导致的消费者购买力的增强和消费结构的转变，他们为消费品市场的繁荣提供了有效支撑。此外，我国快速增长的大众富裕阶层，尤其是白领人群的迅速壮大，

① 2009~2014 年贝恩《中国奢侈品市场研究》报告。

也为我国的奢侈品消费市场的发展打下了良好的客户基础。

1.2.1 宏观经济保持增长

自 2010 年以来中国 GDP 增长速度有所放缓，从 10.4%下降到 2014 年的 7.4%，但是 GDP 总量仍然持续增长。如图 1.1 所示，2014 年，中国 GDP 总量达到 10.36 亿美元，成为继美国之后第二个跻身超 10 万亿美元经济体的国家。同时，我国奢侈品消费市场也从 2010 年的 871 亿元增加到 2014 年的 1150 亿元，中国奢侈品消费占 GDP 比重在 2011 年前呈现增长趋势，但是从 2011 年开始缓慢下降，2014 年的占比仅为 0.18%。由此也印证了中国内地市场奢侈品消费的增速减缓。

图 1.1 2009~2014 年中国 GDP 总量与奢侈品消费占 GDP 比例

资料来源：根据世界银行（2009~2014 年）和贝恩（2009~2014 年）数据整理。

1.2.2 居民可支配收入提高

收入决定消费。居民的可支配收入提高，带动消费能力的增强，从而扩大了消费品市场规模，提升了居民消费层次，也促进了奢侈品消费市场的发展。

近十年，中国城镇居民可支配收入大幅提高，生活必需品的支出占总收入的比重逐年降低。如图 1.2 所示，城镇居民人均可支配收入

由 2008 年的 15780.8 元增长到 2014 年的 28843.85 元，2014 年较 2008 年增长 82.78%。城镇居民恩格尔系数由 2008 年的 37.9%下降到 2013 年的 35%，虽然下降幅度较小，但是仍有逐年下降的趋势。由此可见，我国城镇居民对食物等必需消费品的消费占收入比重在逐年减小，生活水平有较明显提高。

居民可支配收入的提高和生活必需品支出的减少为中国消费者提升生活品质奠定了必要的经济基础。

图 1.2　2008~2014 年城镇居民可支配收入与恩格尔系数

资料来源：《中国统计年鉴》（2008~2014 年）。

1.2.3　消费结构不断改变

随着我国经济的发展，居民收入水平有较大提高，消费结构发生了变化。如图 1.3 所示，1990 年，我国城镇居民在衣食住的基本消费支出占总支出的 72%以上，到了 2013 年这一比例已经降到 55%左右。而家庭设备、医疗保健、交通通信和文教娱乐等方面的消费支出占总支出的比例也由 1990 年的 22%左右增长到 2013 年的 40%左右。由此可见，我国城镇居民的消费重心正在从吃、穿、住等基本消费逐渐向家居条件、交通通信、文教娱乐和医疗保健等高品质生活的消费转移；从简单的商品性消费转向包括各种服务在内的如餐饮、旅游、娱乐、

教育、医疗保健等复杂性的商品消费；从大量的普遍性商品转向注重选择，追求高档的个性化消费，消费者也越来越重视商品的质量、品牌、款式、包装和售后服务等。居民消费已开始由基本生活消费为主过渡到以享乐性和体验性消费为主，出现消费升级。

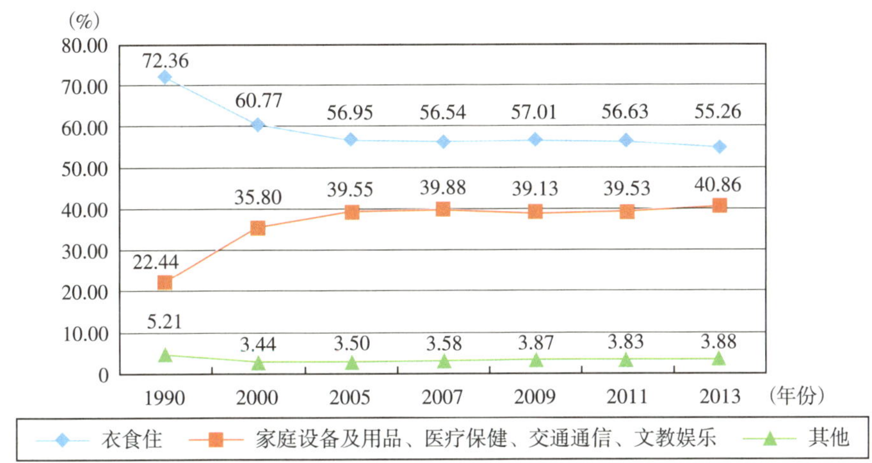

图 1.3 城镇居民各项消费占总消费比例

资料来源：《中国统计年鉴》。

如图 1.4 所示，随着社会消费品零售总额的不断增加，消费品市场步入了快速发展阶段，消费者在国内购买奢侈品的支出在社会消费品总额中所占比例先上升后减缓，其中 2011 年达到峰值 0.58%，随后

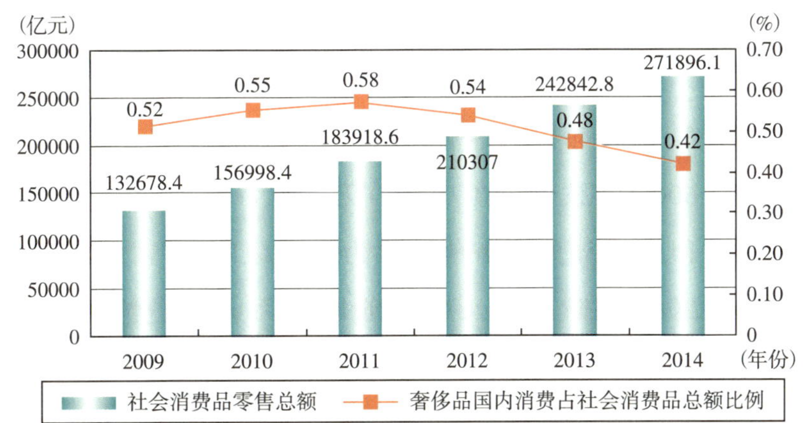

图 1.4 2009~2014 年社会消费品零售总额与奢侈品国内消费占社会消费总额比例

资料来源：根据《中国统计年鉴》(2009~2014 年）和贝恩（2009~2014 年）数据整理。

不断下降，2014 年为 0.42%。原因可能是由于最近几年奢侈品网络销售、海外代购和出国旅游购物的兴起而导致消费者在国内购买奢侈品的比重降低。此外，从图 1.5 也可以看出，消费者在中国内地购买的奢侈品占中国在全球购买奢侈品比例越来越低，即海外代购和出境购物的新兴消费方式正在越来越多地受到大众的欢迎。

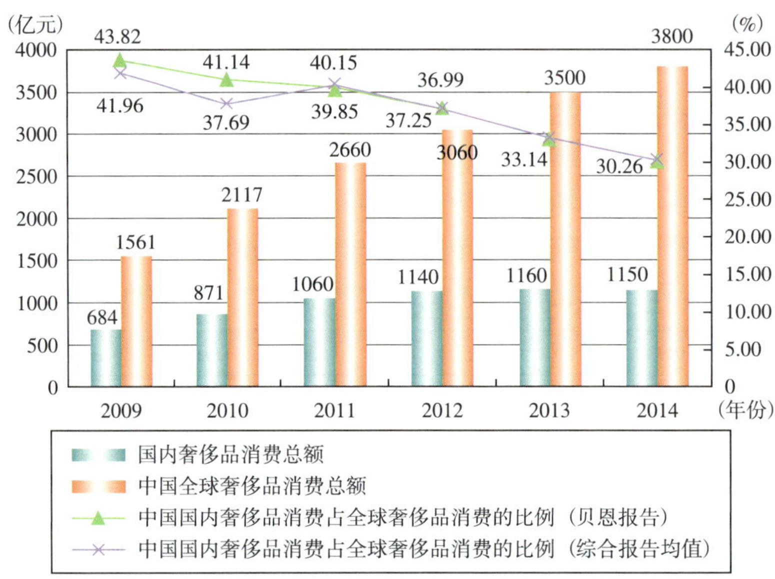

图 1.5 中国消费者奢侈品国内和全球消费总额对比

资料来源：根据贝恩（2009~2014 年）、麦肯锡（2010 年）和益索普（2011 年）数据整理①。

1.2.4 中国大众富裕阶层规模迅速壮大

2015 年，《福布斯》（中文版）联合宜信财富发布了《2015 中国大众富裕阶层财富白皮书》，其中对大众富裕阶层的定义是指个人可投资资产在 60 万~600 万元（约 10 万~100 万美元）的中国中产阶级群体。这部分人群中很大一部分通俗地被称为“高级白领”。如图 1.6 所示，2014 年中国大众富裕阶层的人数达到 1388 万人，增长率为 15.96%，较 2013 年同期下滑近 1%左右，预计到 2015 年底人数将达到 1528 万

① 麦肯锡《2010 年崛起的中国奢侈品市场研究》报告；益索普《2011 年中国大陆奢侈品市场》报告。

人。如图 1.7 所示，2014 年底中国私人总财富约为 106.2 万亿元，增长率为 12.8%，较 2013 年同期下滑约 0.6%，预计到 2015 年底，中国私人总财富将达到 114.5 万亿元。虽然，大众富裕阶层人数和中国私人总财富的增长均在放缓，但是从图 1.7 中可以明显看到，中国大众富裕阶层的财富占中国社会私人财富总额的比例不断上升，2014 年竟达到 17.6%，由此可见中国大众富裕阶层掌握财富量惊人，为中国奢侈品消费提供强大动力。此外，白皮书中还提到，中国 2015 年 40 岁

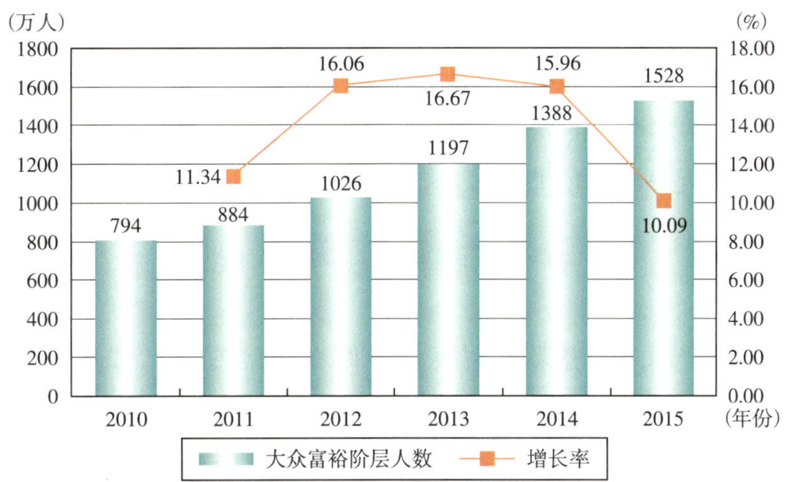

图 1.6 2010~2015 年中国大众富裕阶层人数与年增长率

资料来源：《福布斯》(2015 年)。

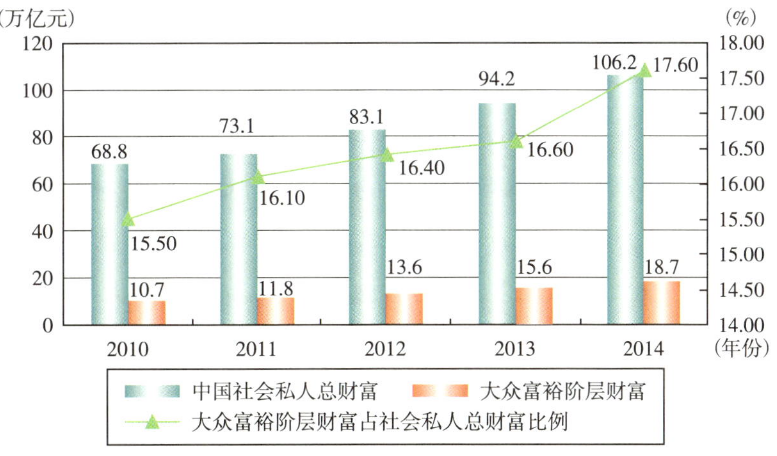

图 1.7 大众富裕阶层财富与中国社会私人财富总额对比

注：私人总财富指个人持有的现金及存款，公开市场交易的股票、基金、债券、房地产等。

资料来源：根据《福布斯》(2013~2015 年) 数据整理。

以下的大众富裕阶层的人数占总体富裕阶层人数的 54.5%，说明中国奢侈品市场的消费者趋于年轻化，所以消费奢侈品的主力军会不断壮大。因此，大众富裕阶层的发展壮大为中国奢侈品市场的发展奠定了坚实的基础。

1.3 中国奢侈品行业发展分析

尽管 2014 年中国国内奢侈品市场首次呈现出负增长，但是这并不意味着中国消费者的消费热情呈现同样的趋势，事实恰恰相反，中国的消费者在全球的奢侈品消费总量仍然保持持续增长。

1.3.1 奢侈品销售渠道多元化

奢侈品传统的销售渠道主要是装修精美的专营店或奥特莱斯等折扣店，由于定价策略的区域性差异和汇率的变化等，在不同国家和地区销售的同类产品存在较大的价差。在中国，由于国际代购和境外直接消费的出现和发展，本地奢侈品价格的偏高，导致中国消费者对奢侈品的旺盛需求向国际市场释放，而本地奢侈品市场不断萎缩。

2014 年我国奢侈品海外代购总规模约在 550 亿~750 亿元，海外代购越来越受到中国消费者的青睐。此外，随着越来越多的中国人有机会出境，而大部分境外地区奢侈品的定价远低于中国内地，因此很大一部分奢侈品消费者选择在海外旅行的过程中购买奢侈品，甚至为了购买奢侈品而顺道去境外旅游，其中目的地市场以中国港澳台地区、日韩和欧美市场为主，而且从日韩市场代购或直接购买奢侈品的现象最为突出。

此外，在今天的高科技信息化环境下，网络无处不在，许许多多的消费者会选择网络渠道购物。如图 1.8 所示，中国的网络购物用户

数量正在迅速增加，2014 年网络购物规模已经达到 3.8 亿人。面对充满机遇与挑战的中国市场，各大奢侈品牌商也在考虑或已经尝试通过电商渠道提升市场销售额。例如，蔻驰（Coach）等轻奢品牌已经着手自建电商平台，博柏利（Burberry）等传统奢侈品牌借助天猫或类似的综合电商平台创建电商渠道，亦有一些奢侈品牌选择在奢侈品垂直电商网站、手机网络移动端进行销售。但是，大部分奢侈品牌商还在观望，其原因或是受制于自身品牌的高端定位，或是受制于物流体系的不可控或不可靠。

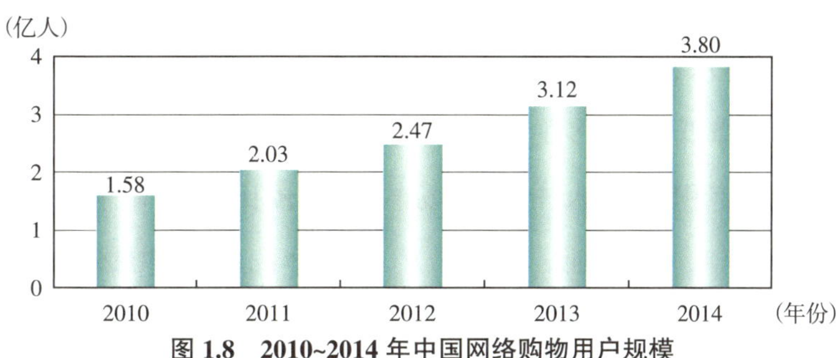

图 1.8　2010~2014 年中国网络购物用户规模

资料来源：中国电子商务研究中心监测数据。

1.3.2　奢侈品热销品类的市场变化

近年来，中国市场上的国际奢侈品牌下的热销品类发生了变化。男性奢侈品销售额年复合增长率呈逐年下降趋势，尤其是腕表和高档男装，腕表降幅最大。与此相反，女性奢侈品牌产品则保持着较好的年复合增长率，成为中国市场上国际奢侈品牌主要的市场增长点，尤其是女性服装、化妆品、鞋履等，说明中国市场国际奢侈品牌的主要消费人群正在从男性主导向女性主导转变。

此外，今天的中国消费者已经逐渐成熟，不再仅仅专注奢侈品大品牌和品牌标志，他们倾向于按照自己的个性和喜好选择更加适合自己的、充满个性的产品。因此，为了应对国际奢侈品牌在中国市场的新变化，寻找到新的增长点，国际奢侈品牌也开始积极推出更加适合

中国消费人群的新产品。

1.3.3 轻奢品牌势头强劲

随着中国奢侈品消费阶层的逐步年轻化的态势，18~45 岁的中青年人群成为购买奢侈品的主要力量，他们注重学习奢侈品品牌知识，并有自己独特的理解，消费特征逐渐由普遍炫耀型向追求个性或时尚型转变。当传统高端奢侈品品牌无法完全满足中国新一代消费者的需求时，这些年轻人开始喜欢上价格较低、品质优良、设计时尚的轻奢品牌。

如图 1.9 所示，2014 年部分传统奢侈品大品牌较轻奢品品牌的开店积极性有所降低，更多的传统奢侈品品牌选择了较为保守的战略。例如，和前几年积极进入中国市场的热情相比，博柏利（Burberry）、路易·威登（LV）、卡地亚（Cartier）等品牌商纷纷放慢了在中国开设新店的步伐，甚至关闭了部分城市的门店，以保证单店的销售额和利润率。2014 年，卡地亚（Cartier）在中国开设了两家新店，但同时也关闭了两家门店。路易·威登（LV）、古驰（Gucci）和阿玛尼（Armani）则在扩张的同时均关闭了一家中国门店。以经营男装为主的奢侈品牌关闭门店的速度更快，例如雨果博斯（Hugo Boss）、杰尼亚（Zegna）等关闭的门店数量远远超过新开门店的数量。

图 1.9 同时揭示，众多奢侈品牌依然在加大对中国市场的投资，例如普拉达（Prada）和蔻驰（Coach），它们于 2014 年分别在中国市场新开设了 7 家和 13 家店面。但与此同时 MCM、迈克·高仕（Micheal Kors）等轻奢品牌在中国开设新店的数量较多，且没有关闭一家门店，这类品牌的市场销售额也在较大幅度的增长。

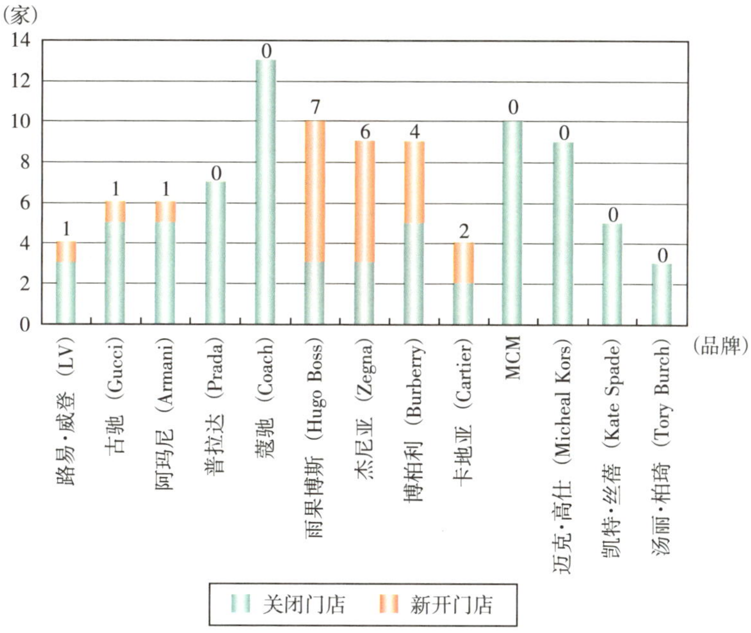

图 1.9 2014 年部分奢侈品牌中国门店变化情况

资料来源：品牌官方网站。

1.4 中国消费者的奢侈品消费行为特点

1.4.1 炫耀性消费不断减少，品牌标识重要性降低

文献显示，中国奢侈品消费群体主要在 18~45 岁，且 35 岁以下的人群占到 75%，而 25~30 岁的年轻人正快速形成一个新型的奢侈品消费群体，其市场发展速度远远超过西方发达国家。如图 1.10 所示，百度发布的《2014 年度奢侈品行业》报告显示，关注并搜索过“奢侈品行业”的人群中“90 后”是规模最大的人群，其中 20~29 岁人群约占 46%，30~39 岁人群约占 38%，19 岁以下约占 10%，而 40~49 岁人群仅约占 6%，呈现出年轻化的趋势。

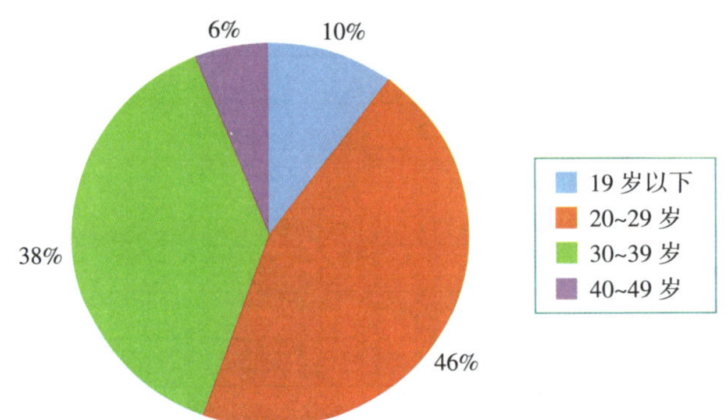

图 1.10 2014 年"奢侈品行业"搜索者人群的年龄分布

资料来源：百度《2014 年度奢侈品行业》报告。

以往的中国消费者在购买奢侈品时会偏爱能够显示富有和较高社会地位的大尺寸品牌标识即 Logo，但是，这种现象正在发生变化。随着中国年轻消费群体购买力的提升和见识的增长，特别是"富二代"消费者，他们中大多有过在欧美求学和生活的经历，他们受到西方文化价值观的影响，会有意识地回避大 Logo 彰显的"土豪"特征。这些富裕的年轻消费者也会向自己的父母传达"更有品位"的奢侈品消费文化。

1.4.2 体验式消费受到追捧

在中国，中产阶级的规模越来越大，越来越富裕，他们对体验式奢侈消费的兴趣也越来越浓厚。2014 年 6 月，胡润研究院与亚洲国际豪华旅游博览（ILTM Asia）联合发布《中国奢华旅游白皮书》，指出旅游是中国高端消费者除美食以外的第二大兴趣爱好，也是他们除健康以外的第二大消费领域。报告显示，中国高端消费者旅游购物消费连续四年蝉联全球第一。

中国消费者对独特的旅行体验有浓厚的兴趣，如南极探险、非洲之旅、定制的 VIP 套餐、纽约时装周上的前排座位或与体育明星亲密接触。水疗、豪华邮轮和其他类型的奢侈服务正在中国迅速发展。旅

游仍然是富豪，特别是亿万富豪的最主要娱乐方式。《中国奢华旅游白皮书》同时揭示，邮轮旅游作为梦想的旅游体验，有 26%的超级旅游者选择，同时有 30%的超级旅游者在未来三年的旅游计划里考虑到了地中海奢华邮轮游。胡润百富研究院发布的《2015 至尚优品——中国千万富豪品牌倾向报告》中提到，富豪对游艇的热情度较上一年上升了 20%，目前有 20%的千万富豪热衷游艇，近一半的亿万富豪已经购买了私人游艇。从“富豪最青睐的娱乐方式”数据来看（见表 1.1），旅游这种典型的体验式消费排名第一，自驾游的排名也有所上升，而美食、钓鱼、游艇等也都进入到体验式消费的前 10 个项目中。

表 1.1　富豪最青睐的娱乐方式前 10

排名	娱乐方式	比例（%）
1–	旅游	24.5
2–	看书	14.5
3–	品茶	11.7
4↑	自驾游	10.6
5↓	家庭活动	9.9
6New	美食	6.8
7New	钓鱼	4.1
8New	游艇	3.5
9↓	SPA	3.4
10↓	品酒	2.4

注：↑：排名比上年上升；↓：排名比上年下降；–：排名与上年一样；New：对比上年新进入前 10。
资料来源：胡润百富《2015 至尚优品——中国千万富豪品牌倾向报告》。

1.4.3　消费更加理性，“最贵的”不再是“最好的”

奢侈品是具有独特、稀缺、珍奇等特点的高端消费品。既是高端，则价格不菲，这是消费者惯有的思维。即使价格昂贵，购买奢侈品的消费者也不会觉得冤枉，存在“买得值”的心理。但随着市场的发展以及信息的透明度增强，消费者的购买心理也逐渐趋于成熟。“最贵的就是最好的”的观念已经发生转变。如今的中国奢侈品消费者更加理性，许多人购买之前会搜寻产品和价格等信息。随着对价值诉求的认

知度和敏感度不断提升，消费者也尝试从多种渠道选择性价比更高的奢侈品。

1.4.4 以更加开放的心态尝试更多的新品牌

随着生活水平不断提高，越来越多的中国消费者尝试新的品牌和风格。相对于传统奢侈品牌，大量涌现的新兴时尚轻奢品牌满足了消费者对于品牌多元化的需求。如图 1.11 所示，巴黎世家（Balenciaga）、迈克·高仕（Michael Kors）、凯特·丝蓓（Kate Spade）等轻奢品牌给消费者留下了深刻印象，并广泛受到中国消费者的欢迎。

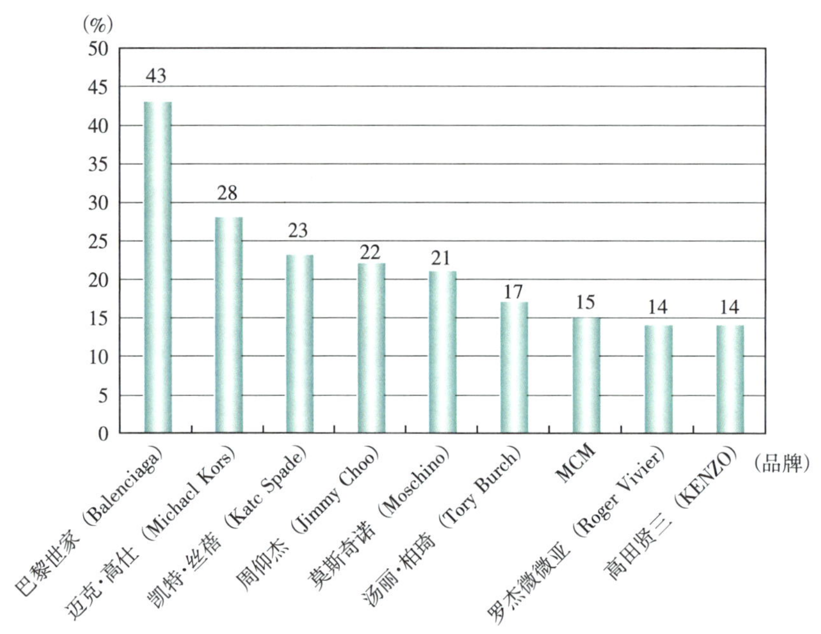

图 1.11 中国消费者愿意购买新兴品牌的比例

资料来源：2014 年贝恩公司《中国奢侈品市场研究》报告。

从中国整体经济发展的大趋势着眼，未来我国宏观经济仍将保持中高速的增长，居民可支配收入仍将不断提高，消费结构将继续优化升级，大众富裕阶层规模不断壮大。因此，从宏观和基本面来看，未来我国奢侈品需求空间和潜能仍然可观，驱动奢侈品消费增长的主要因素没有发生根本性变化。从奢侈品行业发展来看，主要表现在奢侈

品销售渠道走向多元化，热销品类发生改变，轻奢品牌势头强劲。从消费者行为角度来看，主要表现在中国人消费观念更加成熟，消费行为更加理性。

继《2014 年中国奢侈品消费者行为报告》发布之后，我们的研究团队在 2015 年连续对中国奢侈品市场展开调研，目的是从中国市场奢侈品消费者行为的角度研究奢侈品市场的新特点和新态势，并预测该市场未来发展趋势。我们的调研聚焦中国消费者奢侈品消费心理、消费动机、购买决策以及中国传统文化价值观的行为驱动作用等内容，以期对中国奢侈品消费市场做出较为客观、真实和科学的解析和预测。

第2章　研究方案设计

本书的目的是在往年系列报告的基础上，继续报告2015年中国奢侈品市场消费者行为特征及其驱动因素，探索中国消费者奢侈品消费行为的规律性，并对中国奢侈品消费市场态势做出科学预测，图2.1展示的是2015年报告的研究思路和实施路线。

本书采用的研究方法包括文献研究法、问卷调查法、定性研究方法（焦点小组和深度访谈法）、基于社会科学统计分析方法的实证研究方法等。

（1）文献研究法。文献研究主要聚焦奢侈品消费心理学理论（如态度、动机、个性、偏好等）、消费者奢侈品购买决策理论以及文化价值观理论等。

（2）问卷调查法。在文献研究和前期调研问卷的基础上形成2015年度报告的调研问卷，对中国奢侈品消费者采用网上调研和随机拦截访问。

（3）定性研究方法（焦点小组和深度访谈法）。这是一种半结构式的访谈方法，研究人员预先设定好访谈大纲，被调查者在访员的引导下围绕大纲提供相关信息。

（4）基于社会科学统计分析方法的实证研究方法。采用描述性统计分析、多元回归分析方法、因子分析和聚类分析等进行数据分析。

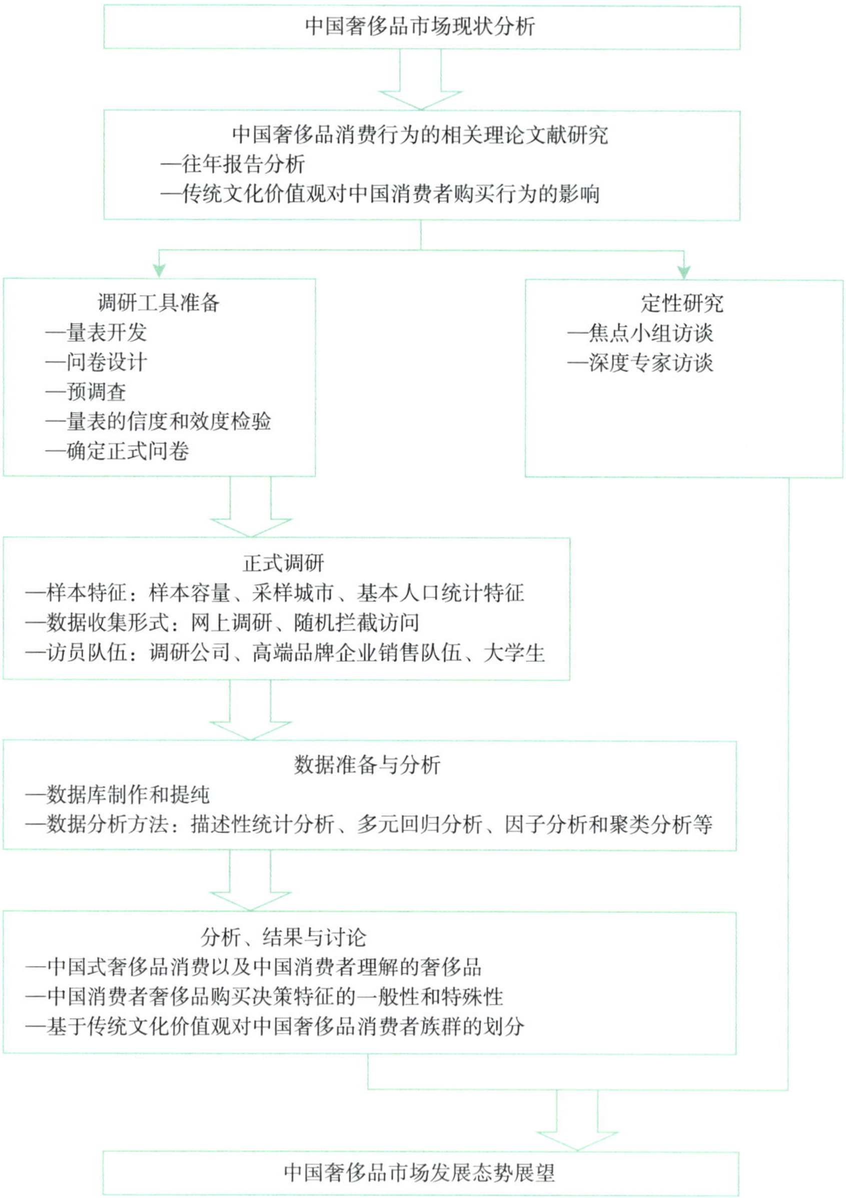

中国奢侈品市场现状分析
中国奢侈品消费行为的相关理论文献研究
—往年报告分析
—传统文化价值观对中国消费者购买行为的影响
调研工具准备
—量表开发
—问卷设计
—预调查
—量表的信度和效度检验
—确定正式问卷
定性研究
—焦点小组访谈
—深度专家访谈
正式调研
—样本特征：样本容量、采样城市、基本人口统计特征
—数据收集形式：网上调研、随机拦截访问
—访员队伍：调研公司、高端品牌企业销售队伍、大学生
数据准备与分析
—数据库制作和提纯
—数据分析方法：描述性统计分析、多元回归分析、因子分析和聚类分析等
分析、结果与讨论
—中国式奢侈品消费以及中国消费者理解的奢侈品
—中国消费者奢侈品购买决策特征的一般性和特殊性
—基于传统文化价值观对中国奢侈品消费者族群的划分
中国奢侈品市场发展态势展望

图 2.1　研究框架逻辑图

第 3 章　正式调研

中国奢侈品消费在经历了持续多年的爆炸式增长之后发展趋向平缓甚至走低，过去人们特别将奢侈品视作彰显个人财富的标志的现象在弱化。奢侈品企业的终极目标也并非仅仅兜售一些消费者可以随身佩戴的显示财富的物件，而是以奢侈品的卓越品质和经典与个性并存来反映或迎合中国消费者新的生活方式。为了系统地、全面地、持续地研究中国奢侈品消费市场，准确把握中国人奢侈品消费心理和消费行为特征及其趋势，反映中国人奢侈品消费行为的变化及其原因，对外经济贸易大学中国奢侈品消费行为研究团队，在往年该课题专题研究的基础上，全面系统地、有所创新地且持续地进行中国奢侈品消费行为跟踪调查，发布年度报告。

问卷设计主要涉及如下内容：奢侈品消费动机、偏好和态度等心理因素；消费或购买决策的社会、经济和文化等影响因素，特别地，中国传统文化价值观的影响作用；品牌来源国效应；奢侈品购买倾向和奢侈品购买力状况等；此外，还包括人口统计变量如性别、年龄、教育背景、收入水平、资产状况、职业以及居住城市等基本信息。

本次调研的对象是中国本土奢侈品消费者，这些消费者分别来自北京、上海、深圳、广州、成都和苏州。数据收集工作由辛迪加专业调研公司、中国高端品牌企业和经过专业培训的在校大学生完成。专

业调研公司采用了线上调查、线下拦截和线下邀约并线上回答的方式，线下地点选在奢侈品销售集中的商业中心，共收集问卷 3200 份。本次调研所采用的数据采集方法以网上调研为主，以奢侈品零售柜台或高端品牌零售柜台前随机拦截访问为辅，网上调研共获得 3100 份问卷；随机拦截访问共获得 400 份问卷。调研共发放并回收问卷 3500 份，其中有效问卷 3347 份，有效答率为 95.6%。无效问卷产生的主要原因是缺失值，为保证统计分析的精确性予以舍弃。有效样本在各个数据采集城市的分布分别为：北京 671 份；上海 629 份；深圳 563 份；广州 563 份；成都 461 份；苏州 460 份。

选取这些城市进行调研主要有以下几个原因：首先，所选取的城市都是家庭年收入比较高的城市，日常基本生活开销在收入中所占比例较小，人们在满足生存需求的基础上，有能力去追求更高层次的物质和精神需求，其中一部分通过奢侈品消费实现。其次，这些城市开放较早，随着国际交流机会的日益增多，人们接触的国际奢侈品品牌也逐渐增加，对品牌价值的认识同样逐渐提高，从而为奢侈品品牌或高端品牌进入这些城市打下了良好的基础，也因为如此，这些城市已经成为各大国际顶级品牌进驻中国的首选市场。再次，随着这些城市的经济发展，越来越多的年轻人选择来这里寻找机会，年轻人更容易接受高端品牌，为奢侈品在华的市场发展提供了肥沃的土壤。另外，选择成都作为本次调研的西部城市代表，是因为西部大开发 10 多年以来，成都是西部经济发展最快的城市之一。作为西部大开发的引擎城市之一，这座城市被誉为中国经济发展“第四极”。事实上，成都的奢侈品消费总额仅次于北京和上海这两个特大型城市，高端品牌在成都的发展远远高于其他二线城市。最后，本调研特意选择苏州作为调研城市，因为一般的奢侈品消费城市报告中较少提到苏州，但是苏州的经济发展与走势一向良好，由此来探索以苏州为代表的中国二线城市的奢侈品消费状况。

3.1 样本分布的人口统计特征

在本次调查中，被调查者的性别比例均衡，年龄集中在18~45岁，占全部被调查者的85.96%。其中，69.88%的被调查者年收入在12万元以上，家庭资产在100万元以上的被调查者占68.99%，个人年收入与家庭资产基本相符合，但是也不乏特殊情况，例如本调研发现存在这样的人群，即年收入在12万元以下者其资产却达到1000万元以上，年收入在100万元以上者其资产却低于1000万元。此外，90.02%的被调查者的学历达到大专以上水平。从职业指标看，企业白领占最大比例，包括国内企业白领（36.06%）与外企白领（16.07%）。下面对样本的人口统计特征做具体报告。

3.1.1 性别

图3.1① 显示，女性被调查者有1779人，比男性被调查者（1568人）多6%，与2014年相比，样本的性别分布较好地反映了人口的客观总体结构。

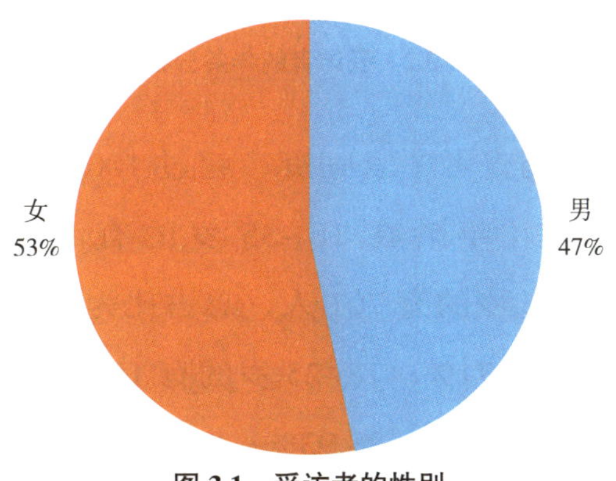

图3.1 受访者的性别

① 在本报告中，所有展示的图表除非有特殊说明，均基于本次调研的原始数据制作。

3.1.2 年龄

图 3.2 显示，被调查者年龄集中在 18~45 岁，共 2877 人，占全部被调查者的 85.96%，18~35 岁是奢侈品的核心目标消费群，总占比为 59.10%，其中年龄在 31~35 岁的人数最多，为 987 人，占比为 29.49%；26~30 岁的有 713 人，占比为 21.3%；18~25 岁的有 278 人，占比为 8.31%。36~45 岁的有 899 人，占比为 26.86%，45 岁以上者共占 13.8%，18 岁以下者占比为 0.24%。样本的年龄分布基本反映了中国奢侈品消费人群的实际年龄结构，与当下中国奢侈品消费主力军的自然规模契合，反映出本调查的样本在年龄指标上有较强的代表性。

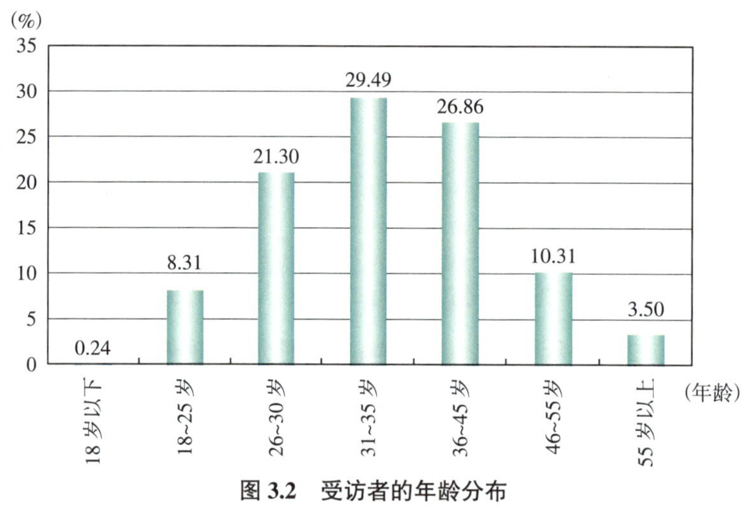

图 3.2 受访者的年龄分布

图 3.3 显示，被调查者中家庭资产超过 100 万元者共有 2309 人，占总人数的 68.99%。年龄在 18~35 岁的有 1306 人，总占比为 56.57%，其中在 31~35 岁的有 701 人，总占比为 30.36%； 26~30 岁的有 455 人，总占比为 19.71%；18~25 岁的有 150 人，总占比为 6.50%；36~45 岁的有 668 人，占比为 28.93%；46~55 岁的有 259 人，占比为 11.22%；55 岁以上和 18 岁以下总占比较少，分别为 3.20%和 0.09%。18~45 岁的主力消费者占到富裕阶层的八成，说明中国奢侈品购买者

中来自富裕阶层的人们呈现年轻化趋势。

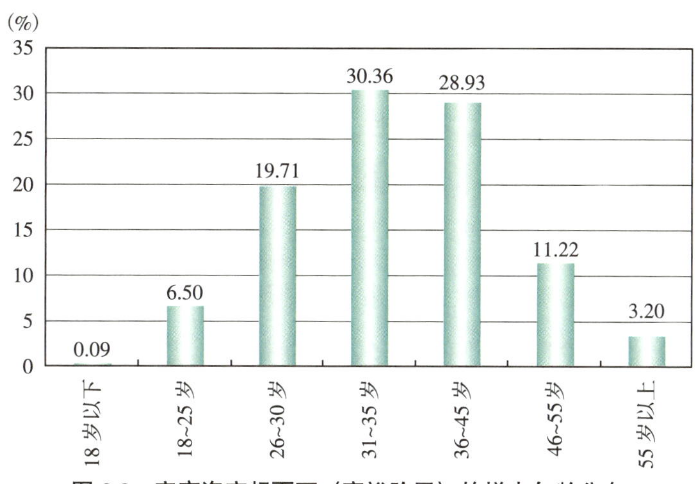

图 3.3　家庭资产超百万（富裕阶层）的样本年龄分布

3.1.3　职业

本次调查按职业将被调查者分成七类，如图 3.4 所示。企业白领人士共计 1745 人，总占比为 52.13%，其中国内企业白领有 1207 人，占比为 36.06%；外资企业白领有 538 人，总占比为 16.07%。专业人员有 738 人，占比为 22.05%。企业主和企业主家属共 378 人，总占比为 11.5%。样本涵盖了主要富裕人群，即奢侈品目标客户群。

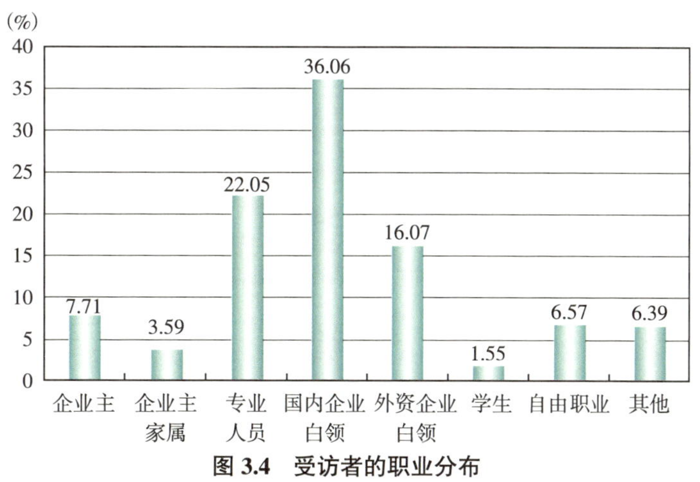

图 3.4　受访者的职业分布

企业主与企业主家属：他们拥有最为丰厚的收入，很高的社会地位，强烈的自尊，丰富的资源，这使得他们在大多数情况下可以随心所欲地消费。他们位于最高层，对于他们来说，个人形象非常重要，可以反映他们的品位、独立和个性。

专业人员：包括律师、医生以及会计师和教师等收入较高的中高端消费人群，这类消费者在地位导向性消费者中拥有较多的资源。他们事业成功，尊重权威和地位，常会选择同伴评价很高的产品和服务。

国企与外企白领：他们拥有较多的资源，是最年轻的群体，平均年龄为 25 岁左右。他们精力充沛，喜爱各类体育活动，积极从事各种社会活动，在服装、快餐、音乐以及其他一些年轻人所喜爱的产品上不惜钱财，尤其热衷新的产品和服务。

学生：他们拥有较少的资源，讲究实际，关注与自己息息相关的事务——学习、工作和娱乐，作为消费者，他们更倾向于选择实际功能型的产品。他们的价值观与白领较为相似，但收入较低，地位较低。他们会模仿所尊重和喜爱人的消费行为。

自由职业者：他们的收入最低，生活在最底层，拥有最少的资源，为满足基本生活需要而奋斗。在经济能力范围内，他们忠诚于自己喜爱的品牌。

3.1.4 受教育背景

图 3.5 显示，被调查者中大专以上人群有 3013 人，占比为 90.02%，其中研究生学历以上的有 540 人，占比为 16.13%。拥有本科及大专学历的有 2473 人，占比为 73.89%，相比 2014 年高出近 20%，是人数最多的人群。高中及中专有 225 人，占比为 6.72%，其他为 109 人，占比为 3.26%。

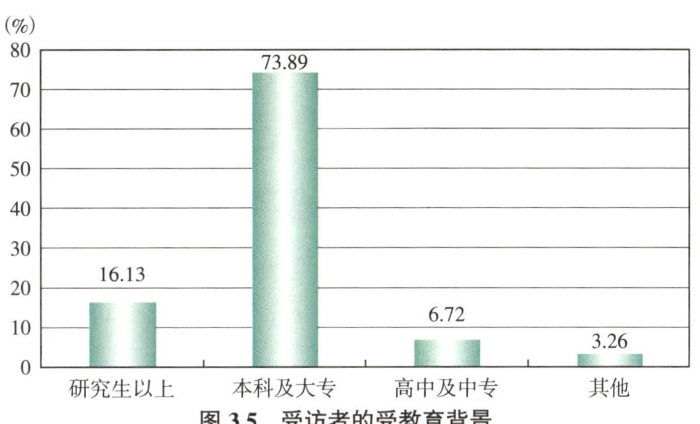

图 3.5 受访者的受教育背景

3.1.5 家庭资产

图 3.6 显示，被调查者中家庭资产在 100 万~500 万元的消费者共有 1283 人，总占比为 38.33%。次之是资产在 100 万元以下者，有 1038 人，占比为 31.01%。500 万~1000 万元的有 680 人，占比为 20.32%，1000 万元以上的有 346 人，占比为 10.34%。数据显示，家庭资产状况越高，奢侈品消费越高。

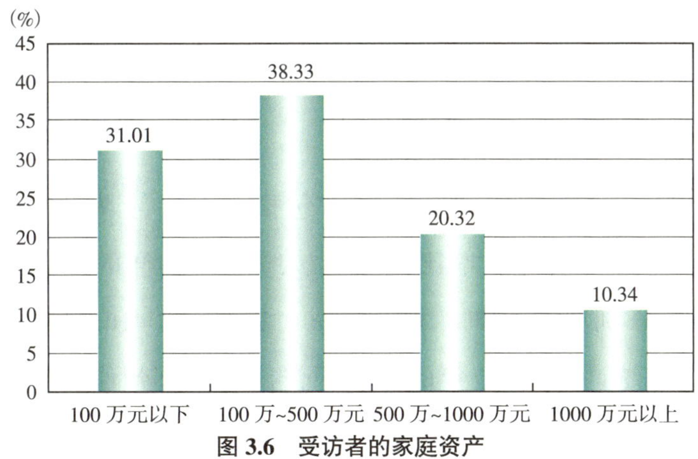

图 3.6 受访者的家庭资产

3.1.6 收入

图 3.7 显示，本年度调查对收入的分层进行了调整，年收入以 12 万元纳税起点为标准。被调查者年收入在 12 万~100 万元的人最多，

有 1310 人，占比为 39.14%，次之是年收入在 12 万元以下的，有 1008 人，占比为 30.12%，年收入在 100 万~500 万元的有 425 人，占比为 12.70%，500 万~1000 万元有 369 人，占比为 11.02%，1000 万元以上有 235 人，占比为 7.02%。显然，被调查者的年收入在 100 万元以下者占到了七成。

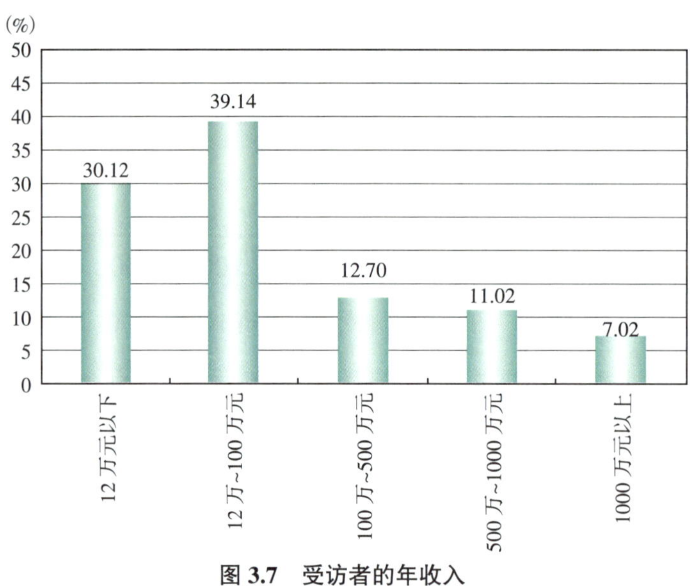

图 3.7 受访者的年收入

3.1.7 居住地

图 3.8 显示，本调研覆盖的城市包括北京、上海、深圳、广州，成都和苏州，各城市的样本比例基本按照配额抽样的原则确定，其样本容量占比分别为 20.05%、18.79%、16.82%、16.82%、13.77%和 13.74%。国家统计局 2015 年的相关报告披露，苏州作为典型的二线城市，在奢侈品消费中有突出表现，反映了国际奢侈品在二线城市的布局调整和市场结果。

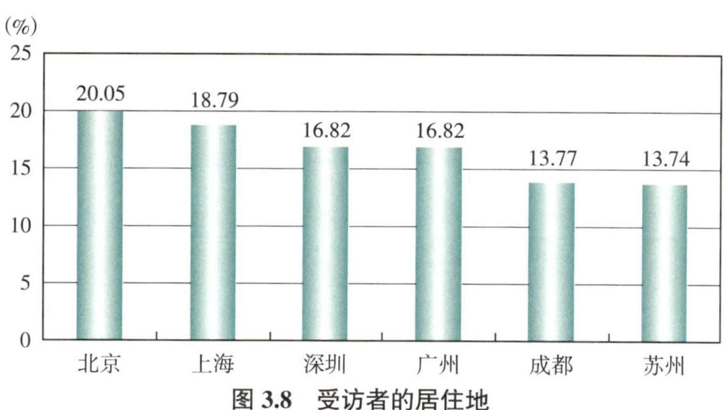

图 3.8 受访者的居住地

3.1.8 奢侈品支出占个人收入的比例

图 3.9 显示，66.23%的被调查者的年奢侈品消费支出占其个人收入的预算不超过 20%，26.69%的消费者个人预算在 20%~40%，6.48%的消费者的个人预算在 40%~60%，只有 0.17%的消费者的奢侈品购买预算超过 60%，不打算购买奢侈品的人只占 0.44%，人数极少。说明几乎所有的被调查者均有奢侈品的财政支出预算，这无疑对奢侈品的市场发展提供了强大的个体财政支出保障。

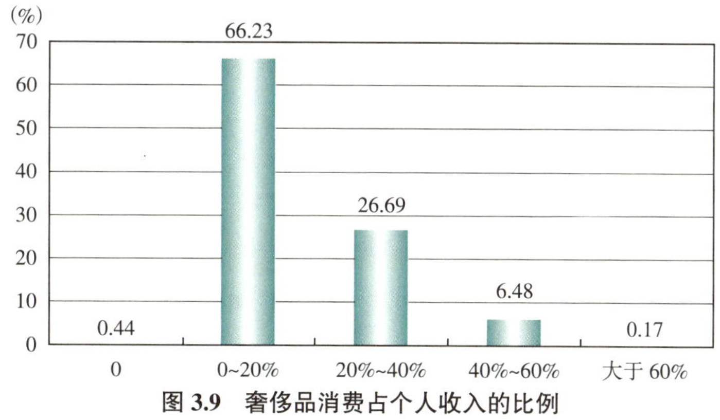

图 3.9 奢侈品消费占个人收入的比例

3.1.9 未来一年奢侈品购买频率预期

图 3.10 显示，53.07%的被调查者在未来的一年会购买 1~2 次奢侈品，34.04%的消费者会购买 3~5 次奢侈品，9.37%的消费者会购买 6~7

次，2.95%的消费者会购买 7 次以上，只有 0.57%的消费者没有购买奢侈品的打算。显然，几乎全部消费者在未来一年均有购买奢侈品的计划，可见奢侈品市场的保持和发展有稳定的需求基础。

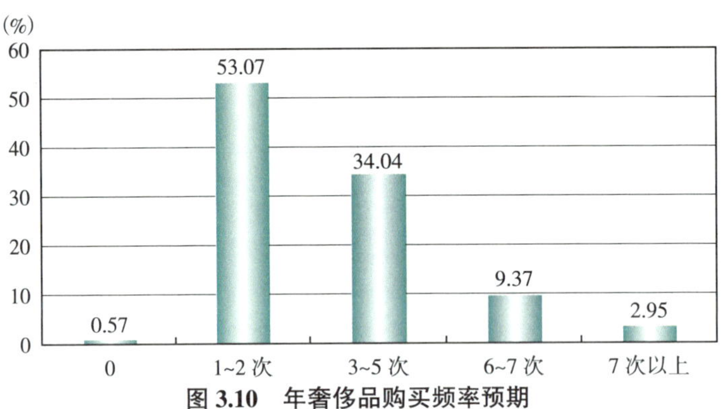

图 3.10　年奢侈品购买频率预期

3.2　问卷题项基本情况

3.2.1　符合自身气质

图 3.11 显示，78.73%的被调查者（共 2635 人）认为，奢侈品应该符合自身的气质。14.04%的被调查者（470 人）对此持中立态度，7.23%的被调查者（242 人）表示反对。在奢侈品牌进入中国市场的初期，许多国人购买奢侈品是为了迎合他人的喜好，盲目跟从，忽视自身需求，不重视奢侈品牌产品与自身气质和形象的匹配。本次调研发现，当今的中国消费者非常在意奢侈品牌产品的风格是否符合个人的气质，这种自身气质主要源于消费者的自我判断，所以其深层的含义是奢侈品牌消费与自我概念的结合，反映出中国人的奢侈品消费行为日趋个性化的特点。

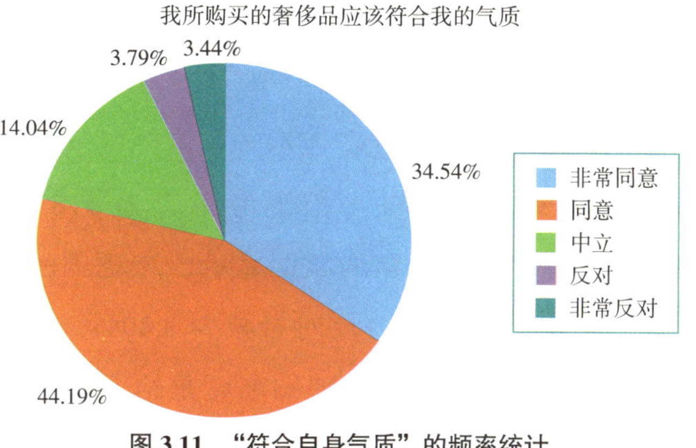

图 3.11 “符合自身气质”的频率统计

3.2.2 在意品牌来源国

图 3.12 显示，有 2176 名被调查者在意品牌来源国，总占比为 65.01%，即超过六成半的消费者在购买奢侈品时在意奢侈品品牌来源国信息，而表示无所谓或不在意品牌来源国的人只占总数的 25.58%，仅有 9.41%的被调查者（315 人）完全不关注品牌来源国。与 2014 年对比，2015 年的数据显示，该题项的支持者增加了 8.81%，中立者减少了 9.60%。上述数据说明，越来越多的中国消费者重视“品牌来源国”信息，换言之，中国消费者对品牌传承及其历史演进更加关注。显然，品牌来源国信息对品牌价值的提升作用不可忽视。

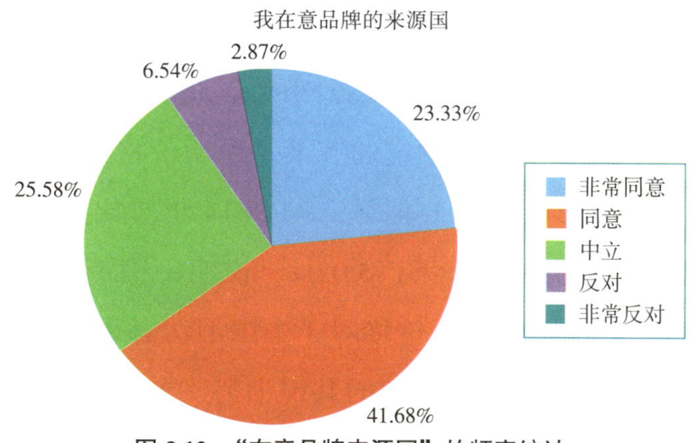

图 3.12 “在意品牌来源国”的频率统计

3.2.3 敏感品牌知名度

图 3.13 显示，2287 位被调查者表示知名度高的奢侈品品牌是他们的优先选择，总占比为 68.33%。拒绝考虑者为 318 人，总占比为 9.50%。与 2014 年对比，2015 年的数据显示，该题项的支持者同比增加 18.41%，中立者减少 14.52%，反对者减少 3.89%，再次印证了品牌知名度是品牌资产的核心要素。品牌知名度是给定品牌较之其他同类竞争品牌被消费者知晓的程度。品牌知名度越高，其在消费者记忆中的烙印就越深刻，对消费者购买行为的影响力就越强大。

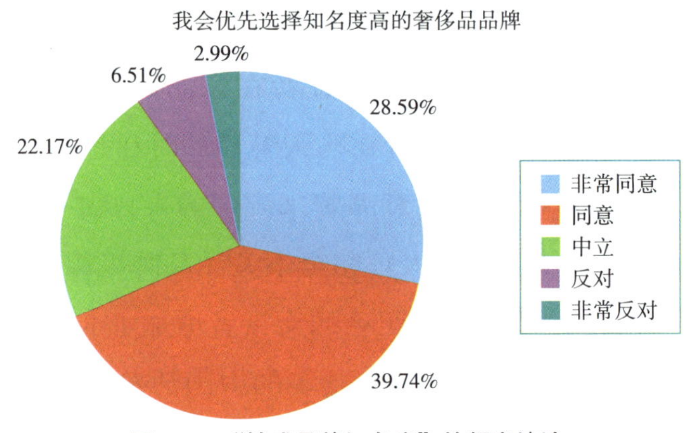

图 3.13 “敏感品牌知名度”的频率统计

3.2.4 关注价格优惠

在被问及奢侈品的优惠信息（如赴海外购买、免税店购物、打折活动等）是否会刺激消费者的购买欲望时，如图 3.14 显示，近七成的被调查者（2389 人）给予了肯定的答案，说明价格因素对中国消费者的奢侈品购买决策影响较大。但是，与 2014 年对比，2015 年数据同时显示，该题项的支持者减少了 5.02%，说明中国消费者的奢侈品价格敏感度有所降低。事实上，价格对于中国消费者是一个复杂的概念。一方面，“一分钱一分货”是大家的共识；另一方面，国际奢侈品牌在中国市场上长期以来的高价格，驱使越来越多的中国消费者利用各种

机会去规避不必要的金钱损失，这是交易的公平原则使然。

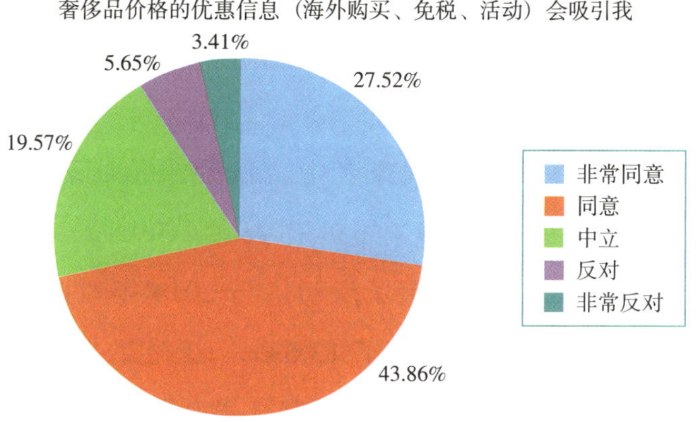

图 3.14 “关注价格优惠”的频率统计

3.2.5 倾听同行朋友

图 3.15 显示，53.66%的被调查者（1796 人）在购买奢侈品时会受同行朋友建议的影响，持中立态度者（1045 人）占比为 31.22%，持反对意见者（506 人）占比为 15.12%。中国素有倾听专家或师长意见的传统，同行朋友或者意见领袖在中国消费者奢侈品购买行为中的影响作用，在于可以保证个体能够在不被集体或圈子排斥的原则下行动，奢侈品消费或购买也不例外，这也反映出中国传统文化价值观中的集体主义观念在其中发挥着作用。与 2014 年对比，2015 年的数据统计

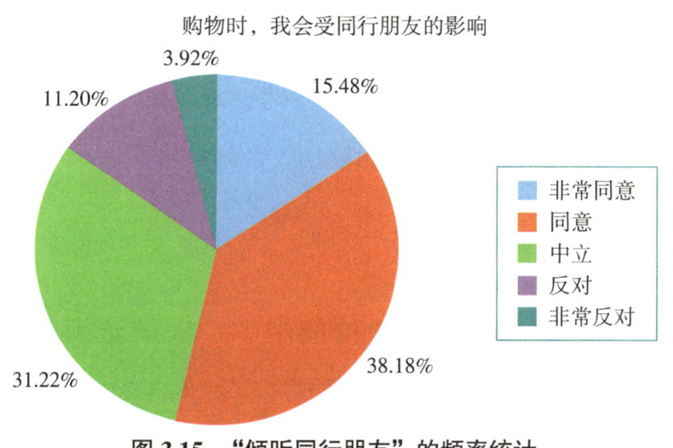

图 3.15 “倾听同行朋友”的频率统计

结果总体变化不大，该题项的支持者增加 1.92%，中立者增加 1.19%，反对者减少 3.11%。

3.2.6 偏爱限量版

图 3.16 显示，在所有被调查者中，偏爱限量版奢侈品者共 1793 人，总占比为 53.57%，29.64%的被调查者（992 人）持中立态度，16.79%的被调查者（562 人）表示反对。与 2014 年对比，2015 年数据显示，该题项的支持者同比增加了 13.63%。上述数据提示，奢侈品市场的分层化应引起特别关注，这是消费高端化趋势在加强的信号，也说明消费者对奢侈品定制需求的进一步增强。小众的限量版代表了设计者或拥有者的独特个性。中国的奢侈品消费者对限量版奢侈品具有明显的规模定制偏好，他们希冀于奢侈品的“稀缺、独特、限量”等产品属性与奢侈品消费“带给使用者独特享受和尊贵地位”的价值主张天衣无缝。

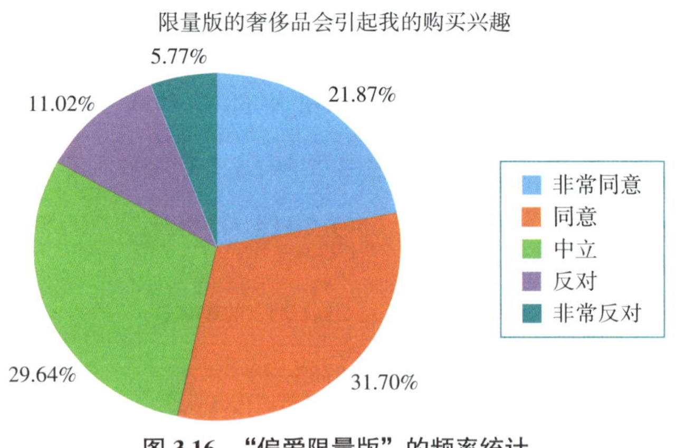

图 3.16 “偏爱限量版”的频率统计

3.2.7 崇尚自然

“崇尚自然”是中国道家文化价值观中“大道至简，无为而至”思想的表达。图 3.17 显示，七成的被调查者（2459 人）表示“崇尚自然”，持中立态度者（656 人）总占比为 19.60%，持反对意见者（232

人）总占比为6.93%。显然，道家思想影响着中国消费者的奢侈品购买行为。但值得注意的是，与2014年对比，2015年数据显示，该题项的支持者减少了7.70%，中立者增加了4.62%，反对者增加了3.07%。该对比数据同样反映出中国奢侈品消费行为的复杂性特征，如何实现“追求独特下的标新立异”与“崇尚自然”的和谐统一将是奢侈品牌在中国市场面临的一道难题。

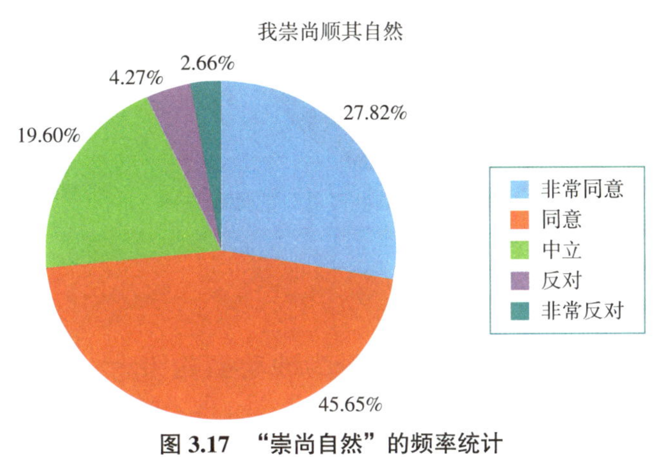

图3.17 “崇尚自然”的频率统计

3.2.8 自我赠礼

此题项用于度量奢侈品消费中的自我赠礼动机。图3.18显示，59.73%的被调查者（1999人）会购买奢侈品来犒劳自己，持中立态度者（892人）总占比为26.65%，持反对意见者456人，总占比为13.62%。这说明西方个人主义价值观已经渗入到中国人价值观体系中，并影响着中国消费者奢侈品购买行为。与2014年对比，2015年的数据显示，该题项的支持者增加了7.00%，中立者减少了7.39%，反对者增加了0.39%。该数据说明，中国奢侈品自我消费水平稳步提升，与国际市场接轨的奢侈品市场的常规化发展走势突出。

这与法国路透社发布的一个报告结果一致。2015年10月，法国路透社发布了针对美国、亚洲和欧洲地区的奢侈品零售商的一次大范

围的调查结果，并披露中国消费者购买奢侈品主要是自用或赠送朋友，而不再是作为给上司或是官员的礼物。

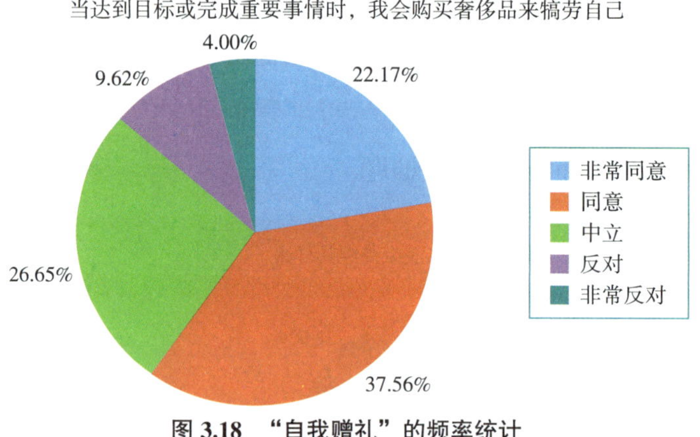

图 3.18 "自我赠礼"的频率统计

3.2.9 关注性价预算比

本题项用来测量被调查者是否为冲动型购买者。所谓冲动型购买者，是指消费者在购物过程中通常是无计划购物，表现为不会在购物时根据收入制定预算，在锁定要购买的商品后，也不会通过不同的渠道货比三家。与此相反，理性购买者会在个人预算、商品品质以及不同渠道提供的价格间做出完美的选择。图 3.19 显示，75.56%的被调查者（2529 人）在购买奢侈品时会做出理性选择。16.97%的被调查者

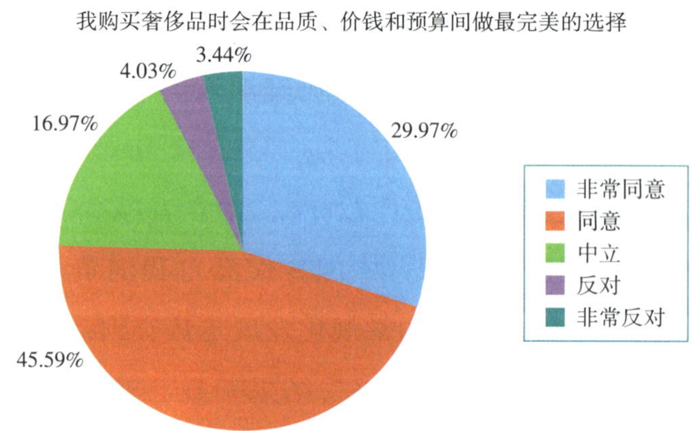

图 3.19 "关注性价预算比"的频率统计

（568 人）持中立态度，持反对意见者为 7.47%（250 人）。由此可见，在中国奢侈品消费人群中，理性消费者占大多数。与 2014 年对比，2015 年数据显示，该题项的支持者减少 4.62%，中立者增加 1.39%，反对者增加 3.23%，总体变化不大。

3.2.10 购买熟悉的奢侈品牌产品

图 3.20 显示，73.80%的被调查者（2470 人）会购买熟悉的奢侈品牌产品，持中立态度者（624 人）占比为 18.64%，持反对意见者有 253 人，总占比为 7.56%。七成以上的消费者会优先选择自己熟悉的奢侈品牌产品，说明品牌熟悉度越高，品牌认可度也越高。

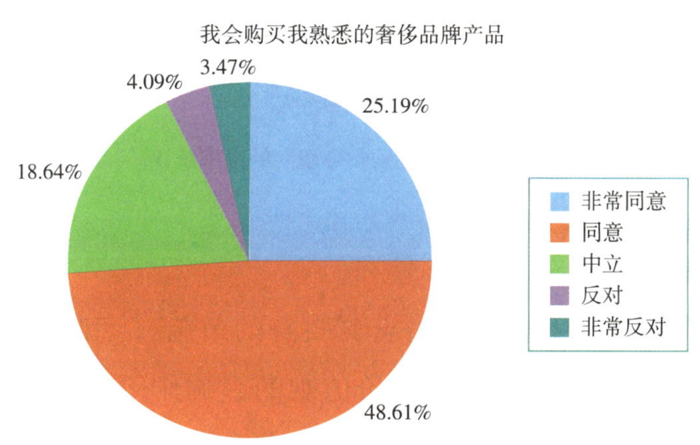

图 3.20 “购买熟悉的奢侈品牌产品”的频率统计

3.2.11 重视购物环境

题项“我在意购买奢侈品时的自在程度（场所、店面与人员）”，是用于调查奢侈品消费者对购物环境的关注度，特别是置身其中的自在程度。一般地，购物环境因素包括购物场所的建筑风格、外部环境、橱窗设计、装修格调以及销售人员的服务质量等。图 3.21 显示，72.06%的被调查者（2412 人）关注购物环境和购买体验，19.90%的被调查者（666 人）持中立态度，持反对意见者为 8.04%（269 人）。与

2014 年对比，2015 年数据显示，该题项的支持者减少了 2.75%，中立者减少了 1.58%，反对者增加了 4.33%，总体变化不大。显然，购物环境和氛围对于大多数奢侈品购买者非常重要，具有良好素质的销售队伍、积极且自在的购物体验以及心理感受会有效地促进奢侈品购买行为。

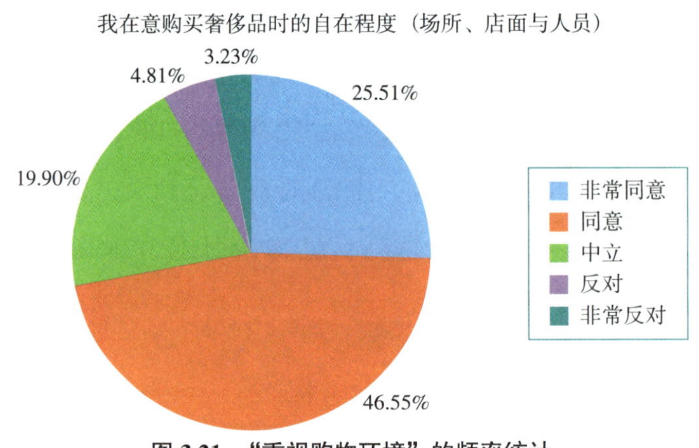

图 3.21 “重视购物环境”的频率统计

3.2.12 行为与角色匹配

题项“人的言行举止必须符合其自身的角色”，用于测量中国消费者奢侈品购买行为来自儒家文化价值观的影响作用的广泛性。文献研究显示，中国传统文化价值观中的儒家文化强调个体在处理个体与社会的关系时要恪守本分，并自觉维护社会秩序，由于奢侈品产品的外在社会符号特征明显，主导中国人处理个体与社会关系的儒家文化对奢侈品购买行为具有驱动作用。图 3.22 显示，78.67%的被调查者（2633 人）认可“人的言行举止必须符合其自身的角色”的儒家文化价值观，14.73%的被调查者（493 人）持中立态度，持反对意见者仅占 6.60%（221 人）。由此可见，儒家文化中的社会角色换言之社会等级观念仍然扎根于中国消费者的价值观之中，且具有不可忽视的广泛性。

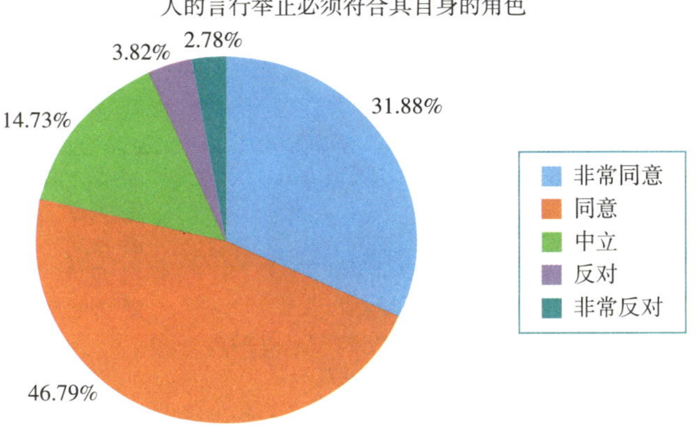

图 3.22 “行为与角色匹配”的频率统计

3.2.13 高价不安感

图 3.23 显示，41.29%（1382 人）的被调查者在购买了昂贵的奢侈品后有购后不安感，并对未来的奢侈品购买行为形成阻力作用；33.55%（1123 人）的被调查者持中立态度，持反对态度者有 842 人，总占比为 25.16%。该统计数据显示，只有占四成的中国消费者在购买了昂贵的奢侈品后有购后不安感，而将近六成的人没有购后不安感，反映出大多数中国消费者的奢侈品购买行为自认为是理性的，并非一时冲动。但是，40%的人群仍然存在购后不安感的事实仍不可忽视，其规模毕竟占到了总人群的 1/3。事实上，由于购买奢侈品的高消费行为与以俭养德、节俭修身的中国传统价值观相悖，导致一部分消费者在购买价格昂贵的奢侈品之后产生内疚感，并影响到其未来的购买行为。从这个意义上进一步分析，发生在一部分人那里的奢侈品消费行为弱化现象，究其原因，不一定总是购买力弱的结果，或许是传统观念作用下的奢侈消费内疚感所致。与 2014 年对比，2015 年数据显示，该题项的支持者增加 4.91%，中立者减少 7.75%，反对者增加 2.84%。对该题项持中立态度的人数的减少，标志着被调查者对该题项有更明确的理解和态度。

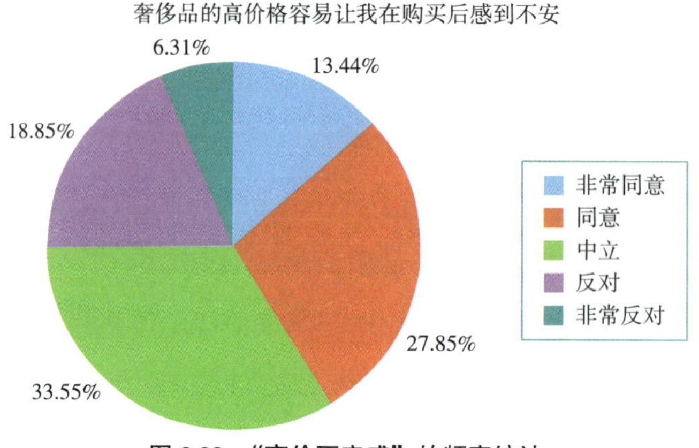

图 3.23 "高价不安感"的频率统计

3.2.14 偏爱经典款

通常奢侈品的经典款式经历了时间和市场的考验，大大降低了消费者的购买风险，从而普遍受到大多数消费者的青睐。相反地，新款产品往往面市时间短，只能获得市场上少数追求标新立异的先锋人士的尝试，不易被大众接受。在本次调研中，如图 3.24 所示，62.89%的被调查者（2105 人）表示经典款比最新款对他们更有吸引力，28.35%的消费者（949 人）选择中立，持不同意者占 8.76%（293 人）。该数据揭示出一个潜在的中国奢侈品消费市场的三元市场结构，即由 62.89%的消费者构成的保守型市场；由 8.75%的消费者构成的先锋型

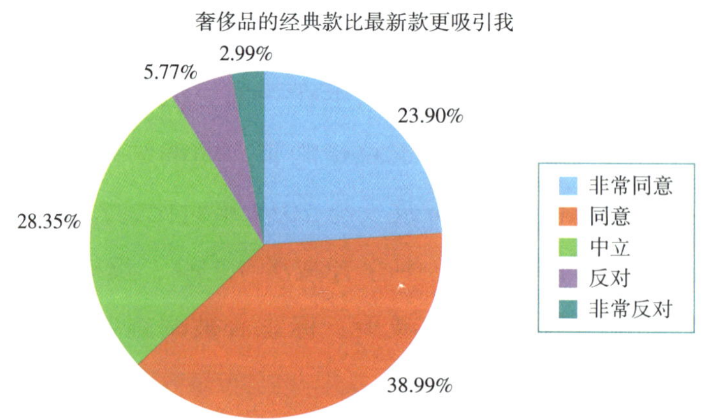

图 3.24 "偏爱经典款"的频率统计

市场和由 28.35%的消费者构成的观望型市场，其市场规模比约为 6：1：3。与 2014 年对比，2015 年数据显示，该题项的支持者增加 1.24%，中立者减少 2.89%，反对者增加 1.64%，无显著变化。两年的对比统计分析进一步揭示，本研究提出的三元市场结构具稳定性特征。在未来的研究中，我们将予以特别关注。

3.2.15 关注保值增值

奢侈品的真正内涵并非总是金钱的价值表达，它更是一种文化现象，体现的是时间的积累和文化的沉淀，因此，有些奢侈品也会被视为抗通胀商品，被认为具有投资性保值增值的功能。图 3.25 显示，61.88%（2027 人）的被调查者在购买奢侈品时会考虑日后升值，26.41%的被调查者（884 人）保持中立，11.71%的被调查者（200 人）并不考虑保值增值因素。与 2014 年对比，2015 年数据显示，该题项的支持者增加 9.83%，中立者减少 6.42%，反对者减少 3.42%。上述数据说明，中国消费者越来越关注奢侈品的保值增值功能，他们对那些具备收藏价值的奢侈品有着越来越浓厚的兴趣。这一趋势显然为奢侈品牌的向上延伸提供了新的思路和通道。

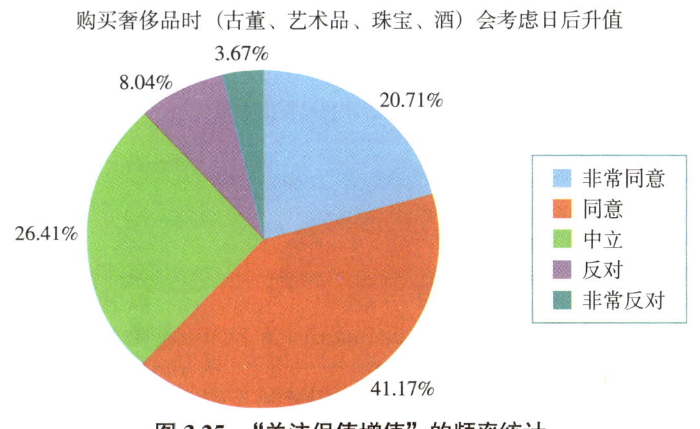

图 3.25 “关注保值增值”的频率统计

3.2.16 提升自信

图 3.26 显示，62%（2075 人）的被调查者希望通过消费奢侈品提升自信，25.90%的被调查者（867 人）持中立态度，12.10%的被调查者（405 人）表示反对。该统计数据揭示，奢侈品牌产品应当兼具双重属性，即消费者通过消费奢侈品达到物质需求和精神需求的双重满足，而通过奢侈品消费提升个体自信就是一种精神满足的体现。

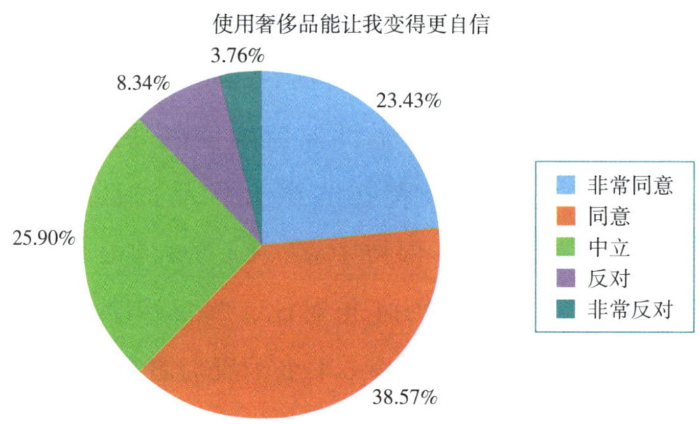

图 3.26 “提升自信”的频率统计

3.2.17 表达尊贵

图 3.27 显示，58.17%（1947 人）的被调查者认为奢侈品象征着尊贵，28.83%的被调查者（965 人）对此持中立态度，13.00%的被调查

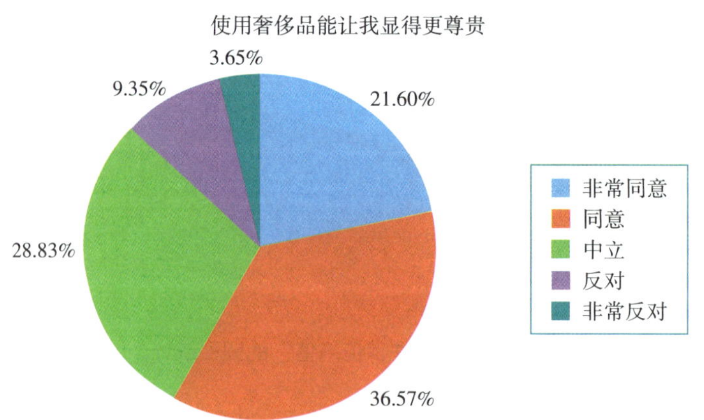

图 3.27 “表达尊贵”的频率统计

者（435人）表示反对。由于奢侈品牌产品具有高品质、昂贵、稀缺等特征，只能被少数人所有，从而使得奢侈品牌拥有了排他性符号价值，成为个体尊贵身份的象征。调研显示，近六成的中国消费者对此表示认同，只有13%的被调查者不予认同，由此可以解释存在于一部分中国奢侈品消费者行为中的炫耀性消费现象。

将图3.26和图3.27中的数据求平均值，与2014年对比，2015年数据显示，支持者增加9.48%，中立者减少10.53%，反对者仅仅增加1.05%。该统计数据说明，一方面反映出中国消费者认同奢侈品有提升自信和表达尊贵的作用，另一方面也反映出中国人奢侈品消费行为的两个重要动机：提升自信和表达尊贵，并且这两大动机越来越普遍。

3.2.18 价高质优

图3.28显示，70.12%（2347人）的被调查者赞同奢侈品的高价位源于其卓越的品质和出色的工艺，21.30%的被调查者（713人）持中立态度，8.58%的被调查者反对。由此可见，大部分中国消费者认可奢侈品的高品质和昂贵价格。与2014年对比，2015年数据显示，该题项的支持者增加0.68%，中立者减少1.62%，反对者增加0.93%，无显著变化，说明价高质优是奢侈品的必要条件。

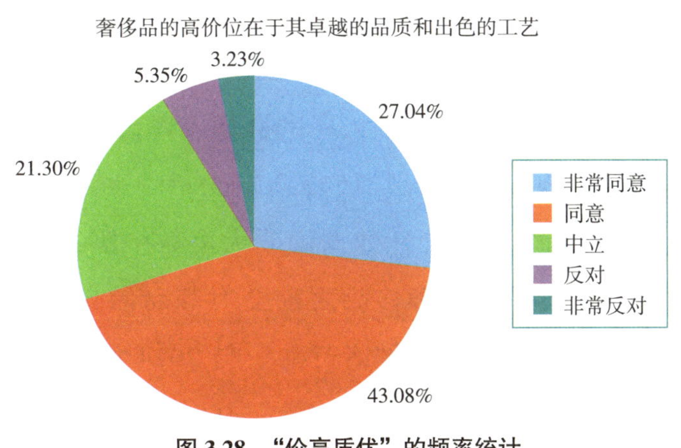

图3.28 “价高质优”的频率统计

3.2.19 导购影响

设置本题项的目的是调查中国消费者奢侈品购买决策行为是否会受导购人员的影响。图 3.29 显示，59.30%（1985 人）的被调查者在购买奢侈品时会参考销售人员的意见，30.06%（1006 人）的被调查者表示无所谓，10.64%的被调查者（356 人）拒绝导购。与 2014 年对比，2015 年数据显示，该题项的支持者增加 16.19%，中立者减少 10.75%，反对者减少 5.40%。上述统计数据表明，导购在消费者购买决策中充当着重要的角色，在门店销售中，训练有素的导购人员将对奢侈品牌商品的销售起到积极的促进作用。

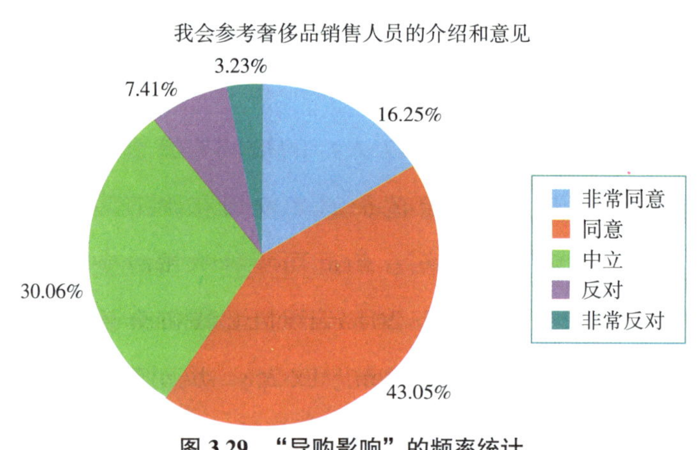

图 3.29 "导购影响"的频率统计

3.2.20 感知划算

图 3.30 显示，75.74%（2535 人）的被调查者会耐心地挑选相对划算的奢侈品，16.52%的被调查者（553 人）表示中立，7.74%的被调查者（259 人）表示反对。该统计数据说明大多数中国人的奢侈品消费行为是理性的，他们在购买奢侈品之前会对商品信息进行比较分析，做出是否划算的判断，然后才付诸行动。与 2014 年对比，2015 年的数据显示，该题项的支持者增加 2.44%，中立者减少 4.28%，反对者增加 1.84%，无显著差异，说明该行为习惯相对稳定。

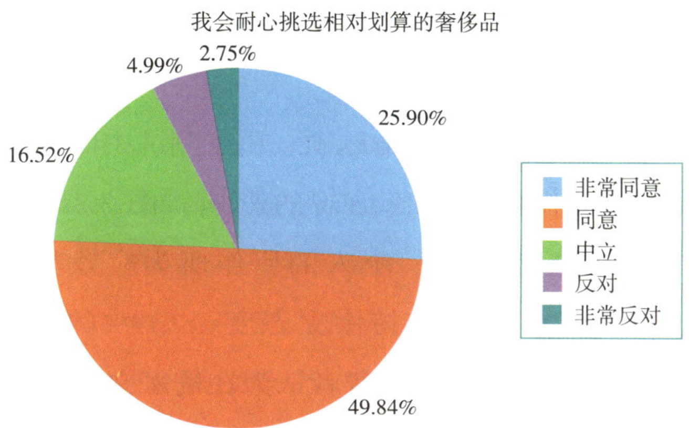

图 3.30 “感知划算”的频率统计

3.2.21 中庸低调

本题项用于测试中国奢侈品消费者在日常生活中是否受儒家文化价值观“中庸之道”的影响。图 3.31 显示，62.27%（2084 人）的被调查者在日常生活中会恪守中庸之道，保持低调不张扬，不被情绪影响而失去中正平和，25.87%的被调查者（866 人）持中立态度，11.86%的被调查者（397 人）表示反对。可见，大部分中国奢侈品消费者深受儒家文化价值观的影响。与 2014 年对比，2015 年数据显示，该题项的支持者减少 10.43%，中立者增加 5.37%，反对者增加 5.05%。说明奢侈品消费高调化趋势增强，奢侈品消费本来就是高调的行为。

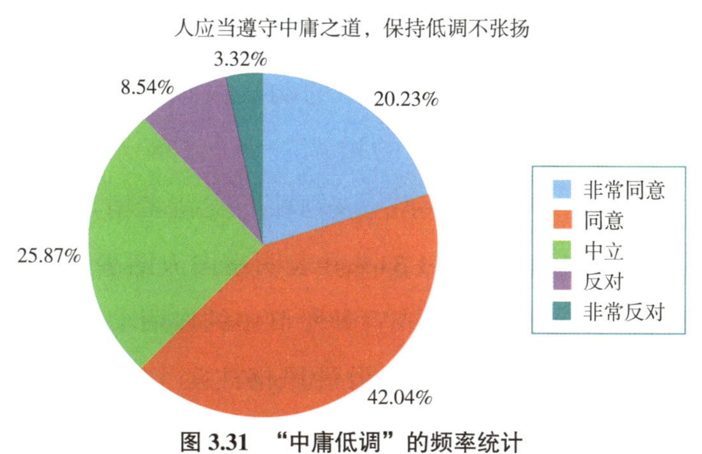

图 3.31 “中庸低调”的频率统计

3.2.22 所作所为与地位符合

本题项是 2015 年度报告新增题项，用于测试中国奢侈品消费者在日常生活中是否受儒家文化价值观的影响。图 3.32 显示，75.92%（2541 人）的被调查者认可一个人的所作所为应该与其地位相符，16.94%的被调查者（567 人）持中立态度，7.14%的被调查者（239 人）表示反对。说明绝大多数消费者认为在儒家文化价值观导向下应注重所作所为与地位相符。

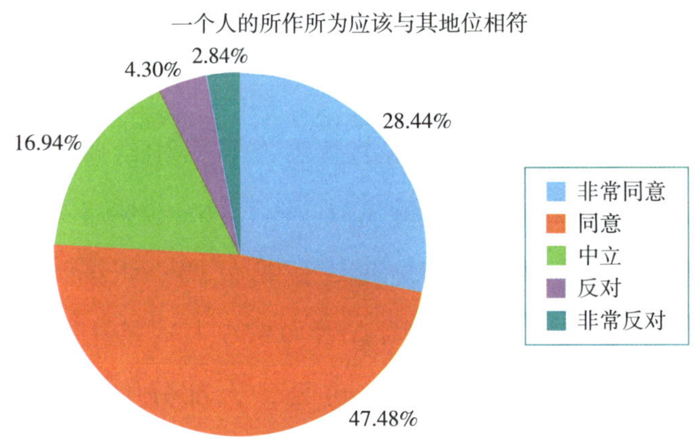

图 3.32 “所作所为与地位符合”的频率统计

3.2.23 从众效应

本题项用来测试中国奢侈品消费中是否存在着从众心理或者迎合圈子的效应。图 3.33 显示，50.80%（1700 人）的被调查者表示他人购买的奢侈品品牌或款式会影响自己的购买决策，33.13%的被调查者（1109 人）保持中立，16.07%的被调查者（538 人）表示不会。与 2014 年对比，2015 年数据显示，该题项的支持者增加 14.18%，中立者减少 2.87%，反对者减少 11.31%。表明中国人对奢侈品的消费越来越受到他人的影响，意见领袖或者参照群体的作用十分重要。

奢侈品昂贵的价格、独特的设计风格注定了它不是大众消费品，只有真正了解奢侈品内涵的少数人才会心甘情愿地负担它的高价格。

而只被小众人群欣赏并拥有的奢侈品经常被当作一个群体的标志或符号，要融入这个群体就必须拥有这样的标志。据悉，2015 年 10 月，路透社发布了针对美国、亚洲和欧洲地区的奢侈品零售商的一次大范围的调查。结果显示，中国的奢侈品消费者的消费习惯和品位正在发生巨大的变化。因此促进了许多新兴奢侈品牌的发展。尽管老牌奢侈品品牌依然广受欢迎，但在许多“意见领袖”如明星们的带动下，许多新兴的轻奢品牌正蓬勃发展。

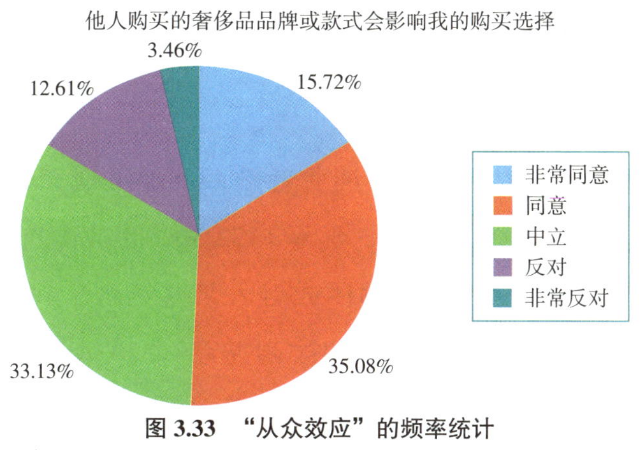

图 3.33 “从众效应”的频率统计

3.2.24 社交关系

本题项用于了解奢侈品购买动机中送礼即社交动机是否存在。图 3.34 显示，60.27%（2017 人）的被调查者认可这样的观点，即购买奢侈品作为礼物赠送他人是一种必要的投资。29.19%的被调查者（977 人）选择中立，10.54%的被调查者（353 人）反对。由此可见，中国人奢侈品消费中存在比较突出的送礼动机，超过六成的人愿意购买奢侈品作为礼物馈赠他人以改善自己的社会关系。显然，奢侈品的属性特征使其成为赠礼的首选，而儒家文化中崇尚礼仪、礼尚往来的价值观会潜移默化地影响使其成为中国人的奢侈品购买行为。与 2014 年对比，2015 年数据显示，该题项的支持者减少 1.46%，中立者增加 2.26%，反对者减少 0.80%。无显著差异。

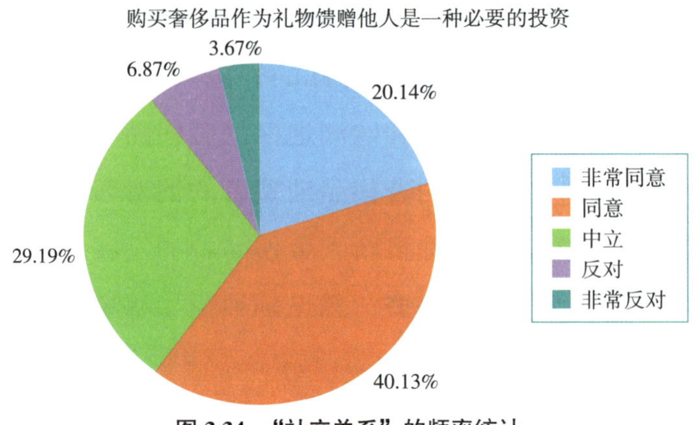

图 3.34 “社交关系”的频率统计

3.2.25 融入圈子

本题项用于调查中国奢侈品消费者是否更加重视“外在自我”，即自己在别人眼中的形象。图 3.35 显示，72.30%的被调查者（2420 人）会适当使用奢侈品以打进某些团体或融入某些场合，19.63%的被调查者（657 人）表示无所谓，8.07%的被调查者（270 人）不认可。可见，在中国的奢侈品消费中，个人消费是为了完成家庭或群体的义务和规范，即身份象征动机在奢侈品消费中比较普遍，说明受到儒家文化中“个体服从于集体”价值观的影响。与 2014 年对比，2015 年数据显示，该题项的支持者增加 13.38%，中立者减少 11.23%，反对者减少 2.14%。支持者的增加说明了奢侈品的群体聚类作用在显著加强。

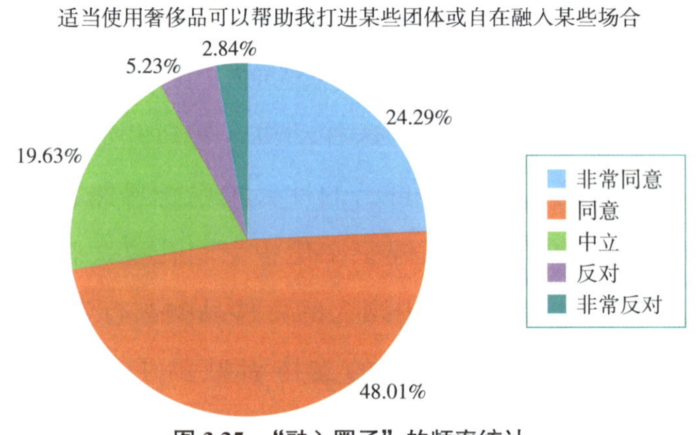

图 3.35 “融入圈子”的频率统计

3.2.26 相信缘分

本题项用于了解中国奢侈品消费者是否受到中国传统佛教文化的影响。图 3.36 显示，75.32%的被调查者（2521 人）认为人生中遇到的人和事都是缘分，17.87%的被调查者（598 人）持中立态度，6.81%的被调查者（228 人）持反对意见。由此可见，大多数被调查者表现出对佛家文化的认同感。与 2014 年对比，2015 年数据显示，该题项的支持者减少 2.44%，中立者增加 0.02%，反对者增加 2.42%。变化不大。

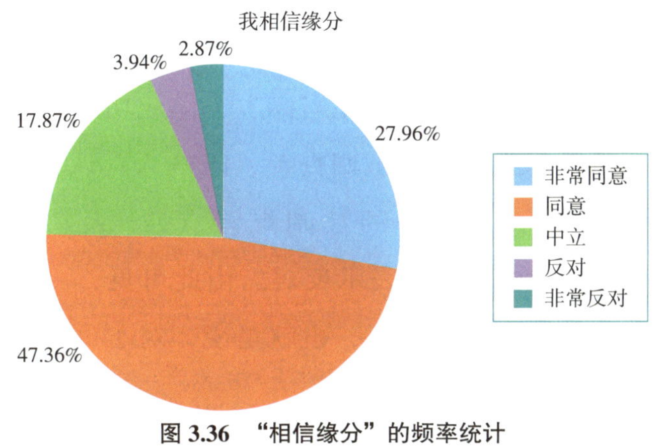

图 3.36 “相信缘分”的频率统计

3.2.27 遵循礼数

本题项用于调查中国奢侈品消费者受到中国传统文化中“遵循礼数”观念影响的程度。图 3.37 显示，79%的被调查者（2644 人）支持为人处事应当遵循礼数的行为准则，14.79%的被调查者（495 人）持中立态度，6.21%的被调查者（208 人）表示反对。由此可见，“礼”文化广泛根植于中国消费者价值观体系中，人们普遍认同礼数在日常生活中的重要性。此外，与 2014 年对比，2015 年数据显示，该题项的支持者减少 9.20%，中立者增加 5.33%，反对者增加 3.87%。说明了在现代生活环境中，传统礼数对个体行为的影响范围有下降的趋势。

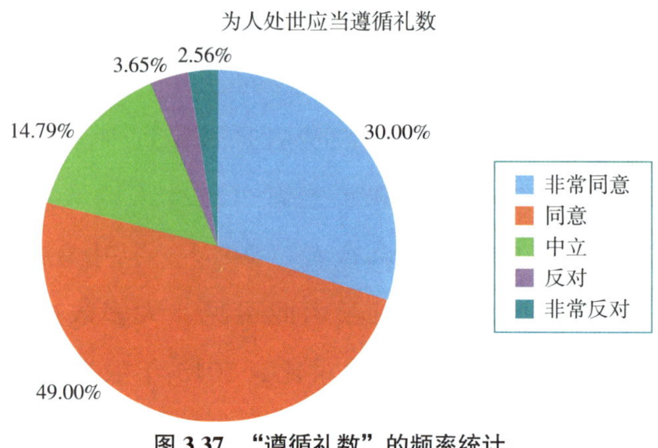

图 3.37 “遵循礼数”的频率统计

3.2.28 象征成功

本题项用于测试奢侈品能否充当标志个体成功的象征符号及其广泛性。图 3.38 显示，55.36%的被调查者（1853 人）认为拥有奢侈品可以作为成功的象征，29.19%的被调查者（977 人）持中立态度，15.45%的被调查者（517 人）表示反对。由此可见，一半以上的消费者将拥有奢侈品作为成功的象征，也就是说，对于这些人，奢侈品是一个人成功与否的外在符号标志。

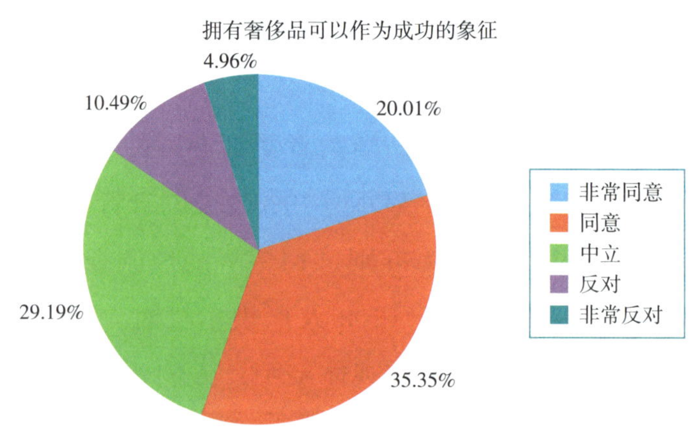

图 3.38 “象征成功”的频率统计

3.2.29 提升品质

图 3.39 显示，63.64%的被调查者（2130 人）认为“人们购买奢侈品是为了提高生活品质”，24.53%的被调查者（821 人）对此持中立态度，11.83%的被调查者（396 人）表示反对。该统计数据说明，大多数中国消费者认为奢侈品代表的是一种高品质的生活方式与消费态度。

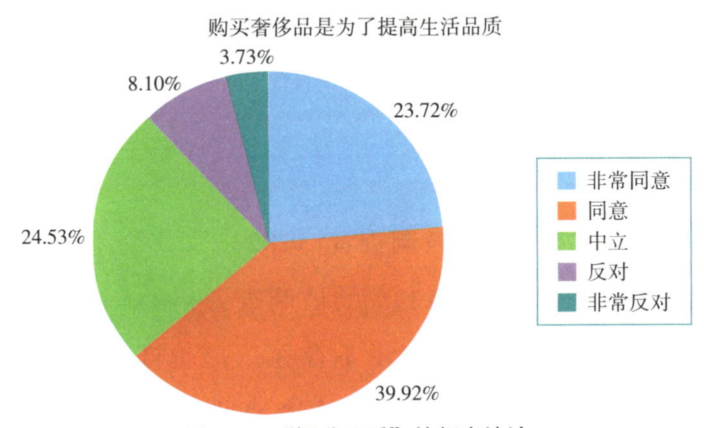

图 3.39 “提升品质”的频率统计

将图 3.38 和图 3.39 的相应数据取平均值后与 2014 年对比，2015 年的数据显示，支持者增加 13.43%，中立者增加 11.11%，反对者减少 2.32%，说明越来越多的消费者看重奢侈品的象征符号意义和对生活品质的提升。

3.2.30 消费行为与地位符合

本题项是 2015 年度报告新增题项。图 3.40 显示，74.57%的被调查者（2496 人）认为一个人的消费行为应该与其地位相符，18.05%的被调查者（604 人）持中立态度，7.38%的被调查者（247 人）表示反对。该统计数据说明，绝大多数被调查者的消费行为受到儒家文化价值观中等级观念的影响。

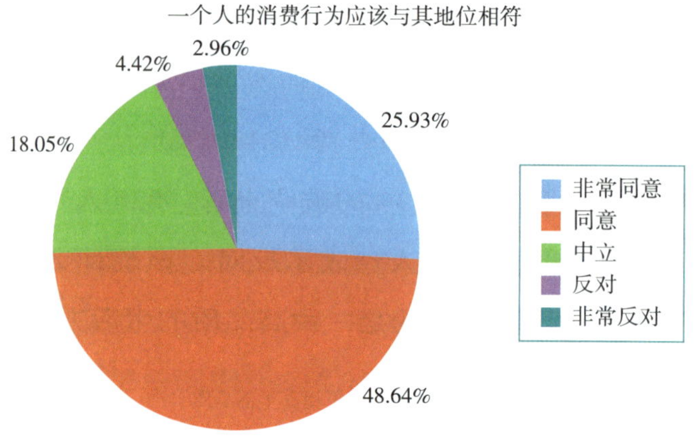

图 3.40 “消费行为与地位符合”的频率统计

3.2.31 舒缓心情

图 3.41 所示，54.47%的被调查者（1823 人）表示会为了缓解心情或宣泄情绪而购买奢侈品，28.11%的被调查者（941 人）持中立意见，17.42%的被调查者（583 人）表示不存在。该统计数据揭示，占半数中国消费者的奢侈品购买行为存在情绪消费现象。与 2014 年对比，2015 年数据显示，该题项的支持者增加 14.22%，中立者减少 0.86%，反对者减少 13.37%。该比较数据说明，为舒缓心情或宣泄情绪去购买奢侈品的人群规模有扩大的趋势。

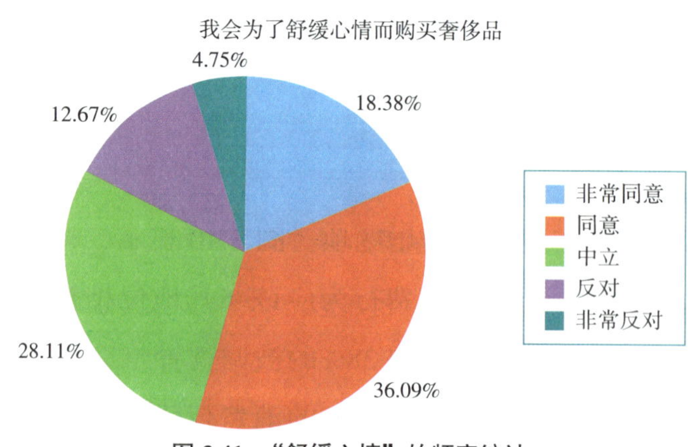

图 3.41 “舒缓心情”的频率统计

3.2.32 倾听他人

本题项是2015年度报告新增题项。图3.42显示，69.76%的被调查者（2335人）认为师长和前辈的话对他们非常重要，23.73%的被调查者（794人）持中立态度，6.51%的被调查者（218人）表示反对。该统计数据说明，近七成的中国消费者有倾听他人的习惯，这些消费者通过向他人学习以达到丰富知识、明智行动的目的。

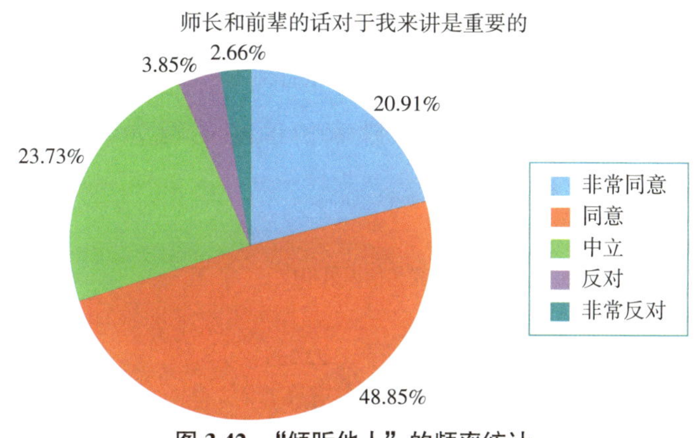

图3.42 “倾听他人”的频率统计

3.2.33 面子文化

图3.43显示，50.37%的被调查者（1386人）表示，当与富有的人逛街时他们会倾向逛高档商店，对此有35.08%的被调查者（1174人）

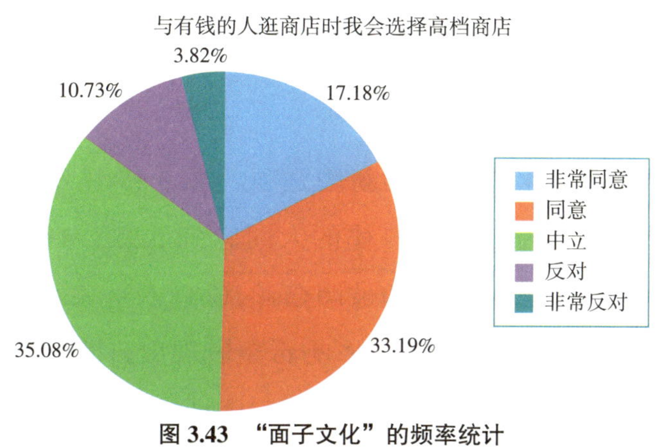

图3.43 “面子文化”的频率统计

持中立态度，14.55%的被调查者（487 人）表示反对。该统计数据反映奢侈品市场存在着追慕虚荣的浮夸现象。

3.2.34 因果报应

题项“相信因果报应”用来测试佛家文化价值观对中国消费者影响的普遍性，这是 2015 年度报告新增题项。图 3.44 显示，65.94%的被调查者（2207 人）相信因果报应，24.77%的被调查者（829 人）持中立态度，9.29%的被调查者（311 人）表示反对。该统计数据揭示，只有不到一成的被调查者明确表示不信因果报应，而相信者或模棱两可者占到了九成之多，这种来自佛家价值观的行为约束力必将反映在中国人的奢侈品消费行为中。

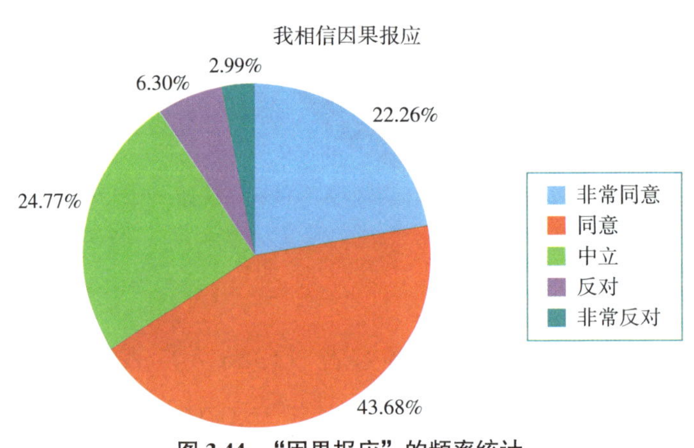

图 3.44 “因果报应”的频率统计

3.2.35 自觉自律

本题项是 2015 年度报告的新增题项。图 3.45 显示，74.82%的被调查者（2504 人）为自己是自律的人而感到欣慰，19%的被调查者（636 人）持中立态度，6.18%的被调查者（207 人）表示反对。此题项表现中国人受儒家文化价值观的影响希望表现出自律的美德。七成的支持者也说明了消费者对自律的认同感，印证出购物的理性态度。

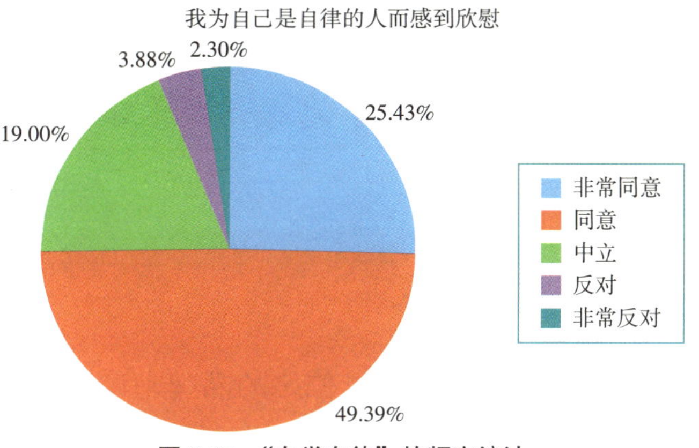

图 3.45 “自觉自律”的频率统计

3.2.36 着装与地位符合

本题项是2015年度报告的新增题项。图3.46显示，74.37%的被调查者（2489人）认为一个人的着装应该与其社会地位相符，18.76%的被调查者（628人）持中立态度，6.87%的被调查者（230人）表示反对。表现了中国人在儒家文化价值观的引导下追求着装与身份和地位相匹配，衣服应该符合个人所处的场合，所以认为着装很重要。

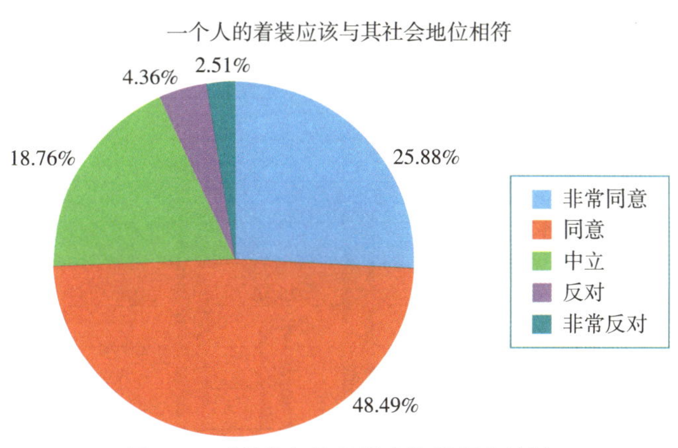

图 3.46 “着装与地位符合”的频率统计

3.3 品牌来源国偏好和渠道选择

3.3.1 品牌来源国偏好

图 3.47 显示，研究中国消费者偏好的品牌来源国，旨在了解哪些国家的奢侈品品牌被中国人熟知、喜爱。问卷中所列选项包括美国、瑞士、德国、意大利、日本、法国、西班牙以及英国，超过九成的奢侈品品牌来自这些国家。统计结果显示，得票率最高的三个国家分别是法国、美国、意大利。法国是中国奢侈品消费偏好第一的国家，59.93%的人选择法国，较 2014 年下滑近 10%；次之是美国，53.93%的被调查者表示偏好美国的奢侈品，意大利排在第三，占比为 53.33%。2014 年的排名依次为法国（71.6%），意大利（68.2%），瑞士（47.0%），美国（28.5%），德国（28.4%），英国（25.0%），日本（13.1%），西班牙（7.1%）。

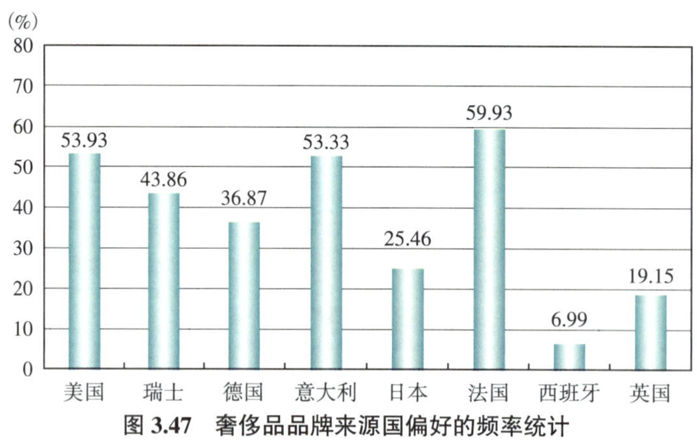

图 3.47 奢侈品品牌来源国偏好的频率统计

3.3.2 品牌来源国偏好的决定因素

图 3.48 显示，在被问及“您对这些国家的奢侈品牌的偏好是基于

哪些因素？（可选三项）”时，86.2%的被调查者选择了品质优良，选择工艺传承和设计美感的被调查者分别为79.0%和76.7%。工艺传承较2014年排名靠前，说明消费者更加注重奢侈品具有的文化内涵。由此可见，在品牌来源国偏好原因上，大多数被调查者的意见是一致的。在中国消费者的眼中，奢侈品就等于卓越的品质、经典工艺的独特传承和独特的设计美感，这三大属性特征在中国消费人群中已经建立起极佳的口碑和信誉。

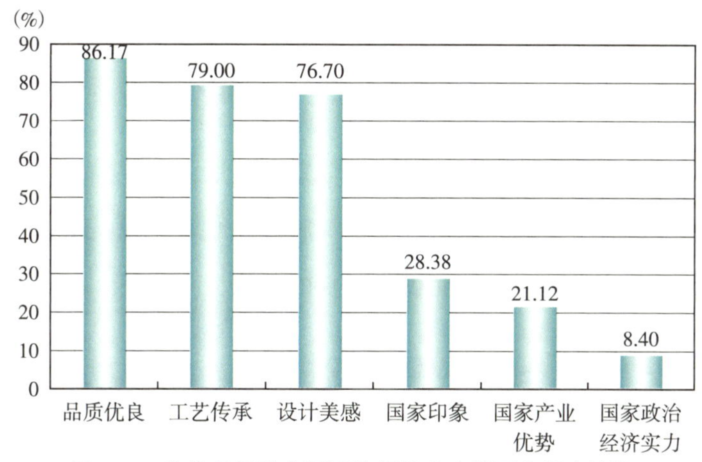

图3.48　奢侈品品牌来源国偏好的决定性因素频率统计

3.3.3 购买奢侈品的渠道

此题项为2015年度报告的新增题项。在问及消费者购买奢侈品“您一般从下列哪些渠道购买奢侈品？（可多选）”时，提供以下选项：专卖店、名品折扣店、朋友代购、国内网购、海淘、出境游购物等渠道。图3.49显示，64.48%的被调查者选择专卖店，53.78%的消费者选择出境游购物，48.88%的选择名品折扣店，剩下排名依次是朋友代购、海淘、国内网购。由此可见，消费者的首选依旧是具有信誉的专卖店，但是随着出境游的热潮涌动和国外相对国内的价格优势，很多消费者在出境游时都会选择购买奢侈品。

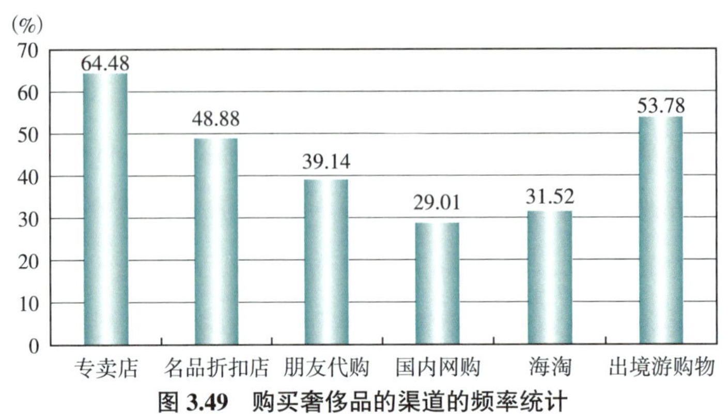

图 3.49 购买奢侈品的渠道的频率统计

3.4 中国式奢侈品消费和中国人理解的奢侈品

基于样本数据的统计分析结果，下面我们对中国式奢侈品消费和中国人理解的奢侈品两个方面做归纳和报告。

3.4.1 中国式奢侈品消费

（1）奢侈品消费行为中集体主义倾向明显。

由于受到中国传统文化影响，中国消费者的群体认同感和归属感特别强烈，使得购买行为通常以群体为单位实现，尤其是典型的高档商品如奢侈品比较明显。“偏爱经典款”、“融入圈子”、“从众效应”的题项均说明了中国人在消费奢侈品的时候非常容易受周围人和环境的影响而决定自己的购买行为。

（2）奢侈品消费行为中理性与冲动并存。

纵观世界各国奢侈品消费的涨跌起伏，奢侈品消费都有一个从非理性增长到理性回归的过程以及从炫耀性消费步入科学消费阶段。因为信息的不对称，所以奢侈品消费行为是理性与冲动并存，是复杂的。例如“关注性价预算比”、“感知划算”、“自觉自律”、“自我赠礼”、“偏爱经典和限量”的题项表现的就是消费者对奢侈品的理性选择。而且

消费者也在逐渐利用奢侈品来满足更深层次的需求，如“提升自信”的题项。因为随着收入的增加、受教育程度的提升和消费者自身素质的改变，他们越来越多地关注自己本身的需要。虽然在中国炫耀消费现象依然存在，例如“表达尊贵”、“象征成功”、“面子文化”的题项，但已有所改善。炫富已成为过去式，消费文化将以低调、有文化、有内涵为主流，此外随着人们对个性的不断追求，消费者的个性化奢侈消费在增加，奢侈品消费将会回归到购买力允许范围且其行为日趋成熟，消费行为也会逐步建立在品牌文化认同的基础上。

如图 3.48 所示，超过七成半的被调查者在选择奢侈品时会更多地考虑“品质优良”、“工艺传承”与“设计美感”因素。回顾奢侈品刚刚进入中国时，人们更多的是用价格衡量奢侈品，这是消费者尚不成熟的表现。本次调查发现，现在的中国消费者不仅关注奢侈品的价格，同时也关注奢侈品的品牌文化与设计风格，如“国家印象”、“国家产业优势”、“国家政治经济实力”。这表明中国奢侈品消费者已经开始从低涉入、低认知的幼稚阶段进入会欣赏奢侈品内涵的成熟阶段。

（3）奢侈品消费逐渐转向体验式消费。

传统的奢侈品消费以典型的炫耀性为特征，新型的奢侈品消费以消费者体验为主要依据，当简单的高品质服务已不能满足高端客户的需要时，体验消费就变得十分重要。“重视购物环境”的题项表明了打造舒适精品的空间是奢侈品品牌商取悦顾客的方法。

（4）偏爱传统渠道且尝试电子渠道。

如图 3.49 所示，消费者购买奢侈品的渠道包括专卖店、名品折扣店、朋友代购、国内网购、海淘、出境游购物等。首选是专卖店，次之是电商渠道。这可以称为是向全渠道模式的转变。全渠道零售是零售渠道从单渠道、多渠道向跨渠道发展演化的高级阶段，由于消费者在购买过程的每个阶段都面临着多种类型的渠道选择，所以以消费者为中心的全渠道零售的实施可以更好地契合新的消费行为，为消费者

带来更高的体验价值。

3.4.2 中国人理解的奢侈品

基于本年度样本数据的统计分析结果并与2014年的相应指标进行对比，发现中国人理解的奢侈品仍然保持“质优价高、保值增值和象征符号”的特征。除此之外，文献研究显示，文化是历史承载的表现和结果，故将2014年报告中的“文化深厚与历史承载”合并为“文化传承”。进一步地，调研的统计结果揭示出三个新的特征，即“限量稀缺、经典与创新并存和意见领袖认知”。

（1）质优价高。

质优价高是奢侈品的首要特征。奢侈品必须有高超的产品设计、优质的原材料和精湛的制作工艺等，以确保奢侈品稳定的高品质。八成半以上的被调查者选择品质优良作为影响其奢侈品偏好的首要因素，次之是工艺传承和设计美感因素。

（2）限量稀缺。

一半以上的被调查者认为，奢侈品是否为限量版和稀缺性是他们偏爱和决定购买的重要原因。事实上，从奢侈品厂商的角度分析，他们为了突出其产品在财富、地位和权利等方面的象征意义，往往也会严格控制奢侈品的出厂数量和面市时间，营造产品的限量稀缺氛围。显然，如果奢侈品具备卓越品质、优质原材料保证和精湛的制作工艺等特点，就自然决定了奢侈品无法被大量生产。奢侈品的这种限量稀缺性价值得到了半数以上中国消费者的认同。从这个意义上看，奢侈品的限量稀缺性才使其为少数人所拥有。

（3）文化传承。

奢侈品牌多为家族企业，服务于贵族，甚至是到皇室御用，历经几代传承，有着悠久的历史。奢侈品可以用来向世人炫耀的关键筹码是其拥有独一无二的显赫身世。奢侈品的价值不仅包含材料和工艺构成的产品本身，更重要的是它代表的品牌理念、精神诉求和人文内涵。奢侈品的消费更是对品牌文化的消费，是对这个品牌的历史、背景和文化的认同。品牌历史、创始人、品牌来源国、传承工艺成为了奢侈品的四大支撑要素。中国消费者重视品牌来源国文化以及品牌来源国对品牌赋予的特殊文化底蕴和内涵。

（4）经典与创新并存。

奢侈品是时代的产物，或者说是在一定的社会经济条件下的产物。随着时间的推移，生活必需品和奢侈品之间并没有一成不变的界限，而随着原材料的不可再生或生产数量的稀少及时间积累等各种因素，过去的必需品也可转变为奢侈品，客观地认知奢侈品是消费成熟的表现。消费者加深对设计的理解，消费观由炫耀性奢侈消费转向个性化的设计消费，凸显对奢侈品创新性的认同。六成以上的消费者偏爱奢侈品的经典款式，是因为奢侈品的经典款式设计独特，功能卓越。此外，调研结果显示中国奢侈品市场的稳定三元结构更加体现出消费者对奢侈品的选择是个性化和经典款相融合的结果。

（5）保值增值。

奢侈品不仅具有使用价值，还具有收藏价值，特别是限量或者定制的奢侈品。对于一些特殊商品如珠宝、手表等，时间的积累、原材料的短缺、工艺的失传等各种原因赋予奢侈品较之一般消费品更加具有保值、增值价值。六成以上的中国消费者在购买奢侈品时会考虑奢侈品的保值增值性。无论是购买奢侈品实物进行收藏以待升值还是利用金融投资手段进行奢侈品理财，都是投资者利用奢侈品进行投资的新渠道。

（6）象征符号。

奢侈品象征符号指奢侈品满足消费者炫耀财富、身份地位和生活方式的象征性意义。在并不成熟的消费阶段，人们热衷于奢侈品消费的一个重要原因是通过奢侈消费显示自己的经济实力和社会地位，或

通过奢侈品消费去创造、维系或拓展个人生存与事业发展的空间。中国消费者比较看重奢侈品的象征价值，是因为他们希望通过奢侈品消费寻求诸如自尊、高端、自信、成功、财富、地位、融入圈子等需要。此外消费同一符号体系的奢侈品可以获得群体内部的认同感与归属感，因此奢侈品象征性的符号价值是明显的。

（7）意见领袖认知。

中国人素有倾听同伴或者专家意见的习惯，因此“意见领袖”成为人际传播网络的重要载体。由于中国的奢侈品消费者的消费习惯和品位已经发生巨大的变化，“意见领袖”效应带动了许多新兴奢侈品牌的发展，也凸显出奢侈品作为一个群体标志的符号象征性。要融入这个群体就必须拥有这样的标志，所以在奢侈品消费中意见领袖的引导作用有着不可忽视的影响。

第 4 章　中国消费者奢侈品购买决策特征的一般性和特殊性

第 4 章是本书基于第 3 章的统计分析结果，总结提炼出中国奢侈品消费者购买决策特征的一般性和特殊性规律，发现以下 15 个因素，即宣泄情绪、自我价值、稀缺限量、自我赠礼、美好生活、卓越品质、购物情境、社交关系、为人本分、意见领袖、融入圈子、偏爱经典、品牌知名度、价格敏感度、品牌来源国是中国奢侈品消费者购买决策的一般性或同质性特征，同时我们还发现，上述 15 个因素又因消费者的人口统计特征差异而有所不同，换言之，这些因素因细分市场的不同而具有特殊性，或称之为异质性。下面将给出具体报告。

图 4.1 是中国奢侈品消费者购买倾向与其决策特征的偏相关回归分析结果，图中决策特征指标由高到低排序。图 4.2 是这些特征的均值条形图，并按照由低到高的顺序排列。

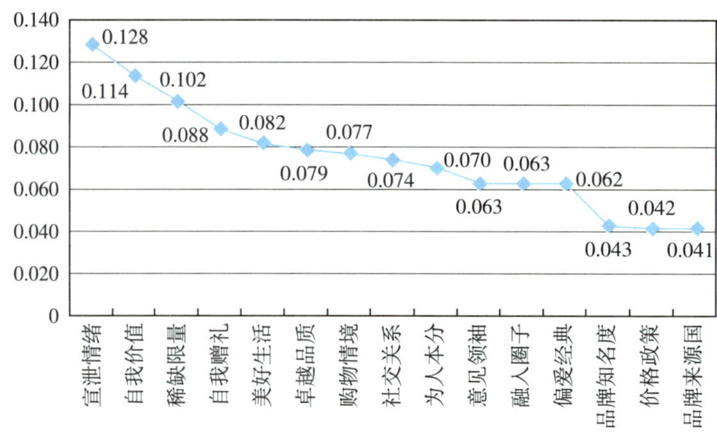

图 4.1　购买倾向与其决策特征的偏相关回归分析折线图

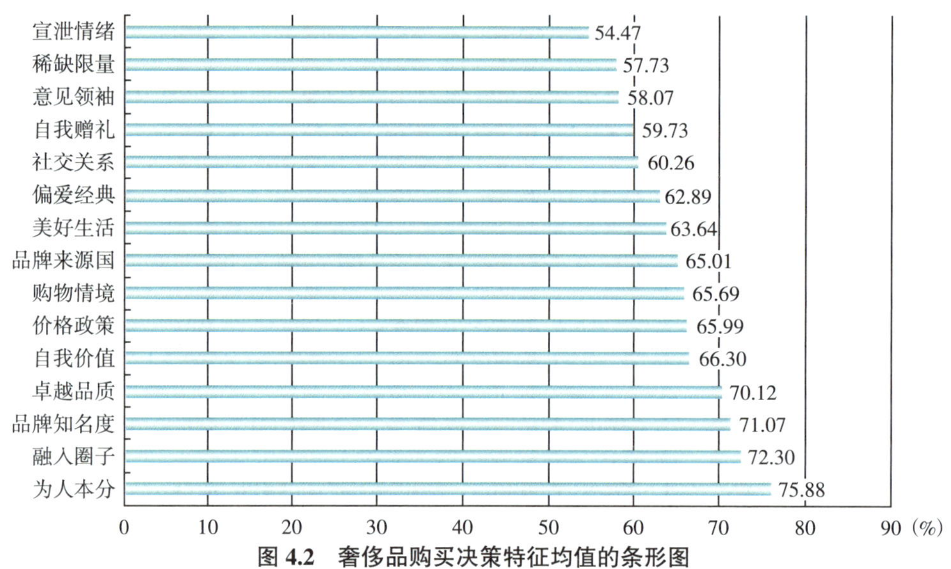

图 4.2　奢侈品购买决策特征均值的条形图

4.1　宣泄情绪

情绪是一种相对难以控制且影响行为的强烈情感，通常指某种可辨认的、特定的感觉。文献揭示，情绪影响消费者购买行为，例如，冲动性购买行为就是情绪化的行为表现，当然，奢侈品购买行为也不例外，甚至更加突出。本调查设计了“我会为了舒缓心情而购买奢侈

品”的题项来测量宣泄情绪对中国奢侈品消费者购买行为的影响程度。

图 4.3 是“宣泄情绪”的性别和年龄差异条形图。该图显示，18~55 岁的人群中，认可奢侈品购买行为有“宣泄情绪”原因的占到 41%~62%，各个年龄群组的女性比男性更情绪化。46~55 岁的人群中，该指标的性别差异最大，超过男性 14%的女性表现为更加容易情绪化。26~30 岁的人群中，该指标差异最小，仅有 3%。在奢侈品的核心目标客户群即 18~35 岁人群中，年龄越大，出现通过购买奢侈品去“宣泄情绪”的情况越频繁，而 36 岁及以上人群却呈现出相反趋势，即年龄与宣泄情绪显示出负相关关系。

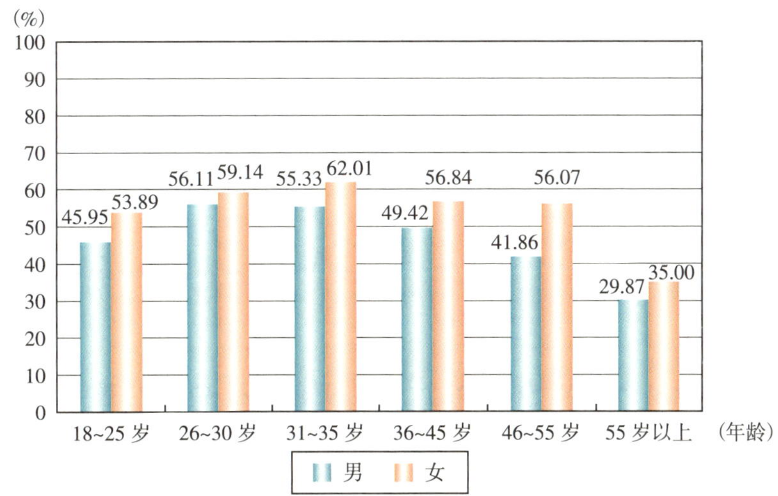

图 4.3 “宣泄情绪”的性别和年龄差异条形图

总体来看，对于各个年龄段的被调查者，女性消费者相对于男性更倾向于利用奢侈品购买来“宣泄情绪”。

考虑到职业压力与宣泄情绪的关系，图 4.4 展示了“宣泄情绪”的职业差异统计结果，外资企业白领是利用奢侈品购买行为宣泄情绪的重点人群，占比最高，达到 62.83%，比其他人群平均高出 5%~10%，其余依次为专业人员、国内企业白领、企业主家属、企业主、自由职业者和学生。外资企业白领由于工作压力大，再加上所在城市的生活

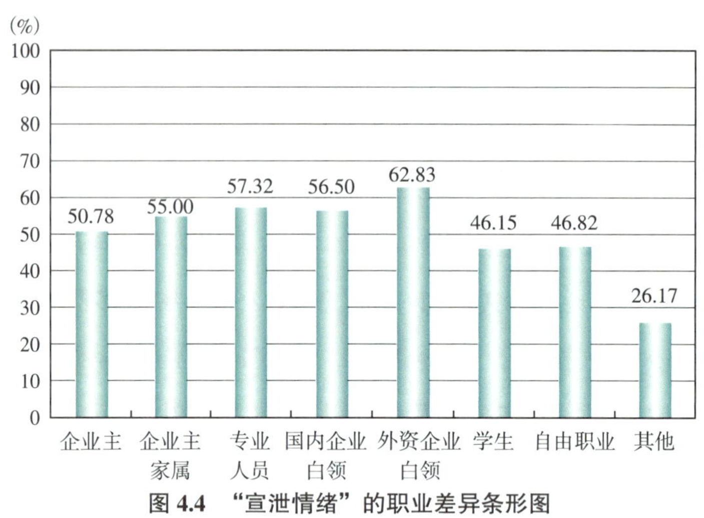

图 4.4 “宣泄情绪”的职业差异条形图

成本较高，他们会通过购买奢侈品去释放工作和生活压力，以达到舒缓心情的目的。

4.2 自我价值

自我价值是个体对自身在个人、家庭和社会中的重要性的主观认知。持久的自我价值认知是一种相对稳定的人格表现，影响个体的消费行为和购买行为。本调查采用以下 3 个题项测量“自我价值”对中国消费者购买奢侈品的影响作用。题项 1：使用奢侈品能让我显得更尊贵；题项 2：使用奢侈品能让我变得更自信；题项 3：我所购买的奢侈品应该符合我的气质。

图 4.5 是“自我价值”的性别和年龄差异条形图，显示 18~55 岁的人群中，认为购买奢侈品能够提升自我价值感的人群比例占到 51%~61%，其中，55 岁以上人群该指标男性高于女性，31~35 岁的男性消费者比女性消费者微弱偏高，其余年龄群组的女性均高出男性。在 46~55 岁的人群中，该指标的性别差异最大，该人群的女性较之男性

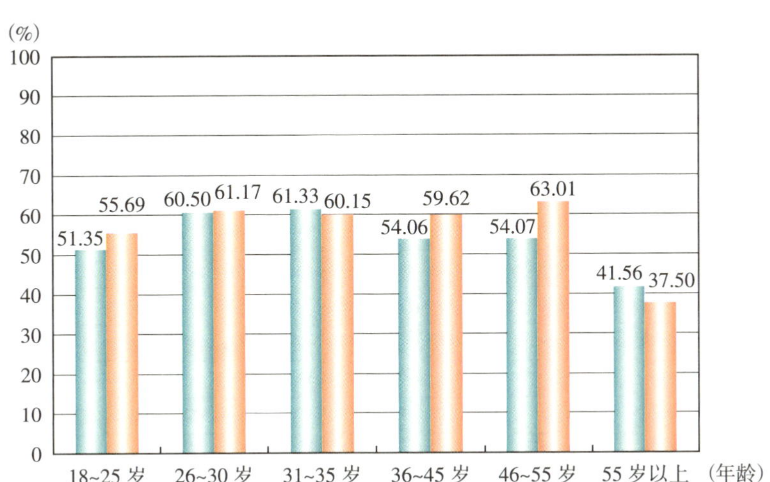

图 4.5 "自我价值"的性别和年龄差异条形图

更加看重自我价值，差异超过 9%。在 26~30 岁的人群中，该指标差异最小，几近相同。在奢侈品的核心目标客户群即 18~35 岁人群中，对于男性消费者，年龄越大，表现为越注重通过购买奢侈品来表达"自我价值"，而 36 岁及以上的男性消费人群则呈现出随着年龄增大而下降的趋势。对于各个年龄段的女性被调查者，在购买奢侈品体现"自我价值"的认知上人员占比呈现出波动性特点。

总体来看，对于各个年龄段的被调查者，除了 31~35 岁和 55 岁以上人群的男性比女性奢侈品消费者更重视"自我价值"之外，在其他年龄组中，女性消费者相对于男性普遍更倾向于利用奢侈品来表达"自我价值"。

考虑到职业差异与自我价值认知的关系，图 4.6 展示了"自我价值"的职业差异，统计结果显示，外资企业白领是通过购买奢侈品来提升自我价值感的重点人群，占比最高，达到 63.94%；国内企业白领、专业人员、企业主、企业主家属的该指标取值约为 57%~60%，差异不显著；自由职业者和学生的该指标取值较低，在 52%以下。由于白领阶层的教育背景普遍较高，思想开放，他们的奢侈品消费行为比

较侧重张扬自我和心理享乐，所以白领阶层往往通过购买奢侈品来彰显自己的高品质生活和时尚品位，展现其个人的气质、自信和尊贵。

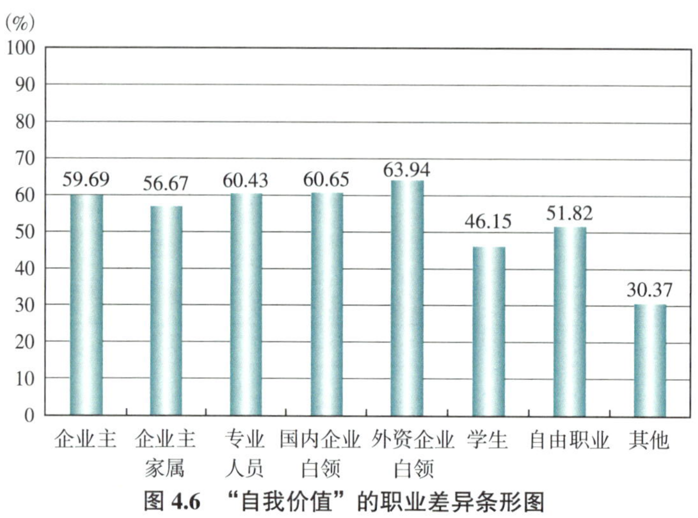

图 4.6 “自我价值”的职业差异条形图

4.3 稀缺限量

经济学的核心内容之一就是挖掘一切“稀缺资源”的溢价效应创造社会财富。本调查采用以下 2 个题项测量中国消费者奢侈品购买行为中产品“稀缺限量”特征的影响作用。题项 1：限量版的奢侈品会引起我的购买兴趣；题项 2：购买奢侈品时（古董、艺术品、珠宝、酒等）会考虑日后升值。

图 4.7 是“稀缺限量”因素的性别和年龄差异条形图。该图显示，18~55 岁的人群中，认为奢侈品购买行为有“稀缺限量”动因的占到 43%~57%，其中，只有 31~35 岁的男性消费者比女性消费者微弱偏高，其余年龄群组的女性均高出男性。在 55 岁以上人群中，该指标的性别差异最大，该人群的女性较之男性更喜欢奢侈品的稀缺性和限量版，差异近 14%。在 31~35 岁的人群中，该指标差异最小，为 1%左右。在奢侈品的核心目标客户群即 18~35 岁人群中，男性消费者呈现

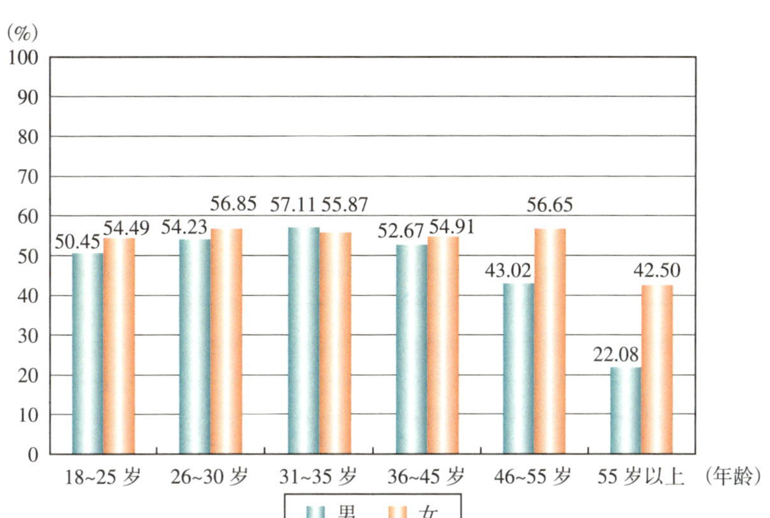

图 4.7 "稀缺限量"的性别和年龄差异条形图

出"年龄越大，越喜欢购买稀缺限量"，而 36 岁及以上人群却恰恰相反，表现为"年龄越大，对奢侈品的稀缺限量特征越不在意"。对于各个年龄段的女性被调查者，注重奢侈品"稀缺限量"属性的人员占比呈现波动性变化的特点。

总体来看，对于各个年龄段的被调查者，只有 31~35 岁的男性消费者对奢侈品"稀缺限量"属性有要求的人员占比相对女性消费者微弱偏高，而其他年龄组均表现为女性消费者比男性更加重视奢侈品的"稀缺限量"属性。

考虑到消费者购买昂贵的稀缺限量版奢侈品受制于其购买力水平，所以，本报告进一步分析不同的收入水平下人们对奢侈品的"稀缺限量"特征的追求是否存在显著差异。图 4.8 展示了"稀缺限量"的个体年收入差异的统计结果，图中的直线表示"随着消费者收入的提升，人们对奢侈品稀缺限量关注度的变化趋势"，该趋势线揭示，被调查者的收入越高，他们对奢侈品"稀缺限量"特征的关注度越高。对该指标关注度的峰值对应收入为 100 万~500 万元的人群，他们的占比最高，达到 65.88%。而年收入在 12 万元以下的人群对"稀缺限量"的

关注度最低，前者的关注度比后者高出近一倍。图 4.8 还显示，年收入高于 100 万元的被调查者对“稀缺限量”均较关注，关注度为 60% 以上。该信息揭示，中国年收入在 100 万元以上的高收入人群对奢侈品普遍有“稀缺限量”的要求。

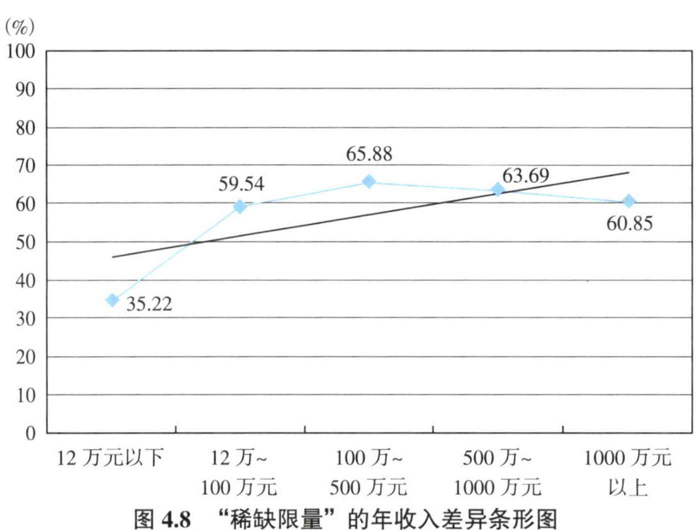

图 4.8 “稀缺限量”的年收入差异条形图

4.4 自我赠礼

购买奢侈品用于“自我赠礼”是中国消费者奢侈品购买行为的一个突出的变化趋势。越来越多的中国消费者通过购买奢侈品褒奖自己或放纵自己。买个礼物送给自己、犒劳一下自己的做法越来越普遍。为了探索发生在中国奢侈品消费者行为中的“自我赠礼”现象，本调查设计了题项“当达到目标或完成重要事情时，我会购买奢侈品来犒劳自己”。

图 4.9 是“自我赠礼”的性别和年龄差异条形图。该图显示，18~55 岁的人群中，消费者认可自己在购买奢侈品时曾经有过“自我赠礼”原因的占到 43%~66%，各个年龄群组的女性比男性更倾向于自我

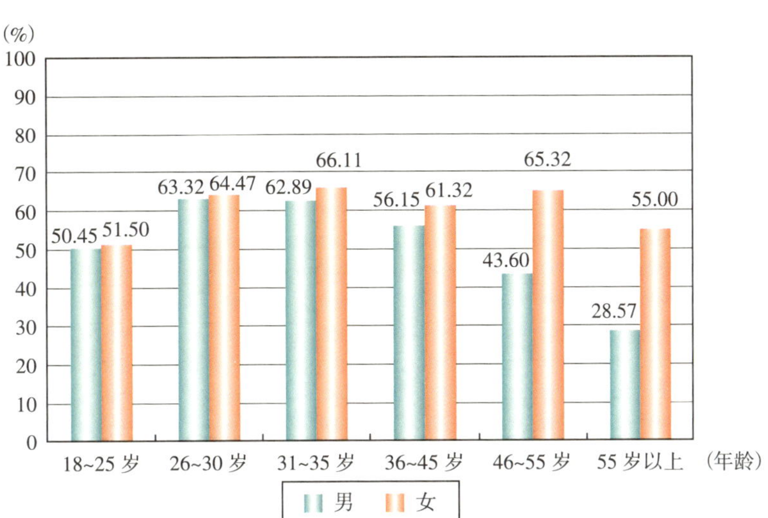

图 4.9 “自我赠礼”的性别和年龄差异条形图

赠礼。在 46~55 岁的人群中，该指标的性别差异最大，女性的得分普遍偏高，达到 22%。在 18~30 岁的人群中，该指标几乎没有差异。在奢侈品的核心目标客户群即 18~35 岁人群中，呈现出消费者年龄越大越会以自我赠礼的名义购买奢侈品，而对 36 岁及以上人群，男性消费者群呈现下降趋势，但是女性消费者群在该指标上呈现波动性变化。

总体来看，对于各个年龄段的被调查者，女性消费者比男性消费者更普遍地存在自我赠礼动机下的奢侈品购买行为。

考虑到不同职业与“自我赠礼”动机之间的关系，图 4.10 展示了“自我赠礼”的职业差异统计结果。该图显示，外资企业白领是选择奢侈品“自我赠礼”的最高人群，占比达到 66.73%，国内企业白领、专业人员、企业主、企业主家属的该指标取值约为 53%~63%，差异不显著，说明他们都喜欢为自己购买奢侈品，由此揭示出在中国的奢侈品市场上存在广泛而高层次的自我赠礼群体。文献研究表明，自我赠礼行为有价格不敏感特征，由此为奢侈品牌商带来的巨大商业价值值得关注。

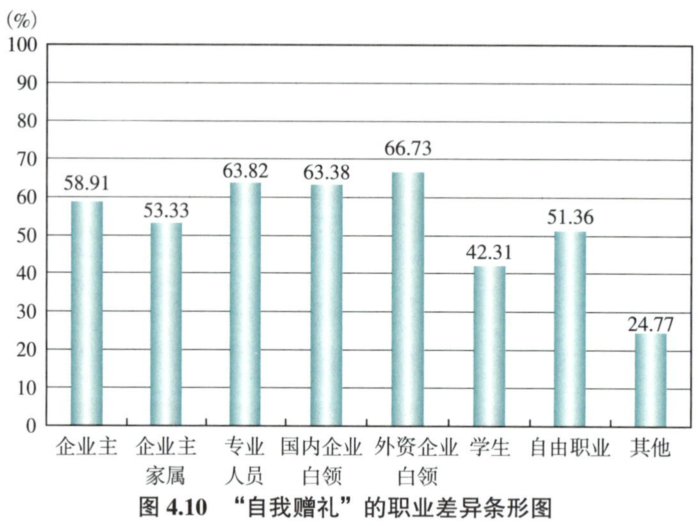

图 4.10 “自我赠礼”的职业差异条形图

4.5 美好生活

高品质生活往往通过高水平的精神和物质消费得以实现，奢侈品通过其卓越的品质、人文价值以及历史价值等能够为人们提供高品质生活。本调查设计了题项“购买奢侈品是为了提高生活品质”来测量中国消费者购买奢侈品的动机。

图 4.11 是“美好生活”的性别和年龄差异条形图。显示 18~55 岁的人群中，认可奢侈品购买行为是为了追求“美好生活”的占到 48%~68%，各个年龄群组的女性比男性更看重奢侈品带来的高品质生活。在 18~25 岁的人群中，该指标的性别差异最大，达到近 14%，说明该人群的女性较之男性更倾向于通过奢侈品消费行为达到追求“美好生活”的目的。在 31~35 岁的人群中，该指标几乎没有差异。对于奢侈品核心目标客户群即 18~35 岁人群，呈现“被调查者年龄越大，越容易通过购买奢侈品来享受美好生活”的趋势，而对 36 岁及以上人群，男性消费者群呈现下降趋势，但是女性消费者群在该指标上呈现波动性变化。

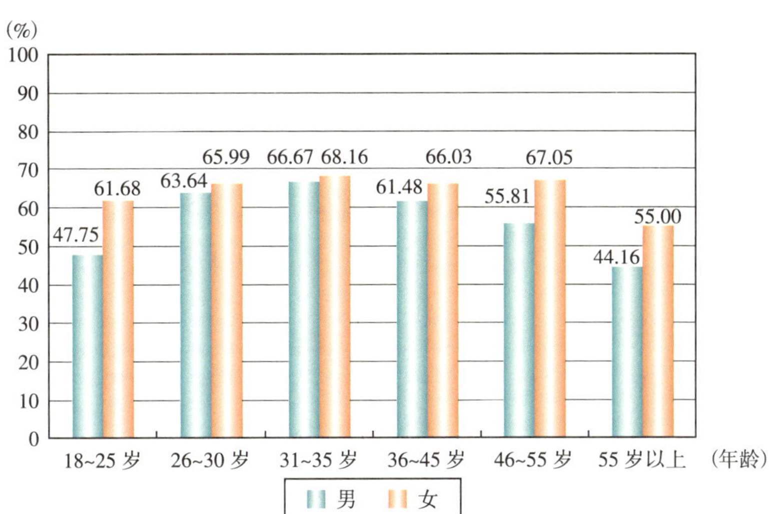

图 4.11 "美好生活"的性别和年龄差异条形图

总体来看，对于各个年龄段的被调查者，女性消费者相对于男性更倾向于通过购买奢侈品达到追求"美好生活"的目的。

考虑到职业差异与奢侈品购买动机即"美好生活"的关系，图 4.12 展示了"美好生活"的职业差异统计结果。外资企业白领最喜欢通过奢侈品享受美好生活，所占比例最高，达到 70.45%，而在专业人员、国内企业白领、企业主中，他们的奢侈品购买行为中的"美好生活"动机差异不大，占比为 60%~68%，自由职业者、学生和企业主

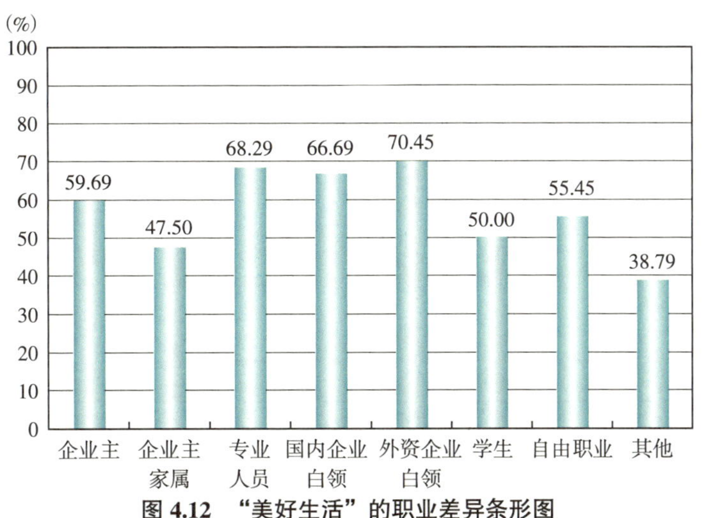

图 4.12 "美好生活"的职业差异条形图

家属对该指标的打分偏低，其中自由职业者的情况比较复杂，需要进一步的研究。但是，通过对学生和企业主家属的统计结果的进一步分析，我们认为，这正反映出他们在奢侈品购买与消费行为中的务实或物质主义倾向特征，这与此类人群的社会自主性相对薄弱有关。

4.6 卓越品质

奢侈品的卓越品质是指奢侈品的品质具有持续性、稳定性和独特性，从而使奢侈品具备完美的产品功能价值。卓越品质是奢侈品的基本属性和必要条件。本调查设计了题项“购买奢侈品是为了提高生活品质”，目的是了解中国消费者对奢侈品品质的态度。

图 4.13 是“卓越品质”的性别和年龄差异条形图。该图显示，18~55 岁的人群中，认可奢侈品必须具备“卓越品质”属性的被调查者占到 61%~74%，其中，除 31~35 岁人群的“卓越品质”性别差异不显著外，其余年龄群组的女性均比男性更苛求奢侈品的“卓越品质”

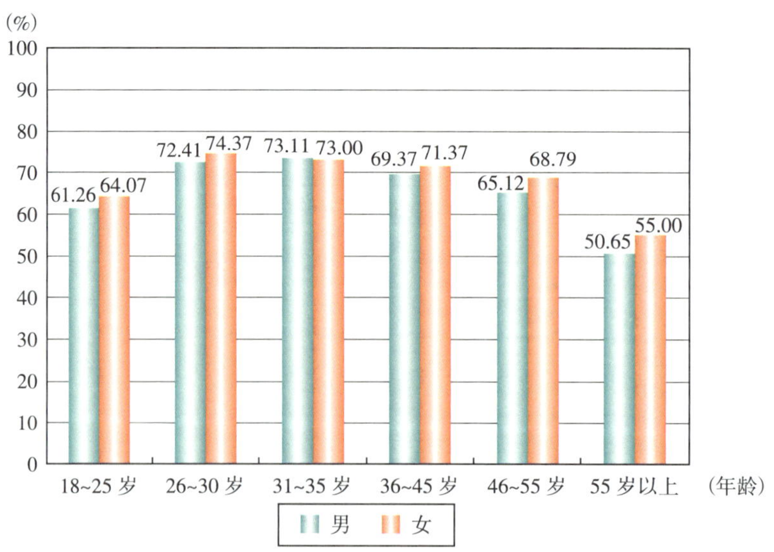

图 4.13 “卓越品质”的性别和年龄差异条形图

特征。在55岁以上人群中，该指标的性别差异最大，为4%。对于奢侈品的目标客户群即18~45岁人群，最年轻群体即18~25岁人群对奢侈品“卓越品质”的占比相对于年长组即26~45岁的人群少10%左右，年长组平均有70%左右的人群十分在意奢侈品是否具备卓越的品质。这种趋势可以延续到46~55岁年龄组。在所有被调查者中，只有55岁以上人群这个指标偏低，但是也占到该人群的50%以上。

总体来看，对于各个年龄段的被调查者，女性消费者相对于男性更苛求奢侈品的“卓越品质”，只有年龄段在31~45岁的人群，男性与女性在对奢侈品“卓越品质”的追求上基本一致。

中国消费者对奢侈品的“卓越品质”诉求是否因所居住的城市的不同而存在差异呢？图4.14显示，深圳、苏州、上海的居民对奢侈品的品质要求最苛刻，均在72%以上，成都、广州、北京的居民在66%左右。特别需要指出的是，苏州作为一个二线城市，这里的消费者对奢侈品的质量诉求与上海这样的一线大城市的消费者一样，说明苏州的奢侈品消费者成熟且理智，不会一味盲目追求奢侈品牌而忽略了对奢侈品的质量要求。

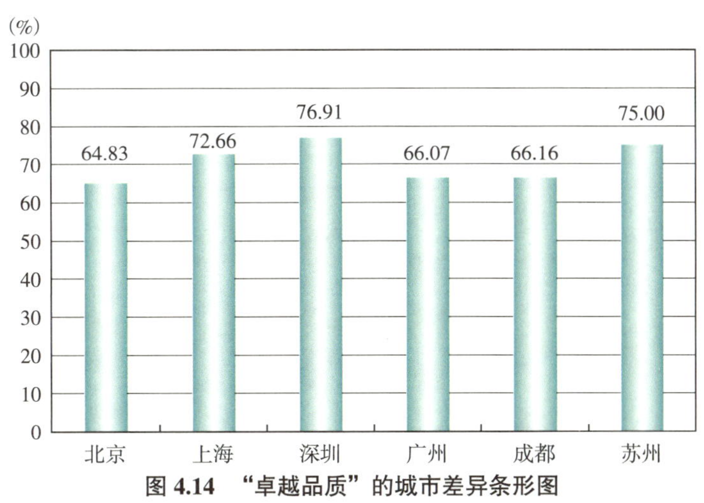

图4.14 “卓越品质”的城市差异条形图

4.7 购物情境

购物情境，是指依赖于时间和地点且与个人或刺激物属性无关，但对消费者当下的行为具有显著和系统影响的因素。消费者行为学中的“刺激—反应”理论揭示，消费者在购物环境的刺激下，随时会改变其购买决策。这类刺激主要包括卖场氛围、现场促销活动、销售导购等。在选择和购买奢侈品时消费者会偏爱自己熟悉和感觉自在惬意的购买氛围，高素质的销售导购能够直接激励消费者的购物信心，并推动或促成交易达成。本调查采用以下 2 个题项测量购物情境对消费者购买行为的影响。题项 1：我会参考奢侈品销售人员的介绍和意见；题项 2：我在意购买奢侈品时的自在程度（场所、店面与人员）。

图 4.15 是“购物情境”的性别和年龄差异条形图。该图显示，18~55 岁的人群中，认可奢侈品购买行为有“购物情境”原因的占到 52%~64%，各个年龄群组的女性比男性更看重奢侈品的购物情境。在

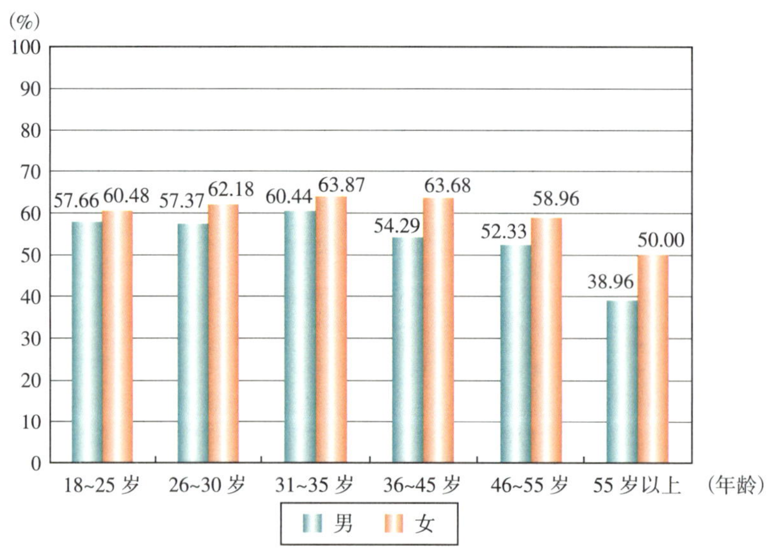

图 4.15 “购物情境”的性别和年龄差异条形图

55 岁以上人群中，该指标的性别差异最大，为 11%，女性较之男性更看重购物氛围或"购物情境"。而 18~30 岁人群中，该指标的性别差异较小，在 3%左右。在奢侈品的核心目标客户群即 18~35 岁人群中，呈现"被调查者年龄越大，越重视奢侈品的购物情境"，而在 36 岁及以上人群中，年龄与购物情境显示出负相关关系。

总体来看，对于各个年龄段的被调查者，女性消费者相对于男性更看重奢侈品的购物氛围或环境。

中国奢侈品消费者对购物情境的要求是否因消费者职业的不同而存在差异呢？如图 4.16 显示，其中 52.33%的企业主、50.00%的企业主家属、63.01%的专业人员、61.31%的国内企业白领、63.57%的外资企业白领、59.62%的学生、56.82%的自由职业者对奢侈品购物情境较为关注，其中外资企业白领最注重奢侈品购物情境，而企业主家属对购物情境的要求最低。由于"购物情境"的职业差异并非十分明显，均在 50%以上，由此得出结论，多数的中国消费者在购买奢侈品时在意"购物情境"，重视奢侈品购物体验。

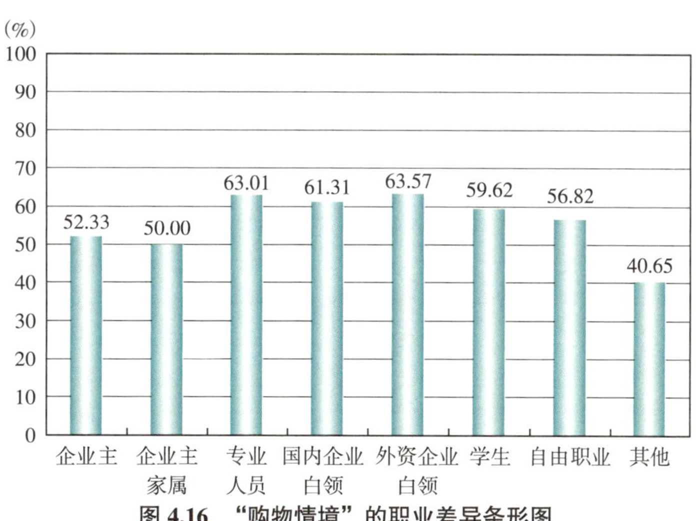

图 4.16 "购物情境"的职业差异条形图

4.8 社交关系

将奢侈品作为礼物赠送他人可以反映送礼者对受礼者的重视程度，或受礼者相对送礼者的社会关系价值。本调查设计如下题项："购买奢侈品作为礼物馈赠他人是一种必要的投资"，来测量中国消费者对奢侈品在维系个人的"社交关系"中的作用。

图 4.17 是"社交关系"的性别和年龄差异条形图。该图显示，18~55 岁的人群中，认可利用奢侈品搭建"社交关系"的被调查者的比例占到 50%~67%，其中，26~45 岁的被调查者中，男性所占比例均高于女性，而 46 岁以上女性的该指标普遍大于男性。46~55 岁的被调查者的性别差异最大，约为 9%，在该人群中，女性消费者比男性消费者更倾向于用奢侈品作为礼物去维系"社交关系"。其余人群的该指标差异均较小。对于奢侈品的核心目标客户群即 18~35 岁人群，表现为被调查者的年龄越大，越倾向于通过购买奢侈品达到维系"社交关系"的目的。

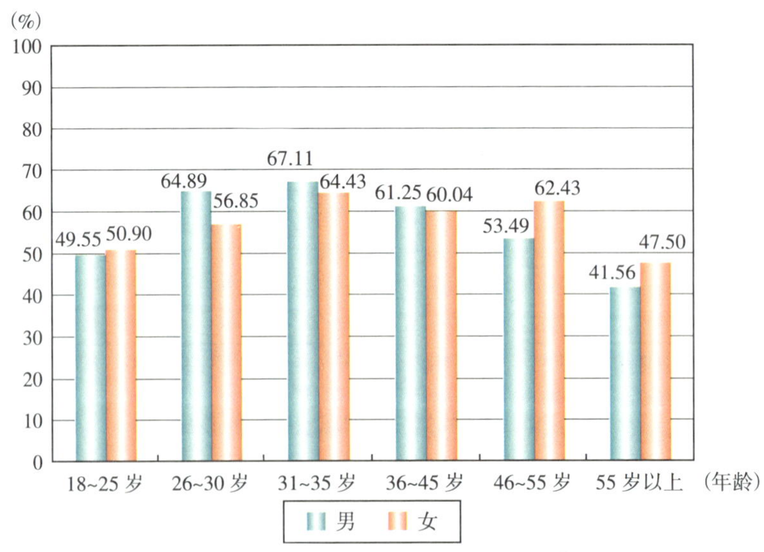

图 4.17 "社交关系"的性别和年龄差异条形图

总体来看，26~45 岁的男性消费者较之女性消费者更愿意通过奢侈品来搭建“社交关系”，而对于其他年龄群组，表现为关注“社交关系”的女性消费者的占比高于男性。

消费者的职业不同，他们对奢侈品在社交关系中的作用的认识也不尽不同。图 4.18 展示了“社交关系”的职业差异统计结果。该图显示，外资企业白领是通过奢侈品来建立“社交关系”的最高人群，占比达到 67.1%，国内企业白领、专业人员、企业主、企业主家属在该指标上的占比约为 59%~65%；学生样本对该指标的打分低于 50%，说明在校学生一般不会拿奢侈品去维系自己的社交关系。对于其他职业的被调查者，他们中有 60%左右的人对该题项表示认同。由于课题组没有对其他这个选项进一步细化，所以很难说明是哪些人偏爱采用奢侈品送礼，有待在未来的报告中做深入研究。

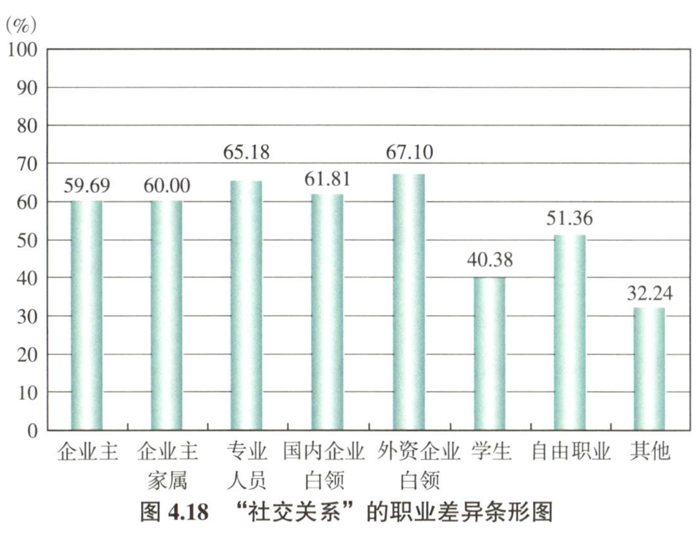

图 4.18 “社交关系”的职业差异条形图

4.9 为人本分

中国人在为人处事方面自觉遵循恪守本分的原则，为人本分是中

国传统文化价值观的重要内容。本调查从个体的言行举止和消费行为层面了解现代中国消费者对为人本分的个人观点。

图 4.19 是“为人本分”指标的性别和年龄差异条形图。该图显示，18 岁以上的人群中，认可个体行为应做到“为人本分”的人群占到 60%~80%，除了 31~35 岁的男性消费者在该项指标上略强于女性消费者外，其余年龄群组的女性均高出男性。在 55 岁以上人群中，该指标的性别差异最大，超过男性约 10%的女性消费者更恪守“为人本分”。在 31~35 岁的人群中，该指标基本不存在差异。统计结果还显示，在奢侈品的核心目标客户群即 18~35 岁人群中，呈现出年龄越大，越注意“为人本分”的趋势，而 36 岁及以上的男性消费人群则呈现出随着年龄增大而下降的趋势。而该年龄阶段的女性被调查者在“为人本分”的传统文化价值观认知上占比呈现出波动性特点。

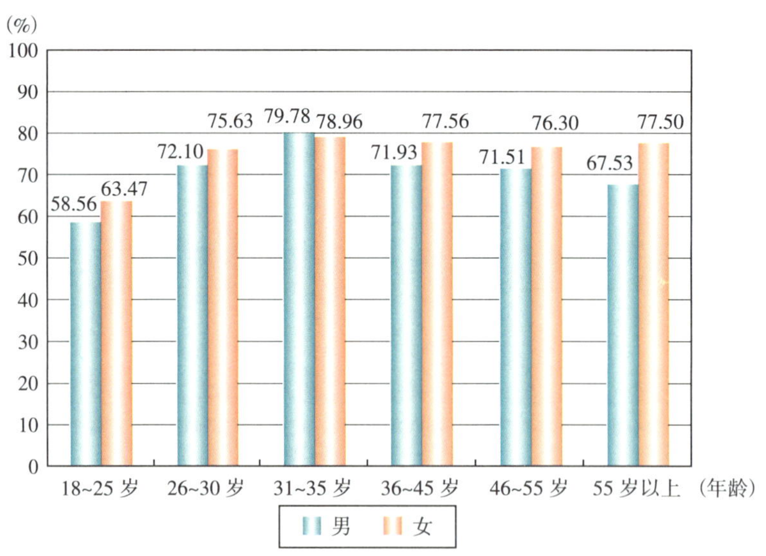

图 4.19 “为人本分”的性别和年龄差异条形图

总体来看，除了 31~35 岁的男性消费者在该项指标上略强于女性消费者外，对于各个年龄段的被调查者，女性消费者相对于男性普遍推崇“为人本分”的传统文化价值观。

本调查希望进一步了解“为人本分”价值观是否因受教育程度的不同而存在差异。图 4.20 展示了“为人本分”的受教育背景差异统计结果。该图显示，研究生以上人群对“为人本分”的关注度为 74.26%，本科及大专人群占 77.32%，高中及中专人群占 62.22%，其他占 39.45%。显然，本科以上学历人群对“为人本分”的认可度均较高，比例在 75%左右，说明中国消费者中高知阶层受到传统儒家文化价值观的影响明显，他们在“为人本分”方面高度一致。

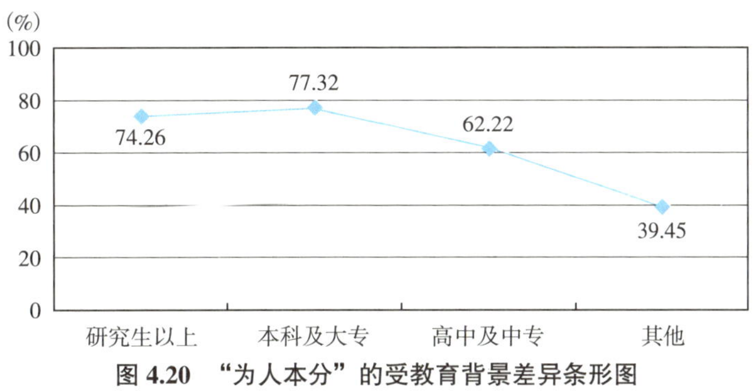

图 4.20 “为人本分”的受教育背景差异条形图

4.10 意见领袖

中国消费者较之西方消费者更在意别人对自己的评价，他们的消费行为不仅是为了满足个人需求，还有迎合他人的看法和获得团队认同的成分。这里，我们希望了解意见领袖和同伴评价对中国奢侈品消费者的影响。意见领袖是在人际传播网络中经常为他人提供信息，同时对他人施加影响的“活跃分子”，他们对大众传播起着重要的中介或过滤作用。同伴评价是陪同消费者购物时的同伴对其所要购买的商品发表的针对商品本身性能、款式、价格等多方面的意见总和。他们的评价不仅包括对商品的认知性见解，还表达了其个人的价值观、态度、信念、情绪等。本调查采用如下三个题项测量“意见领袖”对中国消

费者购买奢侈品行为的影响。题项 1：他人购买的奢侈品品牌或款式会影响我的购买选择；题项 2：购物时，我会受同行朋友的影响；题项 3：师长和前辈的话对于我来讲是重要的。

图 4.21 是“意见领袖”的性别和年龄差异条形图，显示 18~55 岁的人群中，认为在购买奢侈品时受“意见领袖”影响的被调查者占到 50%~67%，其中，26~30 岁和 36~45 岁的男性消费者在“意见领袖”指标上微弱高于女性消费者，其余年龄群组的情况恰恰相反，表现为女性更看重“意见领袖”。55 岁以上人群在该指标上的差异较大，即多于男性消费者近 17%的女性消费者在购买奢侈品时会倾听“意见领袖”。

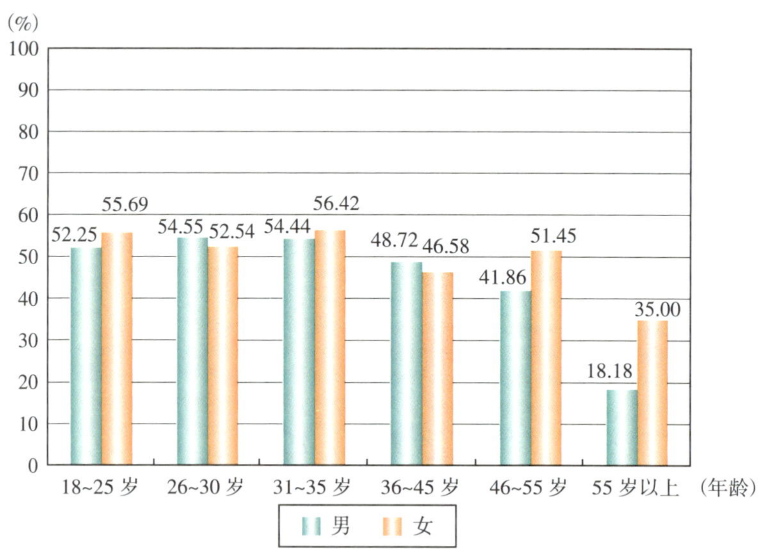

图 4.21 “意见领袖”的性别和年龄差异条形图

总体来看，对于各个年龄段的被调查者，18~25 岁、31~35 岁以及 46 岁及以上的人群表现出在购买奢侈品时女性较之男性更倾向于倾听意见领袖，而其他两组人群则表现为男性消费者较之女性在购买奢侈品时希望得到“意见领袖”的建议。

下面考查意见领袖的职业差异。图 4.22 展示了“意见领袖”的职业差异统计结果，显示外资企业白领是选择奢侈品时最认可“意见领袖”的群体，占比达到 55.95%，国内企业白领、专业人员、企业主、企业主家属的该指标取值为 51%~55%，差异不显著，说明意见领袖对大多数消费者的奢侈品购买行为具有影响作用。我们还发现，自由职业者人群对“意见领袖”的需求程度最低，这可能是因为他们自由且随意的工作性质所致，他们比对照人群更追求自由，享受自由，不太容易受到周围人和事物的影响。

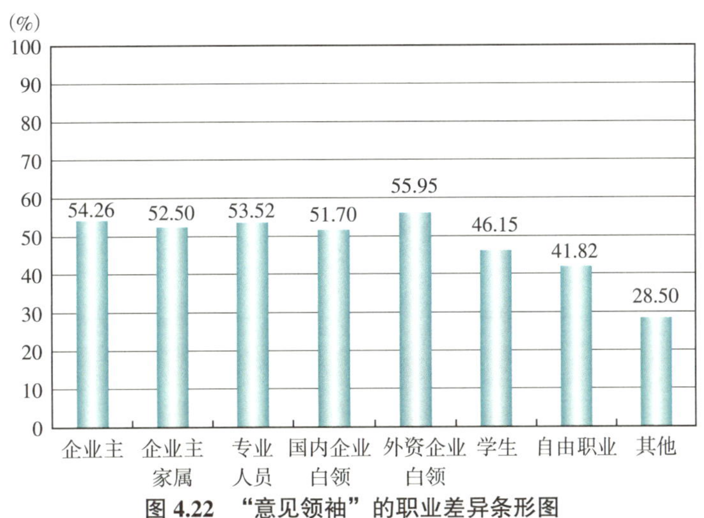

图 4.22 “意见领袖”的职业差异条形图

4.11 融入圈子

圈子是指一群具有共同爱好或共同利益的人所组成的群体。在现代社会中，圈子的形迹渗透到了各行各业，大到国家、社会，小到家庭、单位办公室，圈子无处不在。圈子不仅能够决定一个人的生存空间和范围，而且一个人的圈子影响力又是其在圈子中地位高低的关键。文献研究显示，人们希望借助奢侈品消费反映自己所处的较高的社会

圈子，并以期融入更高层级的社交圈子，从而达到自荐或者获得合作伙伴的机会。如今，圈子营销已成为社交网络的主要营销策略之一，圈子可以网罗忠实消费群体，所以圈子不仅能对企业的品牌传播发展提供有力支持，而且可以降低营销成本，发挥品牌的圈子促销能力。本调查设计了题项“适当使用奢侈品便于融入某些场合或方便沟通”来测量融入圈子对奢侈品购买者的影响程度。

图 4.23 是“融入圈子”的性别和年龄差异条形图，显示 18~55 岁的人群中，认为奢侈品购买行为有“融入圈子”原因的占 63%~78%，其中，只有 26~30 岁和 31~35 岁的男性消费者比女性消费者微弱偏高，其余年龄群组的女性该指标均高出男性。46~55 岁的人群该指标差异最大，仅为 4%。在奢侈品的核心目标客户群即 18~35 岁人群中，呈现“被调查者年龄越大，越容易通过购买奢侈品来融入圈子”的趋势，而 36 岁及以上人群呈现出下降趋势。

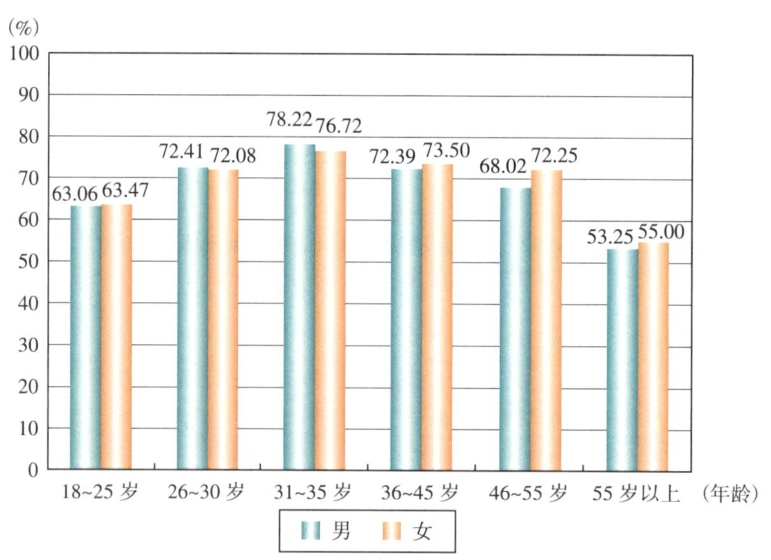

图 4.23 “融入圈子”的性别和年龄差异条形图

总体来看，对于各个年龄段的被调查者，除了 26~35 岁的男性消费者的该指标比女性微弱偏高外，女性消费者相对于男性倾向于更喜欢通过购买奢侈品来“融入圈子”。

中国奢侈品消费者对融入圈子的要求是否因消费者职业的不同而存在差异呢？图4.24展示了“融入圈子”的职业差异统计结果，显示专业人员是选择奢侈品作为“融入圈子”工具的最高人群，占比达到78.05%。专业人员和白领人士对“融入圈子”的认可度也很高，其占比占到75%以上，比企业主和企业主家属人群约高出15%。由此说明，对于在社会中充当重要角色的大多数中产阶级而言，奢侈品消费是必要且重要的，因为他们追求更美好的生活，他们希望进入更有面子的社会圈子，奢侈品消费充当了能够使得较低阶层的人们进入较高阶层“圈子”的桥梁。

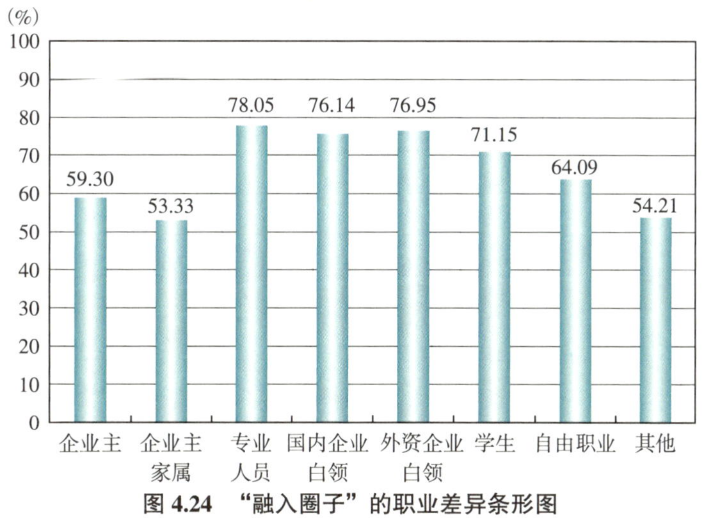

图4.24 “融入圈子”的职业差异条形图

4.12 偏爱经典

相对于奢侈品的时尚款或新潮款，经典款是奢侈品DNA的传承载体，流逝的时间带给它的是历史沉淀后经久不衰的风采和价值。经典款作为奢侈品中的标志性产品具有很高的市场可识别度，并被广泛知晓，它往往与品牌标识有异曲同工的市场效果。本调查采用题项“奢

侈品的经典款比最新款更吸引我”来测量中国消费者对经典款和最新款的偏好程度。

图 4.25 是“偏爱经典”的性别和年龄差异条形图，显示 18~55 岁的人群中，偏好奢侈品经典款式的人群比例占到 53%~67%，其中，18~30 岁的男性消费者较之女性消费者更偏好经典款，而对于其余年龄群组，女性比男性更偏好经典款。在 46~55 岁的人群中，该指标的性别差异最大，为 6%，该人群的女性较之男性更喜欢经典款的奢侈品。在 26~30 岁的人群中，男女的选择结果基本没有差异。在奢侈品的核心目标客户群即 18~35 岁人群中，呈现出“随着年龄增大，偏爱奢侈品经典款式的人群比例越高”的趋势，而 36 岁及以上人群该指标的变化则呈现出下降趋势。

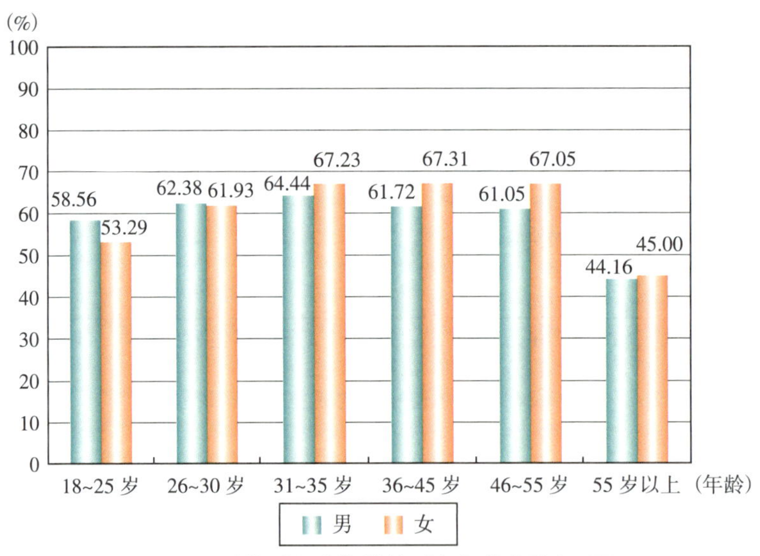

图 4.25 “偏爱经典”的性别和年龄差异条形图

总体来看，18~30 岁的男性消费者较之女性消费者更偏好经典款，而对于其他年龄群组，则表现为女性消费者相对于男性更偏爱奢侈品经典款式。

中国奢侈品消费者对经典款的偏好是否受到消费者家庭资产状况的影响呢？图 4.26 展示了“偏爱经典”的个体家庭资产差异的统计结

果。图中的直线表示“随着消费者家庭资产的增加，人们对经典奢侈品偏爱程度的变化趋势”，该趋势线揭示了被调查者的家庭资产越高，他们对经典奢侈品的关注度越高。但调查结果并没有同趋势线保持完全一致。对应不同的家庭资产，消费者对“偏爱经典”的关注度基本是呈现上升趋势，只是在 1000 万元以上出现下降，我们认为，可能是家庭财富积累更高的消费者对于奢侈品的选择空间更大，也不仅局限于大众认知的经典款，他们会青睐一些限量版的凸显个性品位的奢侈品款式。对“偏爱经典”关注度的峰值对应收入为 500 万~1000 万元的人群，他们的占比最高，达到 68.38%。而家庭资产在 100 万元以下的人群对“偏爱经典”的关注度最低，前者的关注度比后者高出约 13%。该图 4.26 还显示，家庭资产高于 100 万元的被调查者的该指标关注度均在 63%以上。该信息揭示，家庭资产在 100 万元以上的高财富值的消费人群对于经典款式的奢侈品认可度均较高。

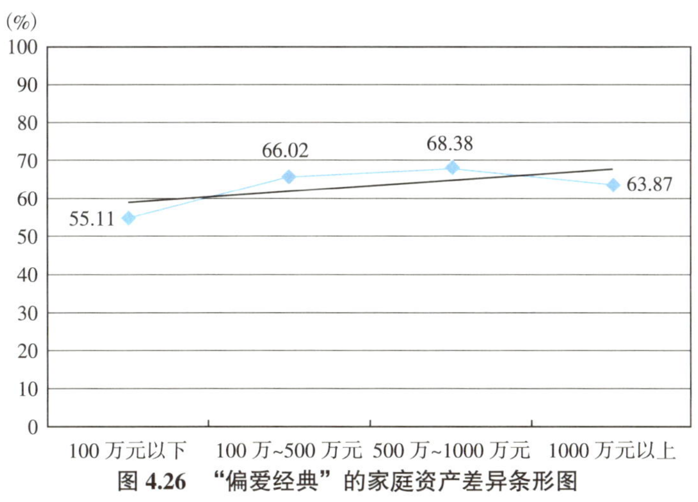

图 4.26 “偏爱经典”的家庭资产差异条形图

4.13 品牌知名度

品牌知名度是消费者认识或回想某一类产品的能力，是消费者在记忆中较强的品牌联结或印象。奢侈品品牌知名度的意义，在于通过人们公认的品牌美誉带给消费者更高的品牌价值感知和美好的品牌联想，为消费购买高溢价奢侈品提供购买理由，从而让消费者感到尊贵和荣耀。本调查采用以下 2 个题项测量品牌知名度对中国消费者奢侈品购买行为的影响作用：题项 1：我会优先选择知名度高的奢侈品品牌；题项 2：我会购买熟悉的奢侈品。

图 4.27 是"品牌知名度"的性别和年龄差异条形图，显示 18~55 岁的人群中，购买奢侈品时考虑到奢侈品的"品牌知名度"的人群比例占到 58%~73%，其中，仅有 55 岁以上的男性消费者比女性消费者偏高，其余年龄群组女性的该指标均高出男性。在 55 岁以上人群中，该指标的性别差异最大，超过女性近 5%的男性消费者更看重奢侈品的品牌知名度。在 26~30 岁的人群中，男女消费者在该指标上的差异不明显。在奢侈品的核心目标客户群即 18~35 岁的人群中，呈现出"年龄越大，越喜欢品牌知名度高的奢侈品"，而 36 岁及以上人群则呈现出下降趋势。

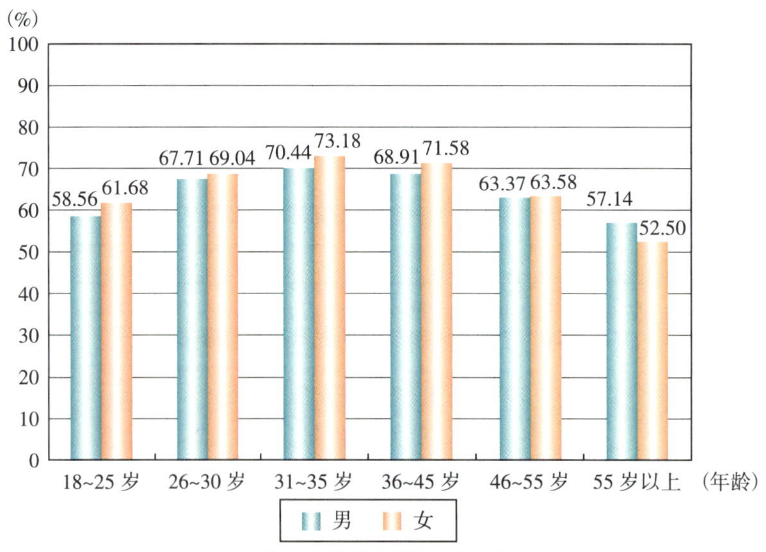

图 4.27 "品牌知名度"的性别和年龄差异条形图

总体来看，在所有被调查者中，18~55岁的女性消费者的奢侈品购买行为比男性更容易受到“品牌知名度”的影响，但是55岁以上关注“品牌知名度”的男性消费者人数占比高于女性。

中国消费者对奢侈品“品牌知名度”的认知是否因所居住的城市的不同而存在差异呢？如图4.28所示，来自深圳、苏州的消费者关注奢侈品“品牌知名度”的人员占比均在73%以上，来自广州、上海、成都的居民该指标在66%以上。在北京，有61.4%的消费者关注“品牌知名度”。

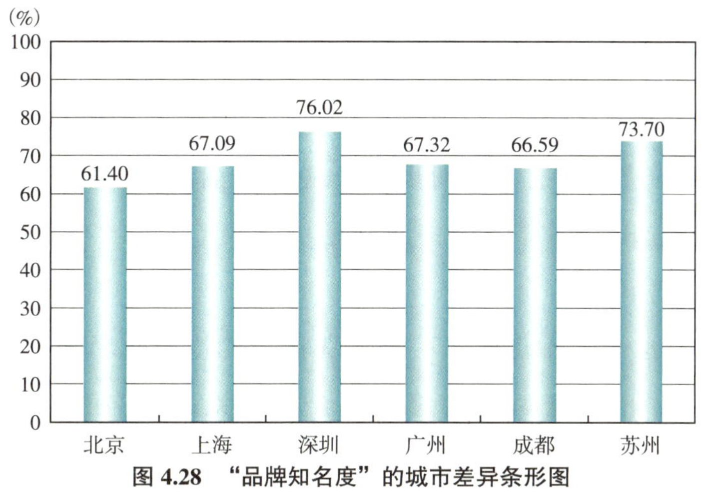

图4.28 “品牌知名度”的城市差异条形图

比较“卓越品质”的城市差异（见图4.14）和“品牌知名度”的城市差异（见图4.28），我们发现来自深圳和苏州的消费者在这两个指标上均有突出表现，这进一步反映出除了“北上广”以外的其他一线或二线城市的消费者对奢侈品的“品牌知名度”均有较为广泛的关注，也说明这类城市的消费者在品牌知识方面与“北上广”呈现趋同效应。

4.14　价格敏感度

奢侈品是高溢价产品，高昂的价格是奢侈品的重要属性特征之一，价格将奢侈品与一般商品区分开来，价格也是不同购买力水平的消费者的区隔鸿沟。但是，奢侈品牌的定位战略将品牌下不同产品进行差异定位，目的是选择更广泛的目标市场涵盖战略，从更多的市场上获利，其市场结果主要表现在价格差异上。本调查采用以下 4 个题项测量奢侈品的价格策略对中国消费者奢侈品购买行为的影响：题项 1：我购买奢侈品时会在品质、价钱和预算间做最完美的选择；题项 2：奢侈品价格的优惠信息（海外购买、免税、活动）会吸引我；题项 3：我会耐心挑选相对划算的奢侈品；题项 4：奢侈品的高价格容易让我在购买后感到不安。

图 4.29 是“价格敏感度”的性别和年龄差异条形图，显示 18~55 岁的人群中，消费者购买奢侈品时会特别关注价格的人群比例占到

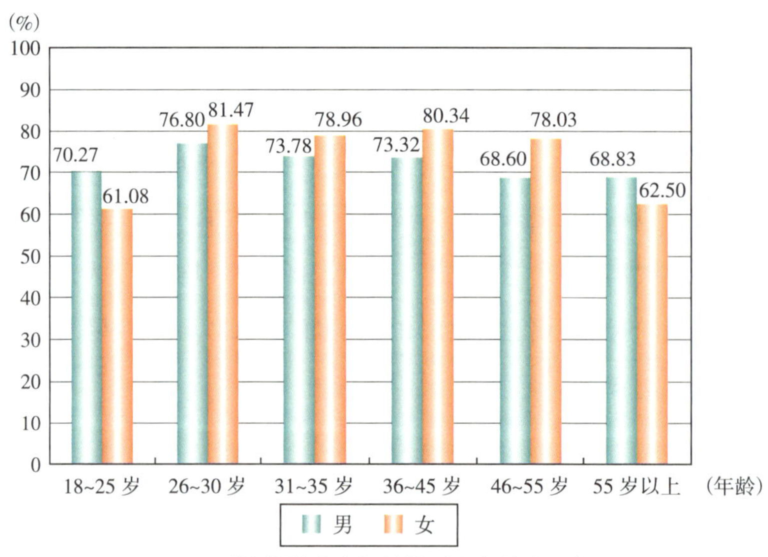

图 4.29　“价格敏感度”的性别和年龄差异条形图

61%~67%，其中，18~25 岁和 55 岁以上的男性消费者比女性消费者更关注价格，其余年龄群组的女性较之男性有更高的价格敏感度。18~25 岁和 46~55 岁的人群的该指标差异均较大，前一个人群中的男性较之女性有更高的价格敏感度，差异为 9%；后一个人群中的女性较之男性有更高的价格敏感度，差异也是 9%。26~30 岁人群的该指标差异最小，为 4%左右。

总体来看，对于各个年龄段的被调查者，最年轻的群体和年龄最大的群体，即 18~25 岁和 55 岁以上的人群中，男性较之女性有更高的价格敏感度，但是其他人群即 26~45 岁的群体则表现出女性较之男性对奢侈品有更高的价格敏感度。

中国奢侈品消费者对奢侈品的价格敏感度是否会随着消费者个人年收入的不同而变化呢？图 4.30 展示了“价格敏感度”的年收入差异的统计结果。图中的直线表示“随着个人年收入的增加，消费者的奢侈品价格敏感度的变化趋势”。该趋势线揭示，被调查者的年收入越高，他们的奢侈品价格敏感度越低。具体地，年收入为 12 万~1000 万元的被调查者均保持对奢侈品价格的高敏感度，价格敏感度较高的人群占到 70%以上。价格敏感度的峰值对应收入为 500 万~1000 万元的人群，他们的占比最高，达到 80.22%。对于年收入在 1000 万元以上的富豪人群，他们中仍然有 57.45%的消费者对价格敏感，只有 40%多的消费者不太关注价格的变化。这说明，即便是富豪人群也会关注奢侈品价格，因为公平是商品交易的基本原则，奢侈品也不例外。富豪人群有更多的机会接触同一品牌下商品的不同价格，这种区域性的价格歧视政策会影响消费者对交易的公平感知，他们自然会选择感知最公平的市场购买奢侈品，如出境游购物或海淘等。

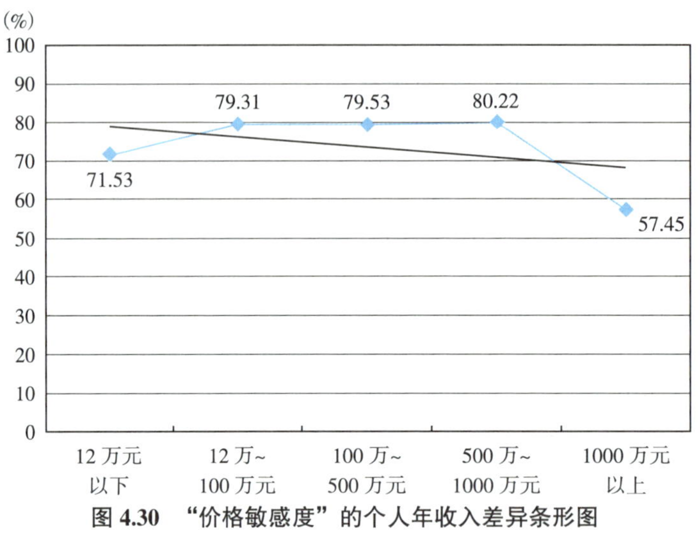

图 4.30 “价格敏感度”的个人年收入差异条形图

4.15 品牌来源国

品牌来源国是指消费者将某一产品视为该品牌所联系的国家或地区，而不论产品本身在哪里生产。当消费者对某个国家或地区的品牌很熟悉时，就会从固定品牌下的产品属性中抽象出该国家或地区的形象，从而形成对该国或地区生产的产品的总体性认知，这种长期形成的对该国的固定印象一旦形成，就会长期影响消费者购买行为。奢侈品消费者往往将奢侈品品牌来源国作为品牌价值的一部分。由于历史的原因，中国错过了若干培育高端品牌的最佳时机，导致国外奢侈品牌充斥中国高端品牌产品市场，也养成了中国消费者对奢侈品品牌来源国的依赖习惯。为了探索品牌来源国信息对中国消费者奢侈品购买行为的影响，本调查设计了题项“我在意品牌的来源国”。

图 4.31 是“品牌来源国”的性别和年龄差异条形图，显示 18~55 岁的人群中，在购买奢侈品时会在意奢侈品的“品牌来源国”的人群比例占到 52%~71%，其中，26~45 岁和 55 岁以上的男性消费者均比

女性消费者高，仅 18~25 岁和 46~55 岁这两组年龄的女性在该指标上高于男性，且 46~55 岁人群的该指标差异较大，超过 16%的女性消费者比男性消费者更看重“品牌来源国”。31~35 岁人群的该指标男女差异最小。在奢侈品的核心目标客户群即 18~35 岁人群中，奢侈品消费者的年龄越大，越关注“品牌来源国”，而 36 岁以上人群在该指标上呈现出波动性特点。

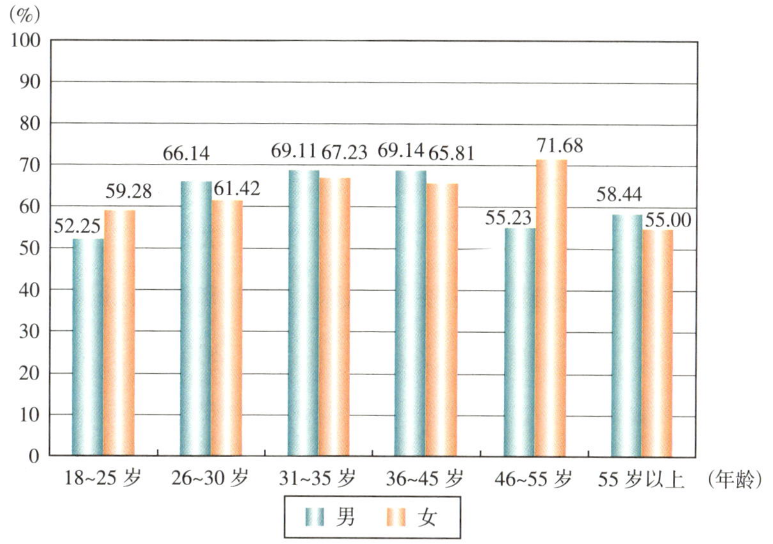

图 4.31 “品牌来源国”的性别和年龄差异条形图

总体来看，只有 18~25 岁和 46~55 岁的女性消费者关注品牌来源国的人员占比高于男性消费者，而其余年龄组的情况恰恰相反，表现为男性消费者关注品牌来源国的人员占比高于女性消费者，但是差异不大。

前文的分析结果揭示，奢侈品“品牌来源国”信息对中国消费者购买行为影响显著，下面课题组进一步分析具体的国家形象的作用。图 4.32 展示了“品牌来源国”的国别偏好差异统计结果，显示中国消费者对奢侈品牌来源国国别偏好由强至弱的排序是：意大利（67.56%）、美国（66.26%）、法国（66.05%）、瑞士（64.78%）、日本（63.50%）、德国（63.13%）、英国（61.78%）和西班牙（56.41%）。与

2014 年报告中的数据统计结果相比发生了变化，2014 年排名第一的国家是法国，第二是意大利，第三是瑞士。2015 年的结果显示美国超过法国成为新兴的奢侈品牌来源国，该现象的出现应与美国新兴的轻奢品牌的蓬勃发展有重要关联，而这也反映出中国消费者的奢侈品购买行为正在发生改变，消费者对来自欧洲的传统老牌奢侈品来源国的刻板印象正逐渐发生变化，人们除了保持对经典奢侈品的喜好以外，也在尝试来自其他发达国家如北美的轻奢品牌，这些轻奢品牌性价比高且时尚充满活力，这是中国奢侈品消费者行为走向成熟且理性的反映。此外，2015 年前三甲以外中国消费者偏好的奢侈品来源国国家由高至低的排序依次为：瑞士、日本、德国、英国和西班牙，但是，这五个国家在“国家偏好”方面差异并不明显，均在 60%左右。2014 年该指标对应的排序依次是美国、英国、德国、日本和西班牙，而这五个国家在“国家偏好”方面差异较大，均值约为 20%，但是极值差达到 21.4%，最高值为 28.5%，最低值为 7.1%。这种“国家偏好”转变的现象反映出在品牌信息越来越透明且信息越来越丰富的网络时代，品牌信息不对称的状况大大改善，奢侈品牌知识越来越容易被消费者获得，这使得各种奢侈品品牌都有了走近消费者的机会，那些较好的迎合了消费者新的生活方式的产品品牌，在多样化和个性化的新型消费

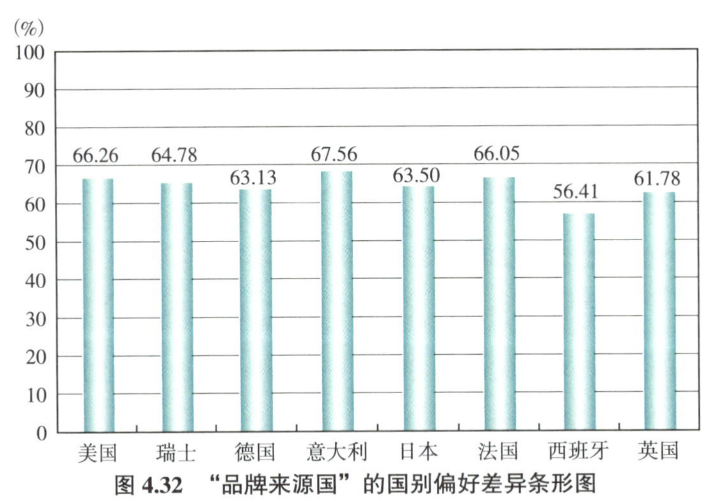

图 4.32 “品牌来源国”的国别偏好差异条形图

浪潮下获得了从未有过的市场空间，因为它们顺应了当今奢侈品消费者与时俱进的消费观念以及对产品偏好多样化和个性化需求的变化趋势。

4.16 中国消费者奢侈品购买决策特征的一般性和特殊性

综上所述，影响中国消费者奢侈品购买决策特征的 15 个因素呈现以下的规律性特点，下面分别基于人口统计变量和奢侈品品牌来源国的差异做总结，其中人口统计变量包括性别、年龄、职业、受教育程度、个人年收入、家庭资产和居住城市。

4.16.1 年龄和性别差异

（1）男性消费者的奢侈品购买决策特征规律性特点的年龄差异。

对于奢侈品核心目标客户群即 18~35 岁的被调查者，在多个因素方面呈现如下规律，即随着年龄的递增，关注人群的规模也在递增，涉及的影响因素有 13 个，分别为宣泄情绪、自我价值、稀缺限量、自我赠礼、美好生活、卓越品质、购物情境、社交关系、为人本分、融入圈子、偏爱经典、品牌知名度和品牌来源国，只有意见领袖和价格敏感度不在此列。

对于奢侈品的高年龄目标客户群即 36~45 岁的被调查者，在除去品牌来源国以外的上述 12 个因素中的变化趋势相反。这种趋势还延伸至 46 岁以上的非目标客户人群。

（2）女性消费者的奢侈品购买决策特征规律性特点的年龄差异。

对于奢侈品核心目标客户群即 18~35 岁的被调查者，在 10 个因素上呈现如下规律，即随着年龄的递增，关注人群的规模也在递增，这

10 个因素是宣泄情绪、自我赠礼、美好生活、购物情境、社交关系、为人本分、融入圈子、偏爱经典、品牌知名度和品牌来源国。

对于奢侈品的高年龄目标客户群即年龄在 36 岁以上的被调查者，在 6 个因素（宣泄情绪、卓越品质、购物情境、融入圈子、偏爱经典、品牌知名度）方面的变化趋势相反，而对除此以外的其他 9 个因素的变化趋势是波动的。

通过对女性消费者的奢侈品购买决策行为影响因素的规律性特点进行分析，可见女性目标客户群在不同年龄阶段的 15 个奢侈品购买动因的群体规模效应与男性有显著不同。此外，上述分析也反映出本次调研的样本在年龄指标上不仅具有代表性，而且 15 个奢侈品购买动因恰当地反映出中国奢侈品消费主力军的购买行为特征。

（3）消费者的奢侈品购买决策特征规律性特点的性别差异。

对于奢侈品核心目标客户群即 18~35 岁的被调查者，随着年龄的增长，消费者购买行为影响因素在群体规模效应方面的性别差异特征有以下三个突出的变化。其一，更多的女性消费者相对于男性消费者需要“自我赠礼”。其二，随着年龄的递增，男性和女性在稀缺限量、美好生活、卓越品质、为人本分、意见领袖和品牌来源国等奢侈品购买动因上的群体规模差异总体呈现减弱的趋势。其三，宣泄情绪、自我价值、融入圈子、偏爱经典、品牌知名度、价格敏感度、购物情境、社交关系等奢侈品购买动因上的男女群体规模差异呈现波动性变化趋势。这种趋势还延伸至 46 岁以上的非目标客户人群。

对于 15 个奢侈品购买动因中的大部分影响因素，较之男性消费者，更多的女性奢侈品消费者在购买奢侈品时会受到这些因素的影响。但是，社交关系和品牌来源国被更多的男性消费者关注。自 2014 年以来，在奢侈品全球市场中男性消费者的购买行为呈现走弱的态势，本调研对此给出了来自该人群购买行为动因的解释。事实上，在中国社会里，男性非常看重自己的社会角色，表现为在社交关系中个体被认可的程度，奢侈品自然地充当着角色符号的作用。但是，随着中国政治和经济环境的变化，以往符号的显性特征需要被“内隐化或内涵化”，这为奢侈品企业制定品牌发展战略提出了新的课题。此外，“品牌来源国”是奢侈品品牌身份的特征，在中国，男性较之女性更在意这种品牌血统，这与一些国际奢侈品牌商出于降低成本的原因，盲目在非品牌来源国不断扩大生产规模的做法形成对立，这或许是男性消费者减少奢侈品购买的另一个内隐。

4.16.2 消费者的奢侈品购买决策特征规律性特点的职业差异

消费者的职业背景影响其奢侈品购买决策行为。我们考察了如下8个奢侈品购买决策动因，即购物情境、美好生活、融入圈子、社交关系、宣泄情绪、意见领袖、自我价值和自我赠礼。我们发现，企业白领的奢侈品购买决策特征受到这8个因素的影响最普遍，特别是外企白领。该结果说明了白领阶层的奢侈品消费动机是复杂的、多元化的。由于他们的工作压力大，所在发达城市的生活成本高，同时他们的学历层次高且思想开放，导致他们需要通过购买奢侈品来满足自己享受生活和表现自我的价值诉求。此外，企业白领和专业人员等一般隶属中产阶级，他们重视奢侈品的符号价值，表现为渴望利用奢侈品来“融入圈子”、维系“社交关系”、享受“美好生活”。作为社会精英的企业主，他们在购买奢侈品时对“购物情境”的关注较低，也较少会通过奢侈品购买来“宣泄情绪”。这种现象或与企业主们丰富且高端的业余生活经历有关，或与他们有更多的机会去宣泄情绪有关。自由职业者人群对“融入圈子”的认可度很高，但对“意见领袖”的关注度较低。这可能是因为他们自由且随意的工作性质所致，他们需要融入更高层次的社会圈子来扩展人脉，但是长期自由化的环境，使得他们不易也不愿受到周围人和事物的影响。学生群体和企业主家属的购

买决策特征也不是十分突出，这可能与他们的社会自主性相对薄弱、务实性较强有关。

4.16.3 消费者的奢侈品购买决策特征规律性特点的个人年收入和家庭资产差异

奢侈品购买动机“稀缺限量”、“价格敏感度”、“偏爱经典”因消费者个人年收入和家庭资产变化的统计结果显示，收入在 100 万元以上的人群，他们普遍重视奢侈品的稀缺限量特征，而年收入在 12 万元以下的人群对“稀缺限量”的关注度最低。所有收入段的被调查者普遍对奢侈品有较高的价格敏感度，即便是年收入超过 1000 万元的富豪人群，他们中仍然有近六成的消费者对价格敏感。因为公平是商品交易的基本原则，奢侈品也不例外。奢侈品的区域性价格歧视现象自然会冲击消费者的公平交易原则，他们自然会选择感知最公平的市场购买奢侈品，如出境游购物或海淘等。无论是哪个收入段的被调查者，“偏爱经典”是共性，这也是奢侈品牌得以延续辉煌的基础。

4.16.4 消费者的奢侈品购买决策特征规律性特点的城市差异

不同城市的消费者对奢侈品“卓越品质”和“品牌知名度”的关注情况：苏州、深圳和成都等城市的消费者表现出对这两个因素的关注度高出“北上广”城市人群的现象，说明中国消费者的奢侈品消费观念普遍更加理性且成熟，且更加在意奢侈品的卓越品质和品牌价值。需要特别提示的是，这种现象已不仅仅存在于“北上广”这样的一线城市。

4.16.5 消费者的奢侈品购买决策特征规律性特点的学历差异

本调研揭示，在中国，高知阶层多“为人本分”，为人本分隶属传统儒家文化价值观体系，这种价值观不仅是中国高知人群的日常行为准则，也指导着该人群的奢侈品消费行为。因此“为人本分”是具有中国特色的奢侈品购买行为的深层次解析。

4.16.6 消费者的奢侈品购买决策特征规律性特点的品牌来源国差异

2015 年，美国首次超过法国成为继意大利之后位居第二的中国消费者偏爱的奢侈品牌来源国，这表明中国消费者不仅偏爱传统老牌奢侈品来源国，同时也欣然接受来自北美的轻奢品牌，这也是中国奢侈品消费者行为走向成熟且理性的标志。

第 5 章　中国奢侈品消费者族群分析

本章我们从中国传统文化价值观对现代中国奢侈品消费者影响的角度切入，探究在中国奢侈品消费的背后，传统价值观对中国奢侈品消费者行为潜移默化的影响，借由价值观来划分消费族群，从而找出中国奢侈品消费者的消费行为特征。

5.1　中国传统文化价值观影响

本调研数据分析结果显示，类似 2014 年，2015 年仍然反映出中国消费者的奢侈品消费动机十分矛盾的特点，表现为他们游离于压抑个性的群体主义和彰显个性的个人主义这两个极端之间，他们兼具浮夸炫富的虚荣外凸显动机和简朴低调的实用功能需求动机，他们并没有极端地偏向任何一端，只是在不同的时间、场合以及不同需求背景下暂时性地表现出某种倾向，从而反映出中国人奢侈品消费行为的多面性、游离性和复杂性特点。这些给深刻认识中国人的奢侈品消费行为带来了很大的困难。

文献研究发现，由于文化价值观兼具时间稳定性和行为导向型特征，对消费者文化价值观的深刻理解，将有助于我们认识中国消费者

消费行为规律性。现代中国人文化价值观体系中有着深刻的传统文化价值观烙印，中国传统文化价值观主要源于儒家、道家和佛家三大文化，其中以儒学为支柱，中国宗教儒释道相浸染，其文化底蕴一以贯之就是“和”。

儒家以仁为本，主张顺应社会，遵循伦理纲常、阶级分际、名分相符、亲疏贵贱、尊卑长幼、重视行为规范和等级秩序。儒家倡导中庸之道，低调内敛、勤俭朴实、温良恭俭让。其核心价值观被概括为“三纲五常”，即所谓“君为臣纲、夫为妇纲”与“仁、义、礼、智、信”。儒学称“礼之用，和为贵，先王之道斯为美”。人人以礼相待，家家以礼相待，社会以礼相待，国国以礼相待，人心则可欣然懿美，家庭则可怡然和睦，社会则可井然有序，世界则可安然和谐。

道家以道为本，主张顺应自然、回归自然；自然无为与自然和谐相处，倡导无欲、无知、无为、“返璞归真”；信奉无为而治，即不要违背自然规律，万事亦无须强求。“道”与“德”紧密相连，“以道相通”，就要“以德相求”：要以德为本、以德为行，抑恶扬善、上善若水，孝敬父母、敬老恤孤，施药治病、怜贫悯疾，助人为乐、助学兴教，谦虚谨慎、慈俭济人，热爱自然、保护环境，劳动自养、自食其力，淡泊名利、和光同尘。“和谐世界，以礼相待”。

佛家以无常为本，主张顺应因缘；“惜缘、随缘和因果循环”，佛家认为，人活着就会结缘，应该珍惜缘分和眼前的人和事物，一切因缘生，一切因缘灭。佛家认为只有内心平和与安定，才有外在的和谐与安宁。内有不和不平的心因，外有不平不和的事缘，相互影响，推波助澜。因而力求“身和同住、口和无诤、意和同悦、戒和同修、见和同解、利和同均”，倡导“心灵环保”。这种“心净则国土净，心安则众生安，心平则天下平”的“内心”与“天下”的关联，来自佛家的“缘起论”。

儒家、道家、佛家虽各有侧重，但是历经不断的演化发展，相济

相补，各取所长，逐渐融合，构成了彼此共存共荣、求同存异的文化格局，长期以来，这种相吸又相斥的形态支配影响着中华民族的精神生活。儒讲存心养性，道讲修心炼性，佛讲明心见性，素有如下说法："儒家治世，道家治身，佛家治心"即"儒家入世、道家隐世、佛家出世"。

本书为了深入探索认识中国传统文化价值观对中国消费者行为的影响，在2014年的调研问卷的基础上又补充了用于度量中国传统价值观的新的题项。数据分析结果如表5.1所示。在3347名被调查者中，共有3238人（总占比96.74%）明显表现出受到中国传统文化观念的影响。进一步地，本书以儒教三种传统价值观作为基础变量，采用聚类分析法将人群聚类，最后获得4个不同的传统文化导向型人群，即儒道导向型、儒释导向型、释道导向型和非传统导向型。

表5.1 基于传统文化价值观的族群构成

	第1类	第2类	第3类	第4类
佛家文化	3.56	4.42	4.26	1.82
儒家文化	4.16	4.12	2.84	1.81
道家文化	4.18	3.08	4.34	1.84
人数（人）	2166	632	440	109
类占比（%）	64.71	18.88	13.15	3.26

5.2 中国传统文化价值观导向的奢侈品消费人群的分类及特征

第1类：儒道导向型。此类人群的规模为2166人，总占比为64.71%，是第一大族群。在第1类人群中，儒家文化价值观导向和道家文化价值观导向的得分均大于4，故将其命名为"儒道导向型人群"。由于儒家文化和道家文化起源于中国，在中国社会中长期保持其

独尊地位，具有包容性、内化性和开放性等特点，对中国消费者行为的影响根深蒂固，本调研结果进一步印证了儒道文化影响的普遍性。消费者通过奢侈品牌消费去彰显个人的社会地位，或通过炫耀式消费去创造和维系有利于个人发展的社会关系网络，其背后的价值观动因是儒家的等级观念（如“行为与地位一致”）和道家的享乐观念（如“追求生活品质”和“崇尚自然”）。关于儒家文化导向，“消费的社会意义”是借助个体消费行为表达和传递某种特定的信息，如消费者的地位、身份、个性、品位、情趣和认同，问卷中的测量题项有：象征成功、面子文化，行为与角色匹配等。关于道家文化导向，“消费的心理满足”是借助个体的消费行为获得“心情、美感、氛围、气派和情调”的心理感受，问卷中的测量题项有：重视购物环境、价高质优和舒缓心情等。所以，儒道文化对中国人群奢侈品消费观的导向作用具有潜移默化的影响（见图 5.1）。

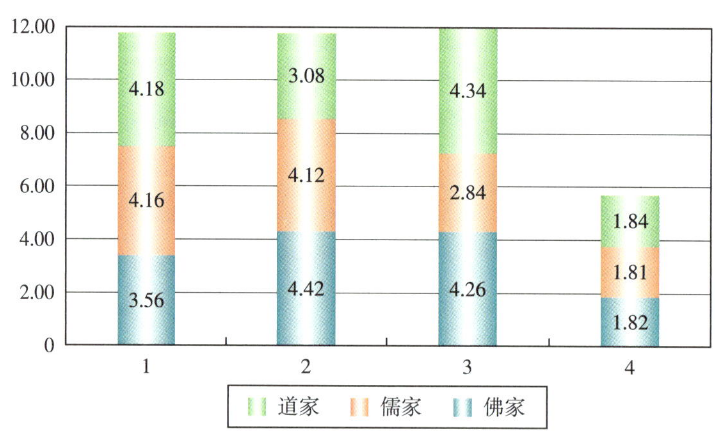

图 5.1　三种价值观在四类族群中的比例分布

第 2 类：儒释导向型。此类人群的规模为 632 人，总占比为 18.88%，是第二大族群。在第 2 类人群中，儒家文化价值观导向和佛家文化价值观导向的得分均大于 4，且后者的得分偏高，故将其命名为“儒释导向型”人群。佛家文化价值观强调命运和缘分，在问卷中的测量题项有：相信缘分。显然，第 2 类人群表现出了中国消费者个

体价值观的多面性特征，即在社会生活中以儒家文化为行为准则，而在个体精神层面则以佛家文化价值观为行为准则。个体消费行为兼具追求奢侈品消费的社会性和功能性产品的实用性。

第 3 类：释道导向型。此类人群的规模为 440 人，总占比为 13.15%，是第三大族群。在第 3 类人群中，佛家文化价值观导向和道家文化价值观导向的得分均大于 4，且后者的得分偏高，故命名为"释道导向型"人群。同第 2 类人群相似，第 3 类人群同样表现出了中国消费者个体价值观的多面性特征，即在个体生活中以道家文化为行为准则，而在个体精神层面则以佛家文化价值观为行为准则。个体消费行为兼具追求奢侈品消费的自我享乐性和功能性产品的实用性。

第 4 类：非传统导向型。此类人群的规模为 109 人，总占比为 3.26%，是第四大族群。这类人群为数较少，但是也具有相当的代表性，他们是新新人类一族，受到西方文化价值观的影响，传统文化价值观在这类人群中有淡化的趋势，但有必要针对这类人群展开更深入的研究。

通过前文的分析可以看出，中国奢侈品消费者行为有文化价值观导向下的潜在市场积聚特征。消费者行为学理论指出，消费者购买行为的最深层且根源性影响因素来自文化价值观的驱动，我们的研究初步进行了中国奢侈品消费者的文化价值观市场细分，显然，对各个细分市场消费行为的进一步研究将是非常重要的。

第6章　业内看新常态下的奢侈品市场发展

在2015北京洪堡论坛和对外经济贸易大学奢侈品研究中心的支持下，课题组就目前奢侈品领域出现的新态势、新特点和新问题与一些奢侈品领域的专家和学者进行了深入探讨。为此，我们进行了用于定性研究的焦点小组访谈和深度访谈。焦点小组访谈的主题是“展望新常态下的奢侈品市场发展”；深度访谈的主题是“奢侈品行业与互联网科技的关系”。两个访谈内容涵盖了奢侈品不同产品领域发展情况、奢侈品市场整体发展情况以及科技在奢侈品行业中的运用状况。访谈结果为本调研报告提供了来自业内职业经理人和专家学者们独特视角下的真知灼见，下面是围绕该主题的定性研究报告。

6.1　焦点小组访谈

6.1.1　焦点小组访谈设计

按照市场调研方法中关于焦点小组访谈法的要求，我们组织了本次焦点小组。焦点小组成员都是来自奢侈品行业、学界的专家或奢侈品方向的研究员，对奢侈品发展状况有深刻的认识和理解。课题组邀

请了一位奢侈品学术研究领域的资深专家作为主持人。小组持续讨论 1.5 小时。焦点小组组成情况如表 6.1 所示。

表 6.1 焦点小组组成

男	首饰珠宝行业职业经理人 A
	马球运动公司专业经理人 B
女	时尚媒体商务总监 C
	奢侈品管理学博士 D
	奢侈品方向研究员 E、F

焦点小组访谈为本课题研究带来了崭新且丰富的一手资料，揭示了当前“新常态”下奢侈品市场发展状况，各位专家学者探讨了当前奢侈品行业面临的诸多问题，提出了解决方案建议，并对未来奢侈品市场发展态势做出了预测。

6.1.2 焦点小组访谈内容

焦点小组访谈由对外经贸大学奢侈品研究中心的专家主持，6 位嘉宾围绕“新常态下的奢侈品市场发展”的主题聚焦 7 个问题掀起头脑风暴，贡献出他们的真知灼见，下面是访谈报告。

问题 1：有这样的观点，“对于奢侈品牌来说，中国似乎再也不是那个可以让他们春风得意的市场”，请问您如何看待目前新常态下中国奢侈品牌的问题？

A：从珠宝行业来说，尽管现阶段珠宝销售额有所下降，但这却是一个好现象。因为税额和利润在同时增加，开单量也大大增加。老百姓珠宝购买量的增加预示着珠宝行业的前景将越来越好。

B：从马产业来说，中国马产业起步较晚，1996 年全国仅有 5 家马术俱乐部，经过将近 20 年的发展，如今全国已有 600 多家马术俱乐部，北京地区也有 120 多家。目前市场对于马的需求越来越多，马运动分工也越来越细，马的价值越来越体现出来，每年我国马的进口量以及有关马运动的参与人群量都在不断增长，市场前景良好。

C：过去十年奢侈品牌在中国走过了一段非常好的历程，虽然现在处于调整阶段，奢侈品商要面临各种新的挑战，但鉴于中国巨大的人口红利，中国仍然是最重要的奢侈品市场之一。

D：中国奢侈品市场之前很容易赚钱，增长速度很快，如今调整一下，经过几年休整期之后会发展得更好。从历史来看，21 世纪初全球奢侈品市场处于发展低迷期，经过几年的调整，到 2005 年市场已实现了 8%甚至两位数的高增长。因此调整是一件好事，未来奢侈品市场的发展将更为积极。

E：目前全球经济都进入了一个调整状态，奢侈品也不例外。在调整阶段出现销量下降、新开门店数下降等情况是正常的。只要积极调整，正面应对挑战，春风自会带动市场新气象。

F：随着经济的快速发展，中国的人均收入水平不断上升，有能力和有意愿购买奢侈品的人群正在逐步扩大。虽然目前中国的奢侈品市场由于受市场环境、品牌定价等因素影响而出现了暂时性的沉寂，但是中国消费人群以及消费特点的变化足以证明中国市场仍然具有巨大潜力，经过合理的调整，中国奢侈品市场仍将春风得意。

小结：2014 年中国内地奢侈品市场首次出现下滑，市场普遍对此表示担忧，认为奢侈品已进入寒冬。曾经高高在上的奢侈品牌开始降价、打折，希望借此来提升销量，然而结果却不尽如人意。中国奢侈品市场进入了一个新的发展阶段：增速放缓，调整不断。实际上市场的这种变化与当前中国宏观经济出现的“新常态”相一致。依照各位访谈嘉宾的观点揭示，大家对“新常态”下中国市场的奢侈品牌发展普遍持乐观态度。具体到行业来说，尽管珠宝行业销售额有所下降但开单量却在增长，这说明有更多的消费者开始购买珠宝。随着人们生活水平的提高，越来越多的人开始参与到马术等与马相关的运动中。马运动的“平民化”不是该行业的衰落，相反却暗示了其未来的繁荣。我们的定性研究显示，这两个奢侈品相关行业有如下相同的变化特征：

参与人群量在不断增长。该现象也与中国的奢侈品市场的一个突出变化相一致，这就是奢侈品消费者不再局限于那些顶级富豪，一般的企业白领也能够拥有奢侈品。普通人群也在追求高品质生活，奢侈品牌已经成为中国消费者对品质生活理解的一种标志和形象认知。

回顾历史，任何经济形式、任何行业的发展规律都有升降交互发生的特点。速度不能代表一切，数字也不能代表一切，只有从质量上做出提升，在方向和体系上做出改进，奢侈品业才能获得健康发展。总之，尽管当下中国奢侈品市场的发展形势并不理想，但这只是一个过渡和调整阶段，调整过后中国奢侈品市场将进入一个更加健康发展的新阶段。

问题 2：如果说奢侈品在中国卖不动了，有人可能不会同意这种想法，因为他们认为这将是奢侈品牌的一次调整，在这之后，好时光仍将继续，请问如何看待这种想法？

A：北京地区珠宝行业由于其自身的特殊性，在市场绩效的统计方面可能会有所遗漏。事实上，很多微商、电商都在卖珠宝，私下里会有很多交易。从珠宝行业的发展来看，目前的销售情况很好。

B：奢侈品在中国销售受阻主要是因为价格。奢侈品在中国的价格明显高于欧美，这是一种掠夺，是奢侈品在中国卖不出去的重要原因。因此，奢侈品牌商如果希望在中国市场继续发展下去，必须调整价格，这是核心问题。

C：奢侈品牌集团化是一个全球性的现象，奢侈品在中国卖不动并不代表中国消费者没有购买，只是没在中国购买。奢侈品牌进入了一个全球性调整的阶段，虽然在中国线下销量下降，但是只要奢侈品牌商能够保持品牌一贯的号召力，消费者还是会响应奢侈品牌的号召，还会继续购买。

D：调整是一件好事情，很多企业是被动地面对和接受中国市场的改变，尤其是消费市场的改变。如果奢侈品牌商能够对市场的改变

做出积极的应对，那奢侈品行业还是很容易赚钱的。

E：调整的过程总是痛苦的，新的发展机遇也在调整中诞生。最近的轻奢、互联网电商都给奢侈品牌商带来了新的启示。前途是光明的，道路是曲折的。

F：任何消费者其实都更倾向于体验性的产品，目前大部分消费者没有在中国购买奢侈品主要还是因为价格，只要各大品牌保持自己的品牌特性，同时调整自己的定价策略，线上线下相结合，相信消费者回归指日可待。

小结：从多家奢侈品牌公布的财报来看，“愁云惨淡”已经成为行业的主流，各家都不约而同地把原因归咎于下滑严重的中国市场。德国奢侈品牌 Hugo Boss、英国时尚产品集团 Burberry 的财报都显示，中国市场销售下滑是业绩欠佳的主要原因之一。从表面来看，中国奢侈品市场确实有“卖不动”的现象。然而通过市场调查以及同访谈嘉宾的交流，我们发现了现象背后更加深层次的信息。其一，我们发现“卖不动”的品类主要是男士服装、腕表，2014 年这两个品类的销量下滑均超过 10%，这是短期现象，从长期来看，市场有望回归理性后再发展，为数众多的中产阶级将成为日益强大的奢侈品消费力量。其二，与传统奢侈品牌不同，许多新兴品牌都获得了快速发展，新开门店数持续增长，销量喜人。另外，访谈嘉宾所谈到的珠宝行业也保持了较快的增长速度。面对新常态下的中国市场，奢侈品牌商必须做出市场战略和策略的调整。

调研结果显示，中国消费者对于奢侈品的需求始终在增长，只是由于价格、产品质量、上新速度等问题导致消费者转换了购买地点：由内地转向海外。如今中国消费者是全球最重要的奢侈品购买群体之一，面对如今巨大的市场需求，奢侈品牌商有必要积极调整中国市场的定价战略，吸引中国消费者回归内地，这样中国的奢侈品牌市场才能重回好时光。

问题3：事实上，从中国经济进入新常态以及政策调整以来，奢侈品在中国市场走弱已经持续了两年多时间，您认为奢侈品公司主要做出了哪些值得关注的调整？

B：价格是最根本的。通过价格调整让消费者不再感受到被掠夺。奢侈品牌商应努力降低价格，实现薄利多销。

C：营销方式的改变。营销方式的改变包括：通过社交媒体和企业网站开辟电商渠道，与中国本土电商平台进行合作，接近更多的中国消费者。跨界也是很有意义的。

D：价格只是调整的一方面，真正有效的调整还应该在产品设计和新产品线上。面对年轻的目标客户群消费偏好的改变，奢侈品牌商应该开发新的产品线，这才是治本的方法，但比较难。

E：降价。继香奈儿之后大批的奢侈品牌如迪奥、卡地亚、范思哲等开始纷纷降价。

F：新产品的推出以及电商渠道的开辟。一年以来，女性服装、鞋履及皮包成为了奢侈品增长的亮点，蔻驰等品牌推出了适应职场女性的手提包等产品以增加销量。此外，电商渠道的开辟也是一项重大的举措。

小结：在前面的问题中我们谈到了目前奢侈品行业的发展状况以及宏观经济与政策变化对奢侈品行业产生的影响。毫无疑问，目前的奢侈品行业发展遇冷，各大奢侈品牌纷纷采取措施试图挽救颓势。根据我们的调查以及访谈嘉宾的发言，我们发现目前奢侈品牌商主要在以下几点做出了调整。

第一，价格方面。价格是市场营销策略中十分重要的一环，价格对消费者的影响是最直接的。今年以来国际奢侈品牌商在中国市场集体刮起降价风，希望借助价格优势激活内地消费市场。从经济学来看，正常情况下，市场需求会按照与价格相反的方向变动：价格上升，需求减少；价格降低，需求增加。奢侈品希望通过降价的方式来吸引消

费者有其经济学原理。然而奢侈品又有其特殊性，很多情况下高价格也会成为其品质的象征而得到消费者的追捧。我们认为，奢侈品在中国实施降价策略，确实能够吸引那些对价格敏感的消费者，增加销量。但更让我们高兴的是，长期以来国际奢侈品牌对中国市场的价格歧视正在得到改善。

第二，产品方面。面对中国消费者强大的购买力，奢侈品牌商越来越重视中国市场，纷纷推出迎合中国消费者偏好的产品，许多奢侈品牌也将中国市场列入新品发布的首发地。

第三，渠道方面。随着互联网技术的日益成熟，许多奢侈品牌都将目光聚焦到线上（Online）。事实上，零售的关键是消费者，哪里有消费者，渠道就要扩张到哪里。如今的消费者已经习惯于互联网生活，尤其是年轻一代，网购早已融入其日常生活。电商渠道的加入是对原有传统渠道的补充，也是未来全渠道构建的一部分。当然奢侈品公司的调整并不局限于价格、产品和渠道，许多其他方面的调整也在进行，调整将是一个长久的、持续的、常态化的过程。

问题4：目前一线市场日趋饱和，请问奢侈品企业下一步会将门店开到哪里？

A：不仅是门店开到哪儿的问题，还有开店形式的问题。以珠宝行业为例，珠宝行业消费渠道59%~60%在大中型综合商业体中，32%左右在专业珠宝市场。北京地区有几十家专卖店，如果开到郊区县，或三四线城市，那么还会有更多珠宝市场。

B：门店应开到有消费能力的地方。奢侈品牌商更应关注目标人群，路虎赞助马球就是因为这里有其目标客户，能够精准地找到目标人群。因此开店应当开到有精准目标人群的地方。

C：一线城市趋于饱和，一线半城市的开店量可能会增加。但开店量只是一个方面，以后奢侈品可能会以跨界合作的姿态出现，如在成都出现阿玛尼公寓。

D：开到线上。在互联网时代，网上店铺增加的数量是十分迅猛的，博柏利在天猫开店就是一个非常好的例子。这是在数字时代吸引年轻消费者的一个很好的方法。

E：现在是“互联网＋”时代，以前是我们找产品，现在是产品找我们。将门店开到网上是很自然的事情，不仅能够降低奢侈品商的经营成本，也能够为消费者带来更多的产品选择。

F：二线城市大幅度进驻的机会不大，从过去几年的数据来看，传统奢侈品牌并没有在二线城市成功扩张，还是应该运用电商平台进行渠道的拓展。

小结：一线城市经济发展水平高、财富积累量大，成为奢侈品牌商登陆中国的首选地，经过 30 多年的发展，如今一线市场已日趋饱和。而中国城市化进程的加快，以及大城市以外地区的财富增长，催生了大量二三线城市的奢侈品消费需求。目前，奢侈品牌在杭州、温州、青岛、大连等东南部，东北二三线城市都有布局；西部地区除了成都、西安、长沙、乌鲁木齐等地，也都成为奢侈品企业布局的新兴城市。因此我们说二三线城市是未来奢侈品商开店的选择。这并不意味着奢侈品牌商在二三线城市复制一线大城市的做法，应该因地制宜，如目前发展较好的品牌集合店模式。我们的焦点小组访谈中也有人对此持保留意见，对此还需要做进一步研究。

在我们的定性研究中，许多被调查者都谈到了线上，这与前一问题中提到的渠道调整变化相一致，互联网成为奢侈品牌商开店的新平台。相信未来会有越来越多的奢侈品牌商愿意尝试适合的电商业务，消费者也将从中获益。跨界合作丰富了奢侈品门店的开店形式，能在无形中加深消费者对奢侈品牌的认识，获取更好的消费体验。当然无论奢侈品门店开在线上还是线下，无论采用何种形式，从根本上说，开店必须开在有消费能力的地方。

问题 5：目前，有些中国消费者对常见的奢侈品大牌的兴趣在下

降，对奢侈品集团下的二三梯队品牌或轻奢品牌来说，这一现象是否意味着新的市场机遇？

C：随着时代的发展，消费者对品牌会呈现多样化的需求，不仅是轻奢品牌，也可延伸至很多中国本土优质新兴品牌，它们也会有很好的市场机会。

D：轻奢在美国发展很好，美国几大轻奢服装龙头企业的年报表现出色。原因有二：其一是这些品牌的底子薄，因此增长快；其二是消费者的年轻化趋势加强，很多20多岁的年轻人都是从轻奢品牌开始涉足奢侈品消费领域，一些奢侈品牌的忠诚顾客也会因轻奢品牌的高性价比而选择这类品牌产品。这是机遇，但也存在很多问题，如年轻人的消费行为并不稳定，且变化特别大，易受参照群体影响。怎样应对年轻群体的改变是一个非常大的挑战。

E：消费者选择轻奢品牌很多是看重轻奢产品的设计多样化，相对于传统轻奢品牌在产品设计和种类上往往更加灵活多样。从数据上看，轻奢在新开门店数上确实远远多于传统奢侈大牌，这是一个新的市场机遇。

F：传统奢侈品牌款式较为传统，且Logo等标志明显，这与现今作为消费主力军的中青年消费者的需求特点并不完全一致。对于追求时尚新奇的年轻一代来讲，具有鲜明时尚特色、个性独立的新兴品牌确实存在优势，也有不可忽视的市场机会。

小结：轻奢品牌设计更为时尚新潮，价格普遍低于传统的奢侈大牌，顺应了如今奢侈品消费者年轻化的趋势，为年轻的奢侈品消费者提供了更多样化的选择，满足了他们追求新潮、喜爱特立独行的个性化消费心理；同时也给传统的奢侈品消费者带来了全新的选择机会，轻奢品牌较高的性价比能够吸引一部分顾客的眼球，因此轻奢品牌包括一些独立设计师品牌在未来具有较大的发展潜力，这给传统奢侈大牌的发展带来了较大的冲击，传统奢侈品牌需要适当地进行调整来迎

接这个挑战。另外，因为轻奢品牌的消费人群更趋于年轻化，消费选择还不够成熟，消费者的品位有局限性，其品牌偏好也容易发生变化，因此如何培育忠诚客户，留住更多的消费者，扩大市场份额，对于轻奢品牌而言极其重要，轻奢品牌需要采取相应的措施来应对这种可能发生的改变。

问题 6：中国人海外购买奢侈品最大原因有哪些？如何唤回中国消费者在国内购买？

A：价格。奢侈品商可以和中国商家合作，同样的产品在中国当地生产，无须运到其他地方售卖，这样成本会降低。其实，现在有很多奢侈品牌商委托中国企业在中国生产，在保证质量的情况下降低成本，把价格合理化不是不可能。

B：价格是核心，奢侈品牌必须冷静面对中国市场，必须承认中国市场的重要性。以前人们在购买奢侈品时比较盲目，现在随着中国消费者越来越成熟，越来越理性，价格必须公道，不然势必会造成奢侈品牌商在华销售额的下降。

C：除了价差还有中国中产阶级或者说富有阶级生活方式的改变。如今中国人在签证上所受的约束越来越小，大家都爱出国旅游，顺便购买奢侈品是很正常的事情。因此，如何唤回消费者在国内购买奢侈品其实很难，这个问题有待进一步思考。

D：最根本的原因是奢侈品牌商对中国市场不够重视，引发的问题是价格歧视和产品歧视，产品更新速度慢。很多人选择海外购买是因为国外的产品上新及时、品种齐全。因此要想唤回中国消费者，奢侈品牌商应对中国消费者给予足够的重视。

E：产品质量问题是一个很大的原因。国内很多奢侈产品，尤其是网购、代购的产品都无法保真。而实体专卖店、专柜的价格往往又过高。想要唤回中国消费者在本土购买，奢侈品牌商必须对其销售渠道进行更深入的管理，打击假冒伪劣产品。

F：境外旅游的兴起在很大程度上拉动了奢侈品的境外消费，但是这根本上也是由国内外同样或同类产品的巨大价格差异所造成的。

小结：中国消费者放弃近在眼前的专卖店，不辞万里地前往海外购买奢侈品，其核心影响且最重要的原因是价格。品牌商的奢侈品价格歧视战略以及国家对奢侈品的高关税政策等，都拉高了奢侈品牌在中国市场的价格，这让越来越理性的中国消费者不辞劳苦地舍近求远，去追求更加合理的价格，导致了中国消费者大规模的海外购买奢侈品现象。此外，由于中国消费者生活水平的普遍提高，特别是中产阶级人数的规模化趋势，加之国人生活方式的巨大转变，以前对于大部分人来说很遥远、很昂贵的出国旅行变成了很方便的选择，因此有很大一部分奢侈品消费者选择在境外旅游的同时在境外购买奢侈品。对产品质量的担忧，国内的奢侈品赝品数量众多，充斥着整个消费市场，并且专柜所提供的正品缺乏完善的售后维修服务，同时价格又缺乏竞争优势，这些都是中国消费者选择境外购买或消费奢侈品的重要影响因素。如果奢侈品牌商希望在中国本土市场唤回中国奢侈品消费者，应当先调整中国奢侈品市场的定价，制定较为公道的价格策略，让中国消费者在面对本土市场上的奢侈品价格时，不会受到不公平的价格歧视对待。次之产品的质量及售后服务方面应形成一套较为完善的服务机制，让中国消费者能够在境内就享受到优质的产品和服务。

问题7：请用一句话来表述未来国际奢侈品牌在中国的发展趋势。

A：方兴未艾。

B：与时俱进，了解中国市场。

C：挑战和机遇并存。

D：市场需要细分。

E：发展是必然。

F：虽然坎坷，但是，道路光明。

小结：虽然现阶段中国奢侈品消费市场的发展出现了停滞不前的

尴尬境况，特别地，2014 年奢侈品消费更是出现了前所未有的负增长，但是焦点小组访谈的结果显示，奢侈品市场只是处于一个短暂的调整期。现阶段的缓慢发展对于尚未成熟的中国奢侈品消费市场而言是一针镇静剂，它让前些年狂热的奢侈品市场稳定下来，认清市场的真实情况和市场快速增长背后存在的问题，并能够进行有针对性的调整，这对于轻奢品牌以及本土的独立设计师品牌而言是一次机遇。我们相信，通过这一阶段奢侈品市场的持续调整，中国的奢侈品消费市场值得期待，未来是光明的。

6.1.3 焦点小组访谈结论

过去几年里中国奢侈品市场呈现出从高速增长到缓慢发展的趋势，在 2014 年，甚至首次出现了负增长，这种新常态下的奢侈品市场发展对于各大奢侈品牌商而言是机遇与挑战并存。一方面，全球性的经济发展放缓拖慢了奢侈品行业发展的脚步，传统大品牌新开门店数下降，奢侈品牌商打折、降价不断，奢侈品行业不再像以往那样“春风得意”。另一方面，也暴露出中国奢侈品消费市场上存在的一些问题，例如奢侈品牌商缺乏对消费者体验的重视，定价偏高，售后服务不完善等，这些对于奢侈品牌商来讲都是亟待解决的问题，是进一步拓展中国奢侈品消费市场的前提条件。

总体而言，新常态下的奢侈品市场发展将机遇与挑战并存。伴随着主流中国消费人群消费习惯的转变，轻奢成为奢侈品行业发展的一个新突破口，将成为奢侈品消费市场的一个强劲增长点。随着互联网在企业经营和市场活动中占据越来越重要的地位，奢侈品行业也一定会充分利用互联网优势寻求新的增长点，有效地整合线下和线上资源，以适应现代奢侈品消费者新的生活方式和消费习惯。调整中国市场定位战略、价格策略和产品策略，同样是奢侈品牌商特别需要考虑并解决的问题，其基础是对目标消费者需求的正确理解。

目前奢侈品牌商所面对的市场调整阶段不是绝对的消极现象，它提示奢侈品牌商必须健康且理智地看待中国奢侈品市场，顺应经济规律和市场规律的逻辑，基于对奢侈品消费者需求的理解，从可持续发展的战略角度运作中国的奢侈品市场，面对中国奢侈品消费者。从这个意义上看，奢侈品行业的好时光永远都在。

6.2 深度专家访谈

6.2.1 深度专家访谈设计和内容

访谈背景：2012 年之前，中国的奢侈品消费增长达到两位数的超速发展，但是之后由于受到国际经济大环境的影响，无论是国内还是国际上大多数奢侈品销售逐年下降。面对日益严峻的商业环境，各大奢侈品牌商开始寻求新的商业模式。历峰集团的创始人 Anton Rupert 曾坦率地向老对手 LVMH 和 Kering 伸出橄榄枝，希望联合起来打造一个全球化的奢侈品牌电商平台，以应对未来的挑战。无论三大奢侈品巨头携手共创电商的理想能否实现，奢侈品行业一定会与互联网联手，未来的奢侈品零售一定是朝着“零售+IT 技术”的方向发展。

访谈目的：随着中国经济进入新常态，中国的奢侈品市场受经济的影响也不可避免地出现了下滑的趋势，在新的背景下，奢侈品品牌纷纷尝试互联网，采用新科技应对市场的变化。课题组采用深度专家访谈的目的，是研究互联网技术对奢侈品行业的影响，以及未来中国奢侈品市场的发展趋势。

访谈时间：2015 年 9 月

访谈城市：北京

访谈问题：

（1）互联网技术对奢侈品行业的影响是什么？

（2）未来奢侈品行业的发展趋势是什么？

专家一：某奢侈品牌中国区前零售总监，有10年的奢侈品行业从业经验，一直就职于一线奢侈品牌企业。

专家观点：我想先分享一下我是如何进入奢侈品行业的。大学毕业时，我在一家基金公司做人力资源工作，当时安永出了一份报告，指出中国奢侈品市场将在2012年达到全球第二。我做了一些研究之后，决定辞职转到奢侈品行业。我从一名营业员做起，跟随中国奢侈品10年发展浪潮，到了2012年中国奢侈品行业真的达到了全球第二。俗话说“春江水暖鸭先知”，如今的奢侈品行业数据下滑，作为一线奢侈品零售管理者的我在2012年已经感受到了，这也是我转行到互联网行业的一个契机。2013年之后，我国宏观经济和政策变化，似乎预示着中国奢侈品行业步入寒冬的开始。

在过去的10年里，中国的奢侈品店员根本“不用面带微笑”就能轻而易举卖出去产品，但是2013年以后，即使是奢侈品店员全程微笑服务，也很难卖出去产品了。坦率地讲，过去10年中国奢侈品是粗放型管理方式，不管是在服务细节上还是在购物体验上我们没有花费很多精力，但是以后奢侈品精细化管理必然是一个趋势。奢侈品精细化管理单单只靠人力是很难实现的，无论是互联网技术、电商技术，还是信息集成化技术都必然对奢侈品精细化技术起到助力作用。另外，之前中国奢侈品市场还是礼品主导的市场，但近几年发生了很大变化。一系列因素导致中国奢侈品市场正从礼品消费转到个人消费，注重消费者个人体验，也就是互联网思维中的用户至上原则。在这两个大的环境背景下，采用手机端和移动互联网技术对零售业务进行智能化管理，是对所有现有零售系统的一个补充。坦率地讲，奢侈品行业并不是一个站在前沿拥抱新技术的行业，更多的还是注重百年传承和手工工艺，对于新技术在某种程度上还是被动接受的。但是，在最近半年

到一年的时间，奢侈品行业对新技术接受非常快。例如，正在跟我们合作的一线奢侈品牌香奈儿正在接受并使用语音等新技术。尽管奢侈品牌商在尝试电商、O2O等，但他们并没有投入太多的精力和资源。奢侈品行业利用互联网技术更多的是在营销和店铺管理。奢侈品牌利用互联网技术对店铺进行标准化、量化和规范化管理；利用移动互联网技术在信息的上传下达方面更加快速有效；一线管理者利用互联网技术随时随地进行管理，全面提高管理效率。未来互联网技术和移动客户端将更多应用于奢侈品市场的管理，这些前沿技术将极大地提高奢侈品牌市场管理效率，节约管理成本，创新管理模式，促进奢侈品市场的发展。我们有理由相信，未来的中国奢侈品市场还有很大的上升空间。

专家二：北京某投资管理公司董事长，该投资公司现已与Gucci、Prada、Nike、Adidas、李宁、探路者等上百个国内外知名品牌建立深度运营关系，与天猫、唯品会、京东、寺库等十余家国内知名电商实现友好合作。

专家观点：我想先说一下和奢侈品的缘分，那还是比较早的，应该是2010年。当时在北京有几家奢侈品精品店，但是经营得不是很好，我们分析了原因，主要是没有一个好的管理团队。他们主要靠奢侈品买手和海外的奢侈品精品店来进行采购奢侈品，加上没有解决库存问题。当时我们在国内做运动品牌线上销售，已经形成了比较大的规模。于是一些奢侈品品牌找到我们做线上销售。我们是第一家在京东做奢侈品的专卖店，第二家在天猫做奢侈品的专卖店。我们在天猫第一个月净售额达到30多万元，可见高价位的奢侈品在网上销售是有利可图的，我们从那时开始做奢侈品网上销售。我们目睹了奢侈品从简单松散的销售到今天数据化的销售，我们更多瞄准的是消费者进行精准化营销，注重寻找和分析线上购买奢侈品的人群，看他们的消费习惯，侧重数据化分析。我们比较少设计产品运营，主要还是抓住线

上购买奢侈品的人群，并及时推送给他们。奢侈品虽然价格很高，但是也有大量库存，于是就给了电商做奢侈品销售的机会。我们在瞄准这些货品的时候，最早进行销售的是过季商品。这些过季商品之所以在中国销售得好，是因为奢侈品品牌像 Gucci、LV 的风格每年不会有太大变化，而且大陆消费者很注重 Logo。但是现在很多奢侈品品牌开始推出具有鲜明特质的商品，也有数据显示现在越来越多人喜欢“去 Logo 化”的消费。

对于奢侈品销售，我们必须严格按照奢侈品公司的规定做，包括折扣、开店区域等。现在很多奢侈品公司开始触网，但是目前网上销售十分惨淡。而中国消费者在海外购买奢侈品大幅增加，主要原因之一是海外价格占优势，二是追求品质。总体来说，未来奢侈品线上发展的机会在于瞄准 20%的人群做定制和限量发行的产品。我们在做的电商平台是很多人可以通过预购、预售的方式购买海外“奢侈品”，甚至可以是澳洲的龙虾，而平台另一端是注册的海外奢侈品店、海外买手等。所以说，未来我们可以利用互联网技术、数据库技术，对线上购买者进行精准化营销，注重寻找和分析线上奢侈品购买人群以及他们的消费习惯，线上销售奢侈品有可能成为未来奢侈品销售的一个亮点。

6.2.2 深度专家访谈结论

经过十几年的迅猛发展，中国的奢侈品市场最近一两年出现增速缓慢或规模缩减，进入到调整期。处于调整期的中国奢侈品市场既面临着机遇也面临着挑战。最大的机遇在于奢侈品行业与互联网技术的结合，利用互联网技术进行线上线下销售，提高顾客全方位购买体验，进行精准化营销和精细化服务，提高品牌管理效率。同时，最大的挑战在于如何更好地利用互联网技术为奢侈品行业创造更多的价值。从长期发展来说，机遇大于挑战。未来奢侈品行业如果能够抓住互联网

技术驱动的市场变革所带来的机遇，将可能得到突破性的市场发展。

6.3 定性研究结论

课题组的定性研究始终围绕“新常态下的奢侈品市场发展”以及“奢侈品行业与互联网科技的关系”这两个主题展开。焦点小组和深度访谈为我们了解和透视当前我国奢侈品市场的发展状况提供了重要的观点和专家视角。同时，我们发现，来自奢侈品市场一线的品牌经理人、专家和学者对该市场的判断，支持了课题组对中国奢侈品市场专题研究的主要结论，也反映了当前中国奢侈品市场的基本运行状况、出现的新特点和新趋势。新常态下的宏观经济环境、互联网科技的运用，是影响中国奢侈品市场未来发展的两大重要宏观环境因素。

第 7 章 中国奢侈品市场未来展望

20 世纪 80 年代初期国际奢侈品牌开始进军中国市场。总体而言，前 30 年是国际奢侈品牌在中国的试水期，2009~2011 年是奢侈品牌在中国市场的春风得意期。2014 年以来情况有所逆转，中国内地奢侈品牌市场首次出现负增长，老牌大奢侈品牌商放缓开店扩张速度，关闭在华门店、减少门店总数的情况屡见不鲜，大规模的调价、打折事件频频出现。与此同时，互联网也在不断改变奢侈品牌在中国的传统经营模式。这些变化是当前我国宏观经济调整的结果，同时也是中国奢侈品消费者多年来购买奢侈品牌产品、学习奢侈品牌和产品知识、不断积累经验、消费行为日趋理性、消费价值观日趋成熟的结果。新常态下的中国奢侈品市场充满了机遇与挑战。

目前中国奢侈品市场仍处于调整转型阶段，在对外经济贸易大学中国消费经济研究院的支持下，对外经济贸易大学“中国奢侈品消费者行为研究”团队继续深入中国各主要一二线城市进行实地专题调研，从中国奢侈品消费者层面着手研究这一特殊转型时期中国奢侈品消费市场的变化，目的是从最基础的奢侈品牌消费动机和最根本的中国传统文化价值观两方面诠释中国奢侈品消费者的行为，并通过与前期研究成果的对比探索中国奢侈品消费者主要族群的特性，据此形成对中国奢侈品市场整体发展状况以及未来发展趋势的判断。

7.1 奢侈品市场调整期仍将持续

基于本年度奢侈品消费者行为研究和2014年奢侈品消费者行为报告研究，结合参考2015年和2014年的国家宏观经济数据、国际知名咨询公司报告、各大品牌官方数据和各种权威新闻资讯，我们做出如下判断：当前中国奢侈品市场仍处于调整期。毫无疑问，2002~2012年国际奢侈品牌在中国市场搭乘中国经济发展的“快车”，经历了非常好的发展阶段，从开店数量到同店销售，包括中国销售在全球所占比重，均有激动人心的业绩表现。然而，随着2008年金融危机波及中国，中国的经济增长速度开始放缓，奢侈品行业也受到了冲击，奢侈品市场走向低迷。2013年，中国内地奢侈品市场增速仅为2%，2014年则出现了1%的负增长。然而应该看到，中国消费者仍是全球奢侈品的最大买家之一。我们认为，2013年是中国奢侈品市场晋升到一个稳定成熟阶段的起点，是中国奢侈品市场从初期的高速增长逐渐走向成熟阶段必经的转型过渡期。2014年至今，中国的奢侈品市场则进入一个以调整为主的过渡期，奢侈品市场的调整性过渡将是一个连续的、相对较长的过程，度过目前这个阶段，奢侈品市场将会复苏并进入健康发展的新阶段。

从各大在华奢侈品牌的门店扩张情况看，奢侈品牌商在中国市场的发展战略呈现出以求稳、求准、求新和求高为特点的长期发展导向型趋势。2013年，大多数一线奢侈品牌开始对扩张新门店持谨慎态度，更多地专注于门店的翻新装修或改造升级，而并非像以往那样一味地追求快速开拓门店。2014年，众多一线奢侈品牌的新开门店数量大大低于2013年的水平。但是值得注意的是，这些奢侈品牌并没有缩减新开门店单店的装修预算，表现出足够的理性和从容，符合奢侈品

牌一贯追求高端品牌形象的宗旨。事实上，过快的市场扩张确实有悖于奢侈品牌以“质”取胜的原则，“稀缺”、“精致”才是其理应坚守的品牌个性。与传统一线国际大牌所持的市场谨慎态度相比，以美国蔻驰（Coach）为代表的众多新奢品牌加快了在中国的开店速度，反映了中国奢侈品牌在整个市场调整阶段中的一个反差特点，即轻奢品牌发展势头强劲。这种发展态势恰恰迎合了中国社会分层的新特点，这就是中产阶级的崛起，城市化带来的城乡消费人群结构的变化，70后、80后和90后成为消费主力军，轻奢是富裕阶层的日常消费，轻奢是年轻时尚一族的个性选择。显然，轻奢品牌的固有特点与今天的中国市场结构相吻合，使其能够在未来拥有持续性发展空间。

2015年，中国的奢侈品市场特别是中国香港地区的奢侈品市场发生了以香奈儿（Chanel）和古驰（Gucci）为代表的大规模降价事件，带动起前所未有的规模性奢侈品降价潮。长期以来，国际一线奢侈品牌商在中国市场的价格歧视战略广为诟病，为数众多的中国奢侈品消费者被国内外市场差异悬殊的零售价格推到海外市场，加之出境旅游市场如火如荼，无形中也为中国消费者选择在海外市场购买奢侈品起到推波助澜的作用，一时间降价成为诸多一线国际奢侈大品牌试图唤回中国消费者的重要举措。但是，我们的调研结果和市场实际表现显示，如果希望通过降价唤回中国的奢侈品消费者似乎并不是最有效的市场策略，奢侈品牌商必须在产品概念等方面苦下功夫，那种轻而易举即可获得中国奢侈品消费者纷纷购买的好时光已经是曾经的故事了。中国消费者面对奢侈品牌已经开始成熟，当然，中国的奢侈品市场也有待更加成熟，尚存在诸多问题，需要持续性调整。

新常态下中国经济的突出特点是“中高速、新动力”，其中新动力指科技创新。在中国的奢侈品市场下滑、增速放缓的同时，中国经济也在经历调整期。奢侈品市场作为中国市场的一个子市场，其市场的调整是符合客观经济规律和市场规律的。新常态下中国经济的大环境

自然也为奢侈品行业带来分享利好价值的机遇，这就是科技创新动力，奢侈品业与互联网科技的互动就是具有前瞻意义的选择，或成为调整期过后奢侈品牌商新的市场增长点。

7.2 经典和创新并进是奢侈品市场可持续盈利的保障

奢侈品的经典款式通常由于其设计独特、功能卓越而被多数消费者认同。本次调研揭示，中国奢侈品消费市场是一个三元市场结构，即由 62.89%的奢侈品消费者构成的保守型市场；由 8.75%的奢侈品消费者构成的先锋型市场；由 28.35%的奢侈品消费者构成的观望型市场，其市场规模比约为 6∶1∶3。比较 2014 年和 2015 年的数据后我们发现，中国奢侈品消费群体的三元市场结构具有稳定性特征。对此，我们特别提请理论界和企业界予以特别关注。

随着中国人群奢侈品消费行为不断走向成熟，中国奢侈品消费风向也正在发生明显的变化。以服装为例，高级定制时装既体现不输于国际一流名牌的设计风格，同时又适合消费者的个性特征，是真正“我的”时装。未来，随着中国消费者生活水平的进一步提高和对个性化消费的追求，中国市场对高端私人定制的需求将越来越突出，高级定制式的高品质生活方式也是一种发展趋势。我们预测未来中国奢侈品消费市场的态势是：高端定制市场蓬勃发展，小众定制市场稳步发展，规模定制市场中长期有望稳步回升。

7.3 奢侈品行业的全渠道模式不断完善

奢侈品主流渠道包括专卖店、名品折扣店、朋友代购、国内网购、海淘、出境游购物等。2015 年的本专题研究显示，中国奢侈品消费者的首选渠道依旧是具有信誉的专卖店，但是随着出境游市场的规模化发展和国外市场较之国内市场的价格优势，中国消费者自然会利用出境游的机会在国外购买奢侈品。同时在互联网技术蓬勃发展的今天，电子商务渠道将成为国际商务活动的一个大的趋势，各大奢侈品牌商也在考虑通过电子商务渠道寻求新的市场增长点。事实上，O2O 等线上线下渠道相结合的新兴商业模式已经开始渗透到传统的奢侈品零售模式中，一些大奢侈品牌先锋企业已经试水电子商务，奢侈品的全渠道零售模式逐渐显现，引起奢侈品业的普遍重视。

全渠道零售是零售渠道从单渠道、多渠道向跨渠道发展演化的新的更高一级的渠道结构。由于消费者在购买过程的每个阶段都要面临多种类型的渠道选择，故以满足消费者渠道需求为目标的全渠道零售模式可以更好地契合现代人的生活方式，为消费者带来更全面的消费体验。伴随着互联网技术特别是移动互联网技术的快速发展，由于消费者的购物时间碎片化，购物地点碎片化，购物需求碎片化与个性化，传统零售渠道已经无法有效地与之相适应，奢侈品牌商必须意识到发生在消费者行为中的这些变化，寻找有效的市场对策，通过整合品牌专卖店、大型购物中心品牌专柜、PC 网店、社交商店、移动商店等多种渠道资源，实现与奢侈品消费者购物需求的无缝对接。目前中国乃至全球的奢侈品业在全渠道模式方面的实践仍然处于探索阶段，这是奢侈品牌商面临的新的市场机遇和挑战，有必要予以重视，提早布局。

7.4 奢侈品理性消费行为下的个性化消费趋势明显

2014 年的奢侈品消费者行为报告曾经预测，中国消费者奢侈品理性消费趋势将日益明显。一年的时间过去了，我们一直关注中国人奢侈品消费行为特征和变化趋势，发现 2014 年的预测是正确的，中国奢侈品消费者的消费行为愈加理性，同时，我们还有新的发现，这就是“中国人奢侈品理性消费行为下的个性化消费趋势明显”。

全球奢侈品市场的跌宕起伏和发展显示，奢侈品消费市场都遵循从非理性增长到理性回归的发展规律，前期炫耀性消费突出，之后炫耀性消费与理性消费并存。在奢侈品进入中国市场的初期，许多国人购买奢侈品是为了迎合他人的喜好，盲目跟从，忽视自身需求，不考虑奢侈品的风格是否与自身的气质形象相匹配。但是，本次调研发现，目前中国消费者购买奢侈品时，非常在意奢侈品的风格是否与使用者的气质相符，这反映出中国奢侈品消费者消费行为正日趋成熟。有七成的被调查者表明自己的奢侈品消费行为是自律的。事实上，随着中国中产阶层收入的提高，其可任意支配收入水平提高，表现为奢侈品购买力水平提高，使得中产阶层有能力购买奢侈品，加之社会生活的开放和丰富，消费者能够广泛接触到各类奢侈品牌，学习品牌知识，了解品牌文化，甄别品牌价值，后者助推了奢侈品消费行为的理想化和成熟化。这是中国奢侈品消费者对奢侈品牌认知的一个突出变化，他们正逐渐从简单的模仿和炫耀行为向个性化和自我认同的消费行为转变。

中国的奢侈品消费者包括一大批 80 后和 90 后，他们在跨出学校大门步入社会之后，成为消费的主力军。这两代人拥有同样的特点：

张扬、自我，比其父辈们更注重生活品质与细节。这些受过良好教育的新富阶层年轻、时尚，比上一代的富豪们更追求个性。我们的调查发现，奢侈品的核心目标客户群即18~35岁人群，对“自我价值”的关注度会随着年龄的递增呈现递增趋势。人们追求个性，且个性化奢侈品牌消费愈加突出，奢侈品消费逐渐回归到购买力允许的范围，且消费行为逐步建立在品牌文化认同的基础上。

此外，特别需要关注的是，中国奢侈品消费者行为有文化价值观导向下的潜在市场集群特征。本调研基于文化价值观划分出四类消费者族群，他们分别是儒道导向型、儒释导向型、释道导向型和非传统导向型奢侈品消费者，其中儒道导向型人群占比超过半数以上。该结论印证了中国消费者受到中国传统文化价值观的影响很大，尤其是来自儒家文化价值观和道家文化价值观的影响。儒家文化价值观中集体主义倾向的价值观导致“注重圈子、社交关系和社会等级差异”的中国奢侈品消费者，将圈子文化、社交和等级观念带到其奢侈品消费行为中，使得消费者通过奢侈品消费实现其对个人社会地位和个体生活品质的追求。所以，通过消费者的行为来判断行为的文化价值观驱动作用，不仅可以解释消费者个性特征的动因，还能更好地对未来的消费者行为进行分析和预测，显然这是认识中国奢侈品消费者不同于西方消费者奢侈品消费行为的最根本的驱动因素。

经过多年的高速发展，中国已经成为名副其实的奢侈品消费大国，先富起来的国人在初期消费奢侈品时还没有理性成熟的消费观，难免出现价格攀比、秀标识等炫耀型消费。新富们在选购奢侈品时愿意通过多种渠道了解奢侈品品牌，在购买过程中也更加注意货比三家，择优购买，选购适合自己的奢侈品。随着人们生活品质的逐年提高，价格已经不再是用户选择奢侈品的首要条件。人们既不会因奢侈品的价格高就炫耀式购买，也不会一味追求价格最低的奢侈品，产品体验和服务才是最关键的。

总之，新常态下的中国消费市场的特点是“新消费”，新消费意味着从以往大规模、同质化、普及型消费，向多样化、差异化、高品质消费者转型，进入从量到质、从有到好、求新求特的新阶段。国家明确指出的新消费中的六个大类中的五个消费，即服务消费、信息消费、绿色消费、时尚消费和品质消费均与奢侈品牌消费正向相关。结合国家新的经济发展政策和本书研究成果，我们的判断是：未来的奢侈品市场的整体发展是大趋势，因为有中国国家发展战略的支撑，有中国市场大环境的支撑，发展是必然的。科技创新驱动的奢侈品市场发展将是未来该市场发展的方向。但是，奢侈品市场需要一个调整期的过渡性发展，也是必需的，因为它符合市场发展的一般规律和逻辑。需要特别指出的是，奢侈品消费不等同于奢侈浪费，奢侈品牌消费要更注重其品质与文化内涵，消费者购买奢侈品牌产品体现的是人类对美好生活的追求。以往发生在中国市场的奢侈品牌价格歧视现象需要改变，奢侈品牌商需要考虑中国市场战略与全球市场战略的一致性和平衡性。面对中国经济的新常态，奢侈品牌商要在适应中国市场大环境和中国消费者奢侈品消费需求特点的前提下谋求可持续发展。

Chapter 1 The Current Status of the Luxury Market in China

1.1 The Chinese Luxury Market of 2014

Mainland China's luxury market maintained high-speed development with five years from 2008 to 2012, among which the first four years averagely grew at double-digit rates. Since 2012, its growth rate began to slow down, with its growth rate down to 7%. In 2013, it further slowed down and the growth rate slowed just to 2% year-on-year. In 2014, mainland China's luxury market fell for the first time, 1% (the market value is 115 billion Yuan) lower than in 2013. In addition, global luxury market's total capacity was 224 billion euros (about 1519 billion Yuan) and Chinese consumers' worldwide luxury consumption amounted 390 billion Yuan, which means that Chinese people bought 25% of global luxury products and demonstrates that Chinese consumers were still one of the largest luxury goods buyers in the world. In 2014, among wristwatches, bags, men's wear, jewelries, shoes, women's wear, accessories and cosmetics, perfumes, and personal care supplies these eight luxury products of interna

tional luxury brands in China market, wristwatch and men's wear dropped most, bags' growth rate was zero, while women's wear and shoes grew fast and become the best-seller in luxury category. Chinese consumers' oversea shopping amount reached 55% of the total consumer spending. In addition, overseas purchasing value was about 65 billion Yuan, about 15%; and purchased products were mainly cosmetics, then leather bags, wristwatches and jewelries (Bain & Company, 2009-2014).

In recent years, China's economy entering into a New Normal makes some effects on the sales of l uxury industry. The sales disclosed by Italian luxury giant Prada shows, the net sales volume in China in April 2015 was 774.1 million euros, a 6.3% drop year-on-year. French luxury brands Louis Vuitton says, in 2014 financial year, the sales in Untied States and Euro-market were strong, but the demand from Chinese consumers was soft. With relative good global sales, the French luxury group Hermes's net profit in 2014 is 1.14 billion dollars, increased by 8.7% compares with last year, however, its wristwatch sales decreased, whose growth rate was only 15 in the former year but dropped by 10.6% in the following year.

We assume that China's luxury consumer market has stepped into "adjusting phase" since 2013, so the slowing down of market's growth rate is foreseeable. Whether suppliers' adjustment or consumers' waiting and seeing, China's luxury market must experience "twinge" from market before it enters into mature stage. In addition, China's emerging consumer group is becoming mature and their purchasing channel is diverse, which both make them have rational demand for and individualistic choice of fashion and luxury goods, and bring chances and challenges to luxury goods companies.

1.2 China Luxury Consumer Market Development's Macro-economic Foundation

Luxury market is only a part of consumer market; domestic consumer market's rapid development will undoubtedly drive luxury industry's fast growth. However, domestic consumer market's rapid development firstly benefits from China's national economy's continuous, steady and rapid growth, then consumer's rising purchasing power and the changing consumption structure caused by urban and rural residents', especially urban residents' increasing income. They lay effective foundation for consumer market's prosperity. In addition, China's rapidly enlarging mass affluent group, especially white collar group's fast growing, also lays a good customer foundation for luxury market's development.

1.2.1 Macro-economy Kept Growing

Since 2010, China's GDP has slowed, from 10.4% down to 7.4%, but gross GDP maintained continuous growth. As shown in Graph 1.1, China's gross GDP reaches 1.036 billion dollars, and becomes the second country with over 10 trillion dollars after the United States. Meanwhile, China's luxury consumer market increased from 87.1 billion Yuan in 2010 to 115 billion Yuan in 2014. China's luxury consumption's proportion in GDP demonstrates increasing trend since 2011, but decreased slowly after 2011 and dropped to 0.18% in 2014, which also confirms that mainland China's luxury consumption's growth slowed down.

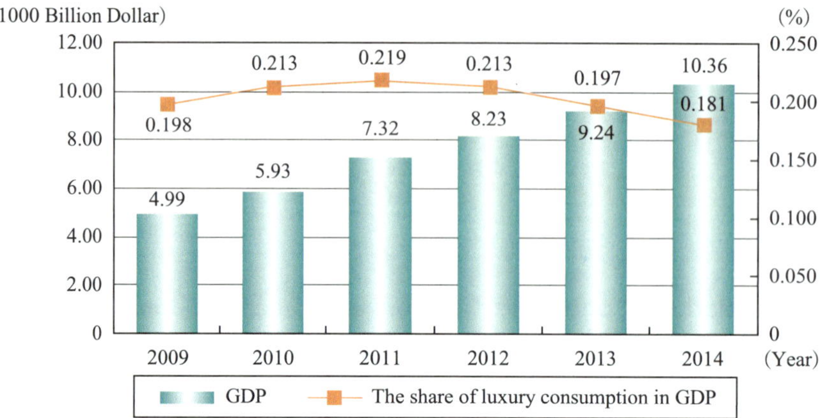

Figure 1.1 China's Total GDP and Ratio of Luxury Goods of GDP 2009–2014

Source: Adept from the World Bank and Bain & Company.

1.2.2 Residents' Disposable Income Was Increasing

Income decides consumption. Residents' increasing disposable income drives consumption ability to grow and further enlarges consumer market scale, lifts residents' consumption level and advances luxury goods market's development.

During recent 10 years, China's urban and rural residents' disposable income has dramatically increased and necessities' spending's proportion in total income has gradually decreased year after year. As shown in figure 1.2, urban residents' per capita disposable income increased from 15780.8 Yuan in 2008 to 28843.85 Yuan in 2014, an increase of 82.78%. Urban residents' Engel's coefficient decreased from 37.9% in 2008 to 35% in 2013. Though the decline range was not large, but it demonstrated annually decreasing tendency. It can be seen that China's urban residents' consumption of food and other necessary goods is taking annually decreasing proportion in income, and their living standard has greatly improved.

The rising residents' disposable income and decreasing necessities' spending lay essential economic foundation for Chinese consumers to improve their life quality.

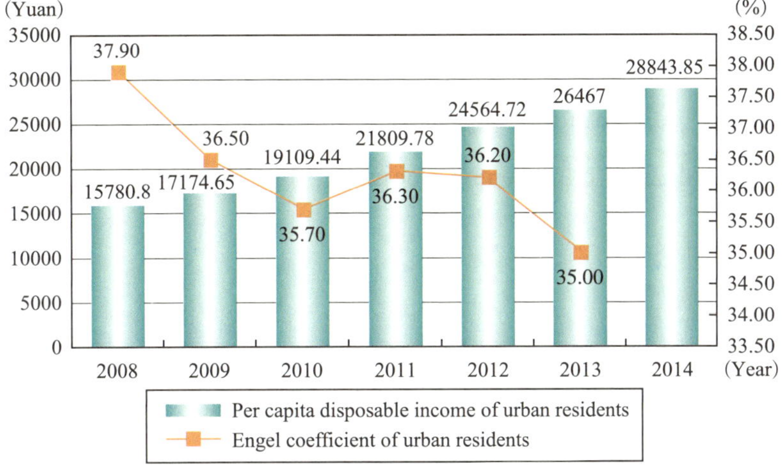

Figure 1.2 Per Capita Disposable Income of Urban and the Engel Coefficient

Source: China Statistical Yearbook.

1.2.3 Consumption Structure Kept Changing

As China's economy grows, residents' income level greatly improves and consumption structure changes. As shown in Figure 1.3, China's urban residents' basic consumption of clothes, food, housing and transporta tion accounted for over 72% of total expenditure in 1990, and in 2013 this proportion dropped to about 55%. In contrast, household equipment, health care, transportation and communication, education and entertain-ment and other consumption's proportion in total expenditurd increased from about 22% in 1990 to about 40% in 2013. It could be seen that China residents' consumption focus was transferring from foods, clothes, housing and other basic consumption to household equipment, transportation and communication, education and entertainment, health care and high-quality life consumption, from simple commodity consumption to complicated commodity consumption including various service such as catering, travelling, entertainment, education, health care, from frequent

common consumption to choice-emphasize, upper-class oriented individualistic consumption; consumers were becoming more concerned on commodities' quality, brands, style, packaging, and after-sale service and so on. Residents' consumption began to transit from basic consumption oriented to hedonic and experiencing consumption oriented and consumption upgrades.

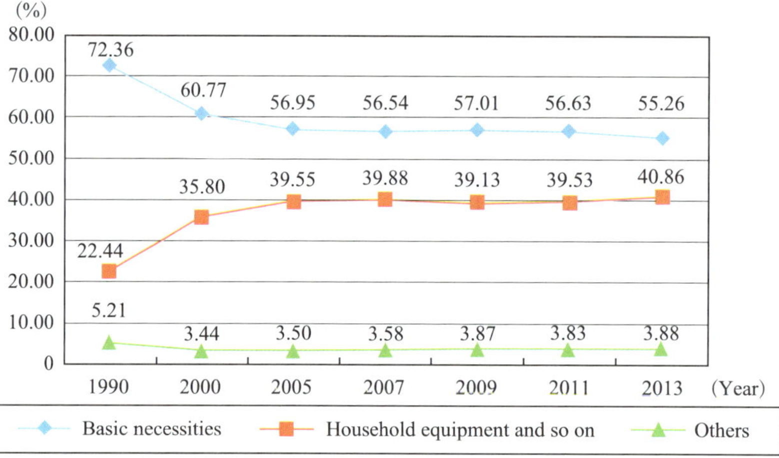

Figure 1.3 Different Consumption Proportion of Total Consumption of Urban Residents

Source: China Statistical Yearbook.

As shown in Figure 1.4, as social consumer goods' total retailing sales kept increasing, consumer market stepped into rapid development stage. Consumers' spending's proportion on domestic luxury goods buying in social consumer goods total sales rose then slowed down; in 2011, it reached the peak of 0.58% then continuously dropped to 0.42% in 2014. The possible reasons may be the luxury goods' online selling, overseas purchasing, and overseas travelling and shopping in recent years cause consumers' domestic luxury purchasing proportion to drop. Besides, from Figure 1.5, we can see that the luxury goods bought by consumers in Chi na mainland accounted for a smaller and smaller rate in Chinese people's

global buying of luxury goods, that means emerging consumptions such as overseas purchasing and outbound traveling purchasing were becoming popular among the mass.

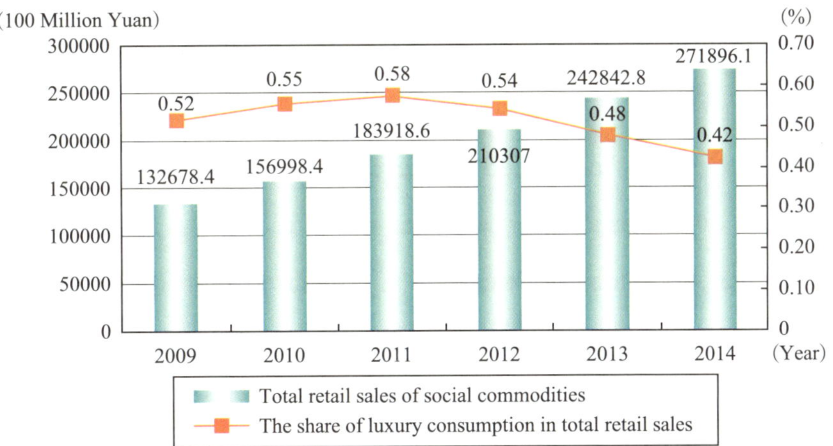

Figure 1.4 The Proportion of Total Retail Sales of Whole Society Commodity and Luxury Goods in Total Retail Sales

Source: Adapt from China Statistic Yearbook (2009-2014) and Bain & Company (2009-2014).

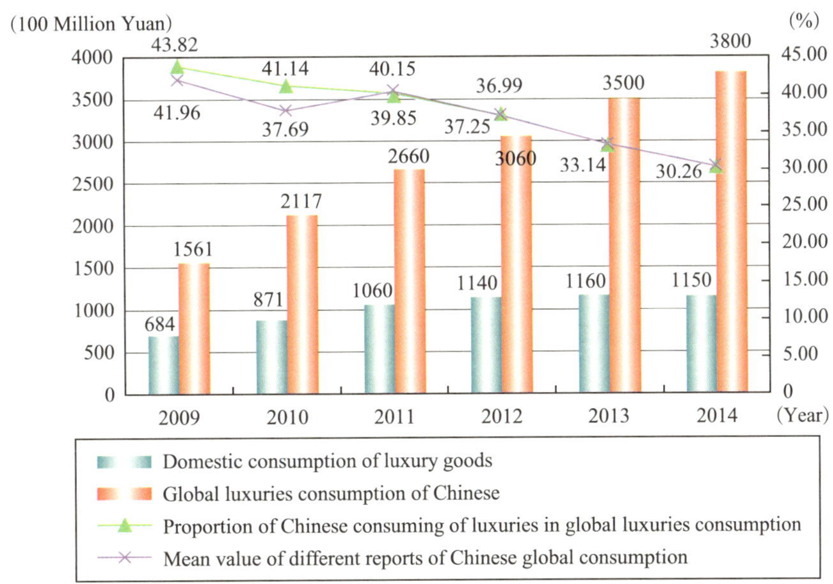

Figure 1.5 The Comparison of Domestic and Global Luxuries Consumption of Chinese

Source: Adapt from McKinsey & Co (2010), Bain & Company (2009-2014) and Ipsos (2011).

1.2.4 China's Mass Affluent Class Was Quickly Growing

In 2015, *China Mass Affluent Report 2015* released by Forbes China and Credit Ease defines mass affluent class as the China's middle class whose personal investable assets is between 600000 Yuan to 6000000 Yuan (about 100000 dollars to 1000000 dollars). A majority of this group is universally called "advanced white collars". As shown in Figure 1.6, the number of China's mass affluent class reached 13.88 million, increased by 15.9%, a drop of nearly 1% compared with the same period of last year, and is expected to be 15.28 million until the end of 2015. As shown in Figure 1.7, China's total private wealth in 2014 was approximately 106.2 trillion Yuan, increased by 17.6%, a drop of about 0.6% compared with the same period of last year. Though the growth of China's mass affluent class and total private wealth was slowing down, we Could clearly see from Figure1.7 that China's mass affluent class's wealth' s proportion in total social wealth was increasing, and reached 17.6% in 2014. So it was self-evident that China's mass affluent class owned amazing amount of wealth and provides strong momentum for China's luxury consumption. In addition, the report also mentions that the number of China's mass affluent people under 40 years old in 2015 accounted for 54.5% of the total number of the rich, which means that the consumers in China's luxury market were becoming younger so the main force consuming luxury goods was keeping growing. Therefore, the expanding of mass affluent group had laid solid foundation for the development of China's luxury goods market.

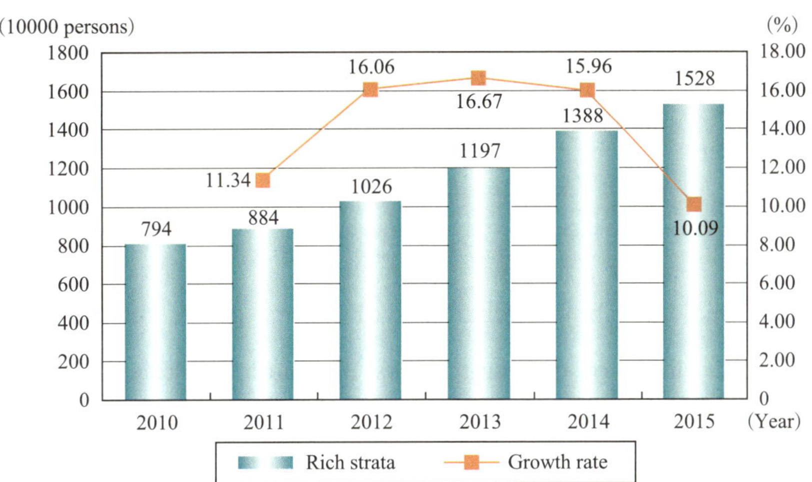

Figure 1.6 Number of the Mass Affluent and its Annual Growth

Source: www. ForbesChina. Com.

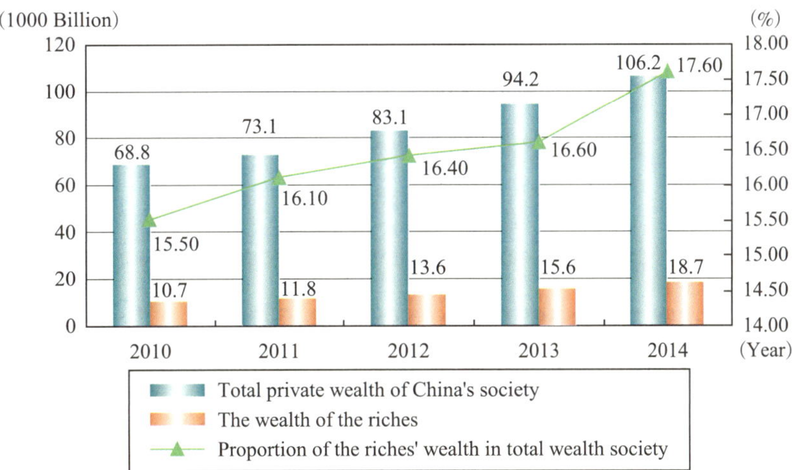

Figure 1.7 Comparison of the Wealth of the Riches and Total Wealth of Private of Chinese Society

Note: Private total wealth refers to cash, deposit, stocks transacting open market funds and bonds possessing by private person.

Source: Adapt from Forbes (2013-2015).

1.3 Analysis of the Development of China's Luxury Industry

In 2014, there was the first negative growth in China's domestic luxu

ry market. However, the same trend did not occur with the consumption enthusiasm of the Chinese consumers, whose global luxury consumption kept growing.

1.3.1 Diversified Luxury Distribution Channels

Traditional distribution channels of luxury goods mainly depend on decorated franchises or discount stores like outlets. Prices of same products vary wildly between different counties and regions because of the differences in exchange rates and regional pricing strategies. In China, due to the emergence and development of overseas purchasing and direct consumption abroad, as well as the little bit higher price of domestic luxury goods, the international markets are meeting Chinese consumers' strong demands for luxury goods, while the local luxury markets keep shrinking.

In 2014, the scale of China's luxury goods overseas reached 55 billion to 75 billion. More and more consumers clearly showed their willingness to buy luxury goods through overseas purchasing in the future. In addition, as going abroad is more and more available to Chinese, lots of consumers would like to buy luxury goods during overseas trips because of the overall lower prices. Some even travel abroad specially for buying luxuries. The target markets are mainly in Hong Kong, Macao, Taiwan, Japan, Korea, Europe and the United States, among which the quite popular are Japanese and South Korean markets.

Additionally, many consumers prefer online shopping under the high-tech information environment with the ubiquitous network. As is shown in Figure 1.8 that the number of China's online shopping consumers was rapidly increasing. By the end of 2014, it reached 380 million persons. Faced with both opportunities and challenges of the Chinese mar

ket, those luxury brand companies were also considering or try ing to boost sales by online channels. For example, affordable luxury brands like Coach had already been setting up their own e-business platform, while traditional luxury brands like Burberry were building online channels on integrated e-business platforms like Tmall. Also, some luxury brands tried to sell on vertical e-business platforms or mobile apps. Most luxury brand companies, however, were still watching because of their upmarket positioning or uncontrollable or unreliable logistics system.

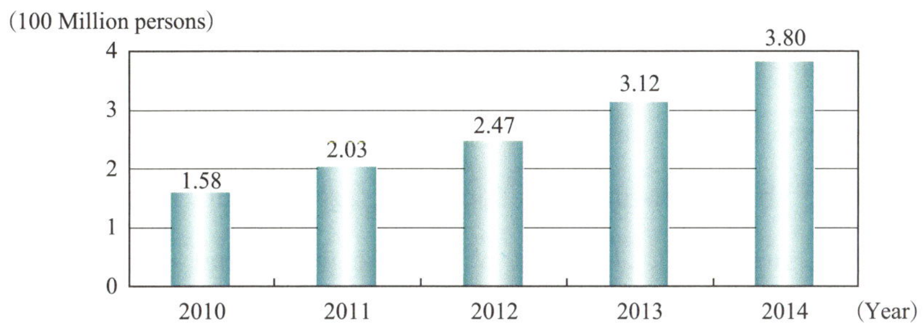

Figure 1.8 The User Scale of Internet Buying in China from 2010–2014

Source: China E-Commerce Research Center.

1.3.2 Changes of the Top Sellers Among the Luxuries Categories

In recent years, there have been some changes of the popular international luxuries in China's market. Men's luxuries sales CAGR decreased annually. In 2013, there was negative growth in men's luxury watches and clothing. On the contrary, the women's luxury products represented by the women's clothing kept good CAGR, and become the major market growth point, among which the market growth rate of women's cosmetics, footwear. This change shows that the dominant consumers of international luxury products in China's market had changed from the male to the fe male.

In addition, Chinese costumers were becoming more experienced, and

they would choose more suitable and personal products according to their own personalities and preferences. Therefore, in order to deal with the new changes in the Chinese market and look for new sales growth points, those international luxuries companies were actively creating new products which were more suitable for Chinese consumers.

1.3.3 Affordable Luxuries Enjoying a Strong Momentum

As Chinese luxuries consumers gradually become younger and younger, the middle-aged and young people from 18 to 45 years old is becoming the main force to buy luxury goods. They pay attention to the study of luxury brands, and have their own understandings. They have been changing their consumption focus to fashion and individual characters instead of simply showing off. When the traditional upmarket luxuries could not meet their consumption demands, they begin to take a fancy to those affordable luxuries with lower price, satisfying quality as well as fashionable design.

As is shown in Figure 1.9, in 2014, part of the traditional upmarket luxuries companies' motivation to open new shops decreased than those affordable luxuries companies', and more of them chose more conservative strategies. For example, compared with few years ago when they were eager to march into China's market, brand companies like Burberry, LV, Cartier slowed down their steps to open new shops. Some of them even shut down few stores in some cities to guarantee the sales amount and profit margin of each shop. In 2014, Cartier opened two new stores, but also closed two. LV, Gucci, Armani also closed one store in China when they were expanding. Those dealing with men's clothing closed stores faster. For instance, Hugo Boss, Zegna had more closed shops than

newly opened ones.

Figure 1.9 reveals some luxury brands were still increasing the investment in China's market. For example, in 2014 Prada opened 7 new shops and Coach opened 13. Affordable luxury brands such as MCM, Michael Kors had more newly opened stores, and none closed shop. And the market sales of these brands also had substantial growth.

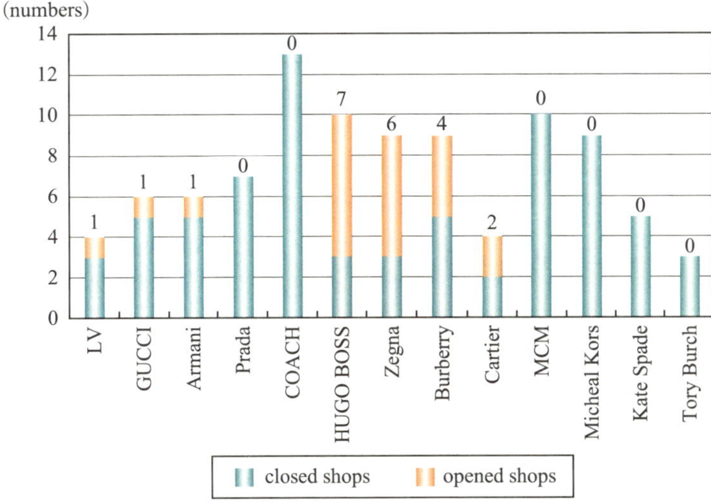

Figure 1.9 The Change of Chinese Stores of Part of Luxury Brands in 2014

Source: Official website of brands.

1.4 Consumption Behaviors of Chinese Consumers on Luxuries

1.4.1 Decreasing Conspicuous Consumption and Brand Awareness

As documents indicate, the ages of China's luxury consumer groups are mainly between 18 to 45 years old, among which consumers below 35

years old accounting for 75% and the young of 25 to 30 years old has been rapidly forming a new consumer group for luxury products, which develops faster than that of the western countries. It shows in Figure 1.10, according to *2014 Luxury Industry* by Baidu, post-90s accounted for the largest percentage among those who paid attention to and searched for "luxury industry", among which 20 to 29 years old accounted for 46%, 30 to 39 accounted for 38%, and those younger than 19 accaented for10%, 40 to 49 accaented for 6%, which indicated a trend towards younger.

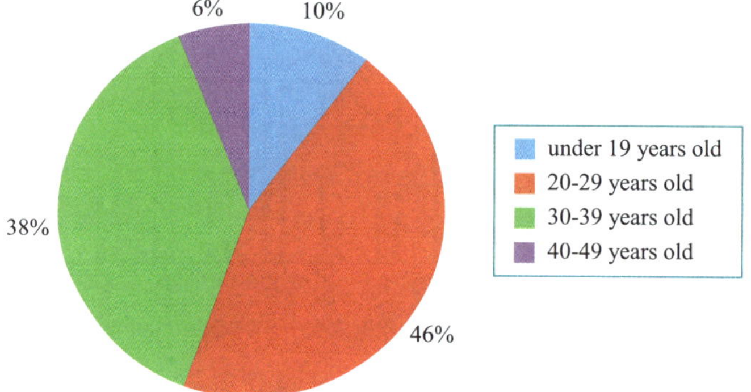

Figure 1.10　Age Distribution of Luxury Industry in 2014

Source: The report of luxury industry in 2014.

In the past, Chinese consumers preferred to buy luxuries with obvi ous large logo to show their wealth and high social status. But now this phenomenon is changing because the growing purchasing power and exp- e riences. The "Rich Second Generation", in particular, will try to avoid big logo with "bounder" characteristics, as most of them have experiences of living or studying in Europe or America, and are influenced by western cultural values. These rich young consumers try to convey "more tasteful" luxury consumption culture.

1.4.2　Experiential Consumption Gaining Popularity

In China, as the growing middle class is richer and richer, they are

increasingly interested in experiential luxury consumption. In June 2014, Hurun Research Institute and Asian International Luxury Travel Expo (ILTM Asia for short) released *China Luxury Tourism White Paper*, saying that traveling was the second most popular hobby of China's upscale consumers except food the second largest hobby after enjoying delicious food, also the second largest consumption domain after health area. According to the report, Chinese upscale tourist consumption has consecutively ranked first for four years in the world.

Chinese consumers have strong interest in unique travel experiences, such as Antarctic expeditions, African trips, customized VIP packages, front seats of New York Fashion Week shows, or close encounter with sports stars. Spa, luxury cruise and other types of luxury services are developing rapidly in China. Tourism is still the main way of entertainment for the rich people especially those billionaires. *China's Luxury Tourism White Paper* also reveals that 26% of the super tourists choose cruise tours as their dream travel experiences, and 30% of the super tourists took Mediterranean luxury cruise tour into their travel plan of the next three years. As mentioned in *2015 Superior Goods—China Multimillionaires' Brand Tendency Report* by Hurun Research Institute, rich tourists' interest in cruise tour increased 20% within one year. Currently 20% of multimillionaires were fond of yacht and half of those billionaires have bought private yacht. Based on the data of the most popular entertainment way for the rich (in Table 1.1), typical experimental consumption such as traveling ranked first, and self-driving's ranking also went up. Enjoying delicious food, fishing, Yacht are also among the top 10 items of experiential tourism.

Table 1.1 Top10 Entertaining Style Adopting by the Riches

Ranking	Entertaining style	Proportion (%)
1-	Travel	24.5
2-	Reading	14.5
3-	Tea-tasting	11.7
4↑	Self-driving	10.6
5↓	Family activities	9.9
6new	Delicious food	6.8
7new	Fishing	4.1
8new	Yacht	3.5
9↓	SPA	3.4
10↓	Wine-tasting	2.4

Note: "↑" represents the rising of rank compared to last year, "↓" represents the decreasing of rank compared to last year, "-" represents the same rank compares to last year, "new" represents entering into top 10 this year.

Source: 2015 Superior Goods—China Multimillionaires Brand Tendency Report.

1.4.3 More Rational Consumption, "The Most Expensive" no Longer Regarded as "The Best"

Luxury goods are unique and rare upmarket products. Consumers always think that upmarket products must be expensive. But luxury goods consumers think high prices "reasonable" instead of "pointless". With the market development and the growing information transparency, consumers' purchasing psychology is gradually becoming mature. The consumption concept of "the most expensive is the best" has changed. Today's Chinese luxury consumers are more rational, and many of them will search for and compare the products and prices. With the growing awareness and sensitivity of value propositions, consumers try to buy luxury goods with higher price-quality ratio.

1.4.4 Trying More New Brands with a More Open Mind

With the continuous improvement of people's living standards, more and more Chinese consumers would like to try new brands and styles.

Compared with traditional luxury brands, the flood of emerging fashion-able affordable luxury brands meet consumers' demands for multiple brands. As shown in Figure 1.11, affordable luxury brands like Balenciaga, Michael Kors, Kate Spade had impressed the consumers a lot and were very popular among Chinese consumers.

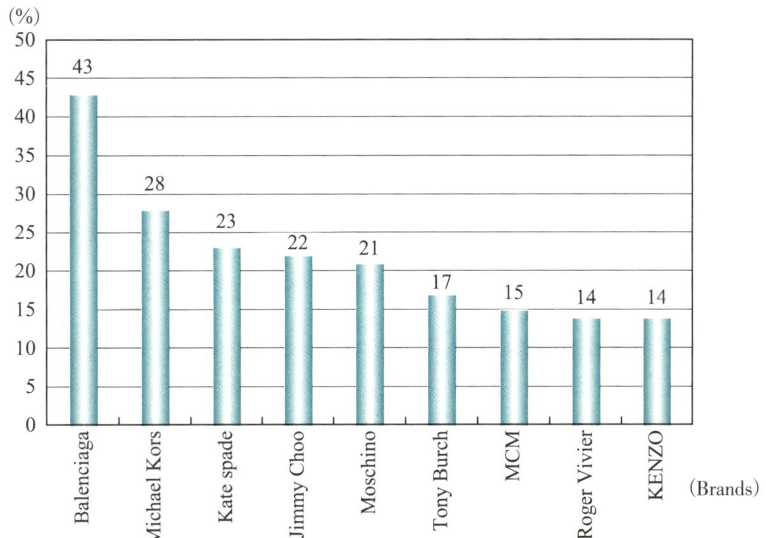

Figure 1.11 The Proportion of Willing to Buy New Brands of Chinese Consumers

Source: Report of Bain & Company.

Taking China's overall economic development trend into consideration, China's macro economy will remain a moderate or rapid growth in the future, with residents' disposable income keeping increasing, consump tion structure being optimized and upgraded, and the mass affluent class growing. Therefore, from a macro and basic point of view, there are still considerable market demands and potential of domestic luxury goods in the future, and the main factors driving the growth of luxury consumption have not changed fundamentally. From the perspective of the development of the luxury industry, it is shown that luxury goods sales channels are diversifying, popular brands are changing, and affordable luxury brands are

enjoying a strong momentum. From the perspective of consumer behaviors, it is shown that Chinese consumers' consumption concepts are becoming more mature and their consuming behaviors more rational.

Following the *China Luxury Good Consumer Behavior Report 2014*, our research team continued carrying out investigations on China luxury goods market, in order to study the new characteristics and trends of the luxury market from the perspective of China's luxury goods consumers' behaviors, and to predict the future development trend of this market. Our researches focus on the Chinese consumers' psychology, consumer motivation, purchasing decision and the driving function of Chinese traditional cultural values, and so on, so as to make objective, factual, and scientific analysis and prediction.

Chapter 2 Research Framework

The purpose of this study is to reveal the Chinese luxury goods market consumer behavior characteristics and driving factors, to explore the regularity of Chinese luxuries consuming behaviors and then to forecast luxury goods market trend according to the series of reports of former years. Figure 2.1 shows the research approach and implementation process of the report of 2015.

This study adopts various research methods including literature survey, questionnaire, qualitative research method (focus group interview and deep interview), empirical analysis method based on statistical analysis and so on.

(1) Literature research method. This method focuses on the theory of luxuries consumption psychology (eg. attitude, motivation, personality and preference), luxuries consumers purchase decision theory and cultural values theory and so on.

(2) Questionnaire. After the preliminary literature research and former questionnaires, questionnaires for the report of 2015 are formed. Later we mainly use the online research and the random selected interview.

(3) Qualitative research method (focus group interview and deep in-

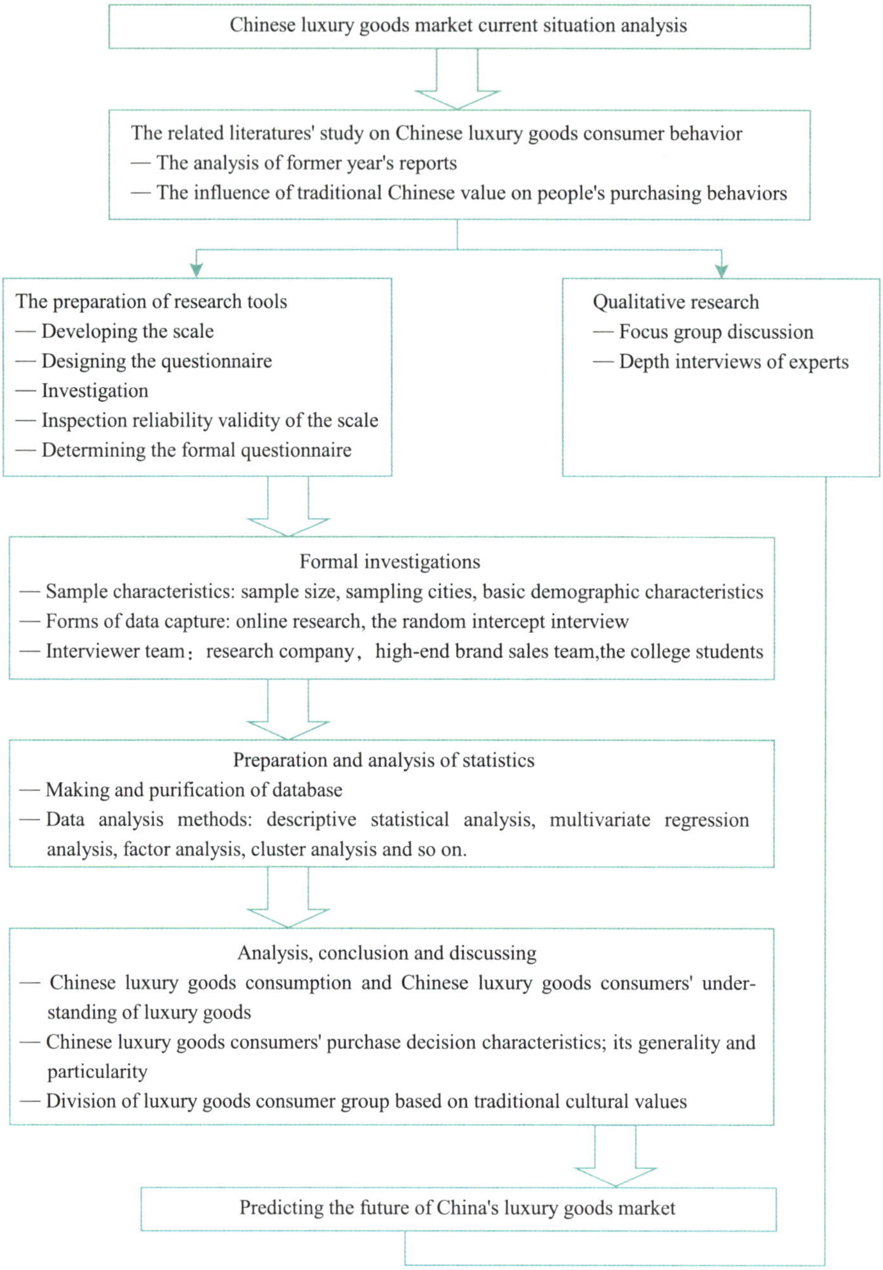

Chinese luxury goods market current situation analysis

The related literatures' study on Chinese luxury goods consumer behavior
— The analysis of former year's reports
— The influence of traditional Chinese value on people's purchasing behaviors

The preparation of research tools
— Developing the scale
— Designing the questionnaire
— Investigation
— Inspection reliability validity of the scale
— Determining the formal questionnaire

Qualitative research
— Focus group discussion
— Depth interviews of experts

Formal investigations
— Sample characteristics: sample size, sampling cities, basic demographic characteristics
— Forms of data capture: online research, the random intercept interview
— Interviewer team：research company，high-end brand sales team,the college students

Preparation and analysis of statistics
— Making and purification of database
— Data analysis methods: descriptive statistical analysis, multivariate regression analysis, factor analysis, cluster analysis and so on.

Analysis, conclusion and discussing
— Chinese luxury goods consumption and Chinese luxury goods consumers' understanding of luxury goods
— Chinese luxury goods consumers' purchase decision characteristics; its generality and particularity
— Division of luxury goods consumer group based on traditional cultural values

Predicting the future of China's luxury goods market

Figure 2.1 Research Process

terview). This is a kind of semi-structured interview. In particular, researcher use predefined interview outline and respondents provide related information under interviewer's guidance.

(4) Empirical analysis method based on statistical analysis. It analyzes data by adopting descriptive statistical analysis, multivariate regression analysis, factor analysis, cluster analysis and so on.

Chapter 3 Researches and Descriptive Statistics

China's luxury consumption goes through years of explosive growth and then gentle development and now a downtrend. The phenomenon of specially regarding luxuries as personal wealth is weakening. The ultimate goal of luxury goods companies is not just to sell some wearable items showing wealth, but to reflect or cater to Chinese consumers' new life style with luxuries' superior quality and the coexistence of classic and specific characteristics. Based on the past monographic studies, UIBE research team on Chinese luxury goods consumer's behaviors releases this annual report under innovative and comprehensive follow-up investigations. The purposes are to study Chinese luxury goods market continuously, systematically, and comprehensively, to grasp the psychological characteristics of Chinese luxury goods consumers and their behaviors accurately, and to reflect the changes of Chinese luxury consumers' behaviors and its reasons.

The questionnaire mainly involved the following contents: psychological factors such as luxuries consumption motives, preferences and attitudes; other influencing factors on purchasing such as social, economic and cultural factors; specially, the influences of Chinese traditional cultur-

al values; preference of the original producing countries; purchasing power of tendency; and other basic information variables such as gender, age, education background, income level, assets status, occupation and residential city.

The research targets were Chinese local luxury consumers from Beijing, Shanghai, Shenzhen, Guangzhou, Chengdu and Suzhou. Data collection was completed by Xindijia, a professional survey company, upmarket brand enterprises in China, and specially trained college students. The professional research company used online survey, and offline interception investigation and interviews. The offline research was carried out mainly in luxury goods business center, and altogether collected 3200 questionnaires. Data collection was based on online survey with 3100 questionnaires, and supplemented by random interception interview with 400 questionnaires. Among all the distributed 3500 questionnaires, 3347 were valid, which makes the effective response rate 95.6%. The main reason of invalid questionnaire is the Missing Value, which is discarded to ensure the accuracy of statistical analysis. The distribution of effective samples in each data acquisition cities were: Beijing (671), Shanghai (629), Shenzhen (563), Guangzhou (563), Chengdu (461), Suzhou (460).

The main reasons to choose these cities were as follows:

Firsly, the selected cities had relatively high household income, with a relatively small percentage of daily basic living expenses. After meeting the basic survival needs, they had the ability to pursue material and spiri tual comforts of higher levels, partial of which were realized by buying luxuries. Secondly, these cities carried out the reform and opening-up policies relatively earlier than other cities. As citizens there had increasing chances for international communication, they had more and more contact with international luxury brands, so they had increasing understandings for the brand values, which laid a good foundation for luxury or upmarket brands to come to these cities. Therefore, these cities had become the first choice of different international top brands to enter into China's market. Besides, as the economic development of these cities, more and more come here seeking opportunities. It was easier for them to accept upmarket brands, which would provide a fertile soil for the growth of the luxury brands in Chinese market. In addition, the reason to choose Chengdu as the representative western city was that Chengdu was one of the fastest-growing cities after more than 10 years' "Western Development". As the engine of "Western Development", Chengdu was known as the "Fourth Pole" of economic growth in China. In fact, Chengdu's total luxury consumption was just less than the two megalopolis cities—Beijing and Shanghai. The development of upmarket brands in Chengdu was faster than other cities. Lastly, although Suzhou was seldom mentioned by reports on luxury goods consumption cities, Suzhou had been enjoying a good development trend. Thus Suzhou was particularly chosen as the research target city to explore the luxury consumption status in China's second-tier cities represented by Suzhou.

In particular, all the figures and tables in the present report are original data except for a special remark.

3.1 Demographic Characters of Respondents

In this survey, the sex ratio of the respondents was proportional, with the age between 18 and 45 years old, accounting for 85.96% of all re-

spondents. Among them, 69.88% had the annual income of more than 120000 yuan. 68.99% had more than 1 million yuan of household assets. Basically, their personal income and family assets were consistent. But there were still special circumstances. For example, we had found that there were some people whose annual income was below 120000 yuan but their family assets were above 1 million. Also, there were some people whose annual income was more than 1 million but their assets was less than 10 million yuan. In addition, 90.02% of the respondents had the education background of college degree or above level. From the occupational indicators, corporate white-collar workers accounted for the largest proportion of them, with 36.06% domestic corporate white-collar and 16.07% foreign white-collar. The following is the detailed report of the sample demographic characteristics.

3.1.1 Distribution of Respondents by Gender

It shows in Figure 3.1 that 53% of the respondents were females (1779 persons), 47% of the respondents were males (1568 persons). The samples' distribution of gender can better reflect the objective and overall structure of population.

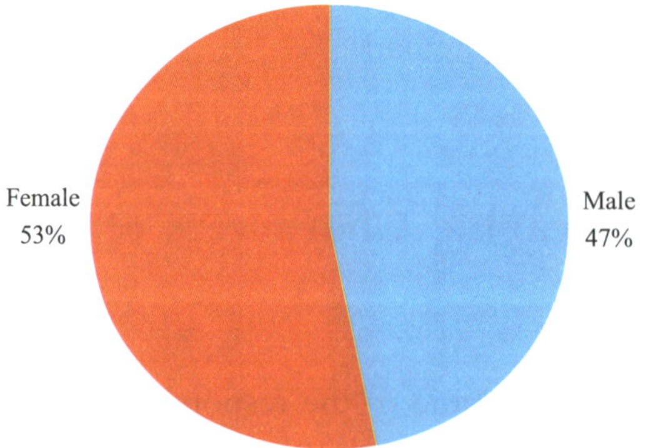

Figure 3.1 Distribution of Respondents by Gender

3.1.2 Distribution of Respondents by Age

As in Figure 3.2, 2877 respondents were between the age of 18 and 45, accounting for 85.96% of the total. Respondents between the age of 18 and 35 were the chief consumer group, accounting for 59.10% of the total. 987 respondents were between the age of 31 and 35, which contribute the largest to the percentage. 713 respondents were between the age of 26 and 30, accounting for 21.30% and 278 respondents were between the age of 18 and 25, accounting for 8.31%. The respondents between the age of 36 and 45 accounted for 26.86%. The number is 899. 14% of the respondents were under 18 years old or over 45 years old. The distribution of respondents by age reflected the luxury goods consumers' age structure in China. This was fit to the natural scale of main force of luxury goods consumers and reflected the sample in this survey having strong representation.

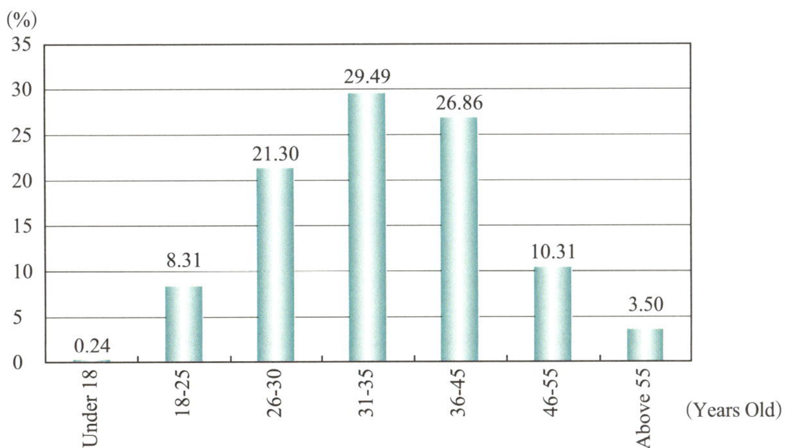

Figure 3.2 Distribution of Respondents by Age

In the survey, there were 2309 respondents who had more than 1 million Yuan of assets, including 1306 participants who were aged be-

tween 18 and 35 accounting for 56.57%, 701 participants aged between 31 and 35 accounting for 30.36% of the total, 455 participants aged between 26 and 30 accounting for 19.71% of the total, 150 participants aged between 18 and 25 accounting for 6.5%, 668 participants aged between 36 and 45 accounting for 28.93%, 259 participants aged between 46 and 55 accounting for 11.22% and the respondents under 18 years old or over 55 years old accounted for no more than 4%. It shows Chinese rich people who buy luxury goods tended to be younger than before.

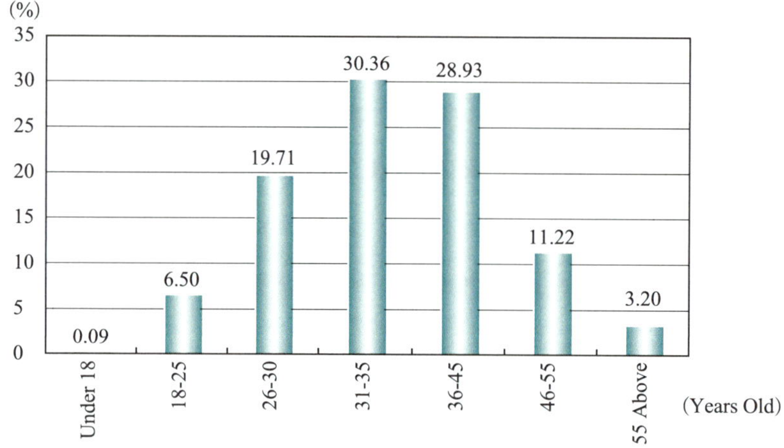

Figure 3.3 Distribution by Age of Wealthy Luxury Consumers Who Had more than 1 Million Yuan of Assets

3.1.3 Distribution of Respondents by Profession

The respondents in this investigation could be divided into seven categories according to their occupations. 1745 respondents were white-collars including white-collars who work in state-owned enterprises (1207 persons) and white-collars who work in international enterprises (538 persons), accounting for 52.13% of the total. There were 738 professionals, accounting for 22.05% and 378 respondents were entrepreneurs, accounting for 7.71%. The samples covered most of the riches who were the target customers of the luxury goods.

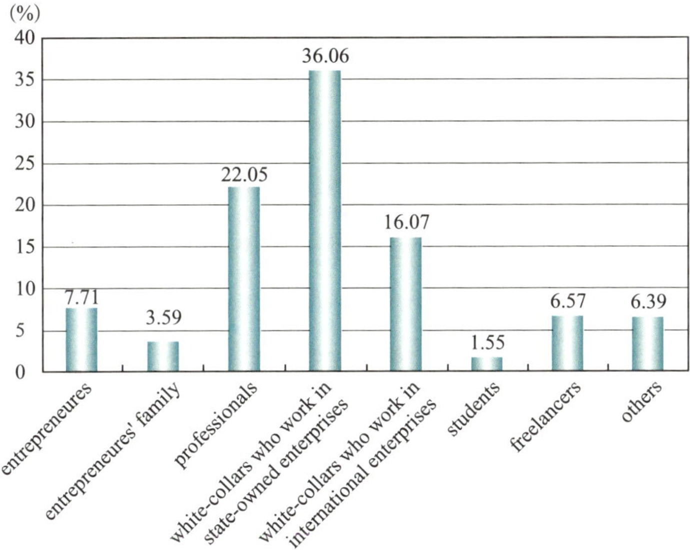

Figure 3.4 Distribution of Respondents by Profession

Entrepreneurs' and their family members: These two kinds of consumers have the highest income, very high social status, a strong sense of dignity and rich social resources, which enable them, in most cases, to afford what they want to buy. They are among the top classes. Personal image is very important for them because it shows their taste and personality.

Professionals: They are lawyers, doctors and accountants with high income who can afford luxury goods. In our classification by occupations, they have richer social resources than other categories except the above group. They have politically conservative and respect authority and status. They often choose products and services that are thought highly of by their peers.

Staffs of state-owned enterprises and foreign companies: This kind of consumers has high income and sufficient social resources. They are the youngest group, with an average age of 25. They are energetic, love all

kinds of sports, and are actively engaged in various social activities. They spend much money on clothing, food, music, and other young people's favorite products, and are particularly keen on novelty products and services.

Students: This kind of consumers has lower income and fewer social resources. They are practical, and their attention is closely related to their own business, including study, work and entertainment. As consumers, they prefer more practical and functional products. Their values and outlooks are similar to the white-collar workers, but with lower income and lower social status. They tend to imitate the consuming behavior of the people they respect and love.

Freelancers: They have the lowest income. They are living in the bottom of the society, with the least amount of resources, and strive to meet basic living needs. They are loyal to their favorite brands which they can afford.

3.1.4 Distribution of Respondents by Educational Background

As it is showed in Figure 3.5, most of respondents had a bachelor, master degree or higher, accounting for 90.02% of the total, among which 540 respondents had a master degree or higher accounting for 16.13%. The number of respondents who had bachelor is higher than that of year of 2014, which had 2473 respondents accounting for 73.89%. 225 respondents had a degree of high school or technical secondary school, accounting for 6.72%.

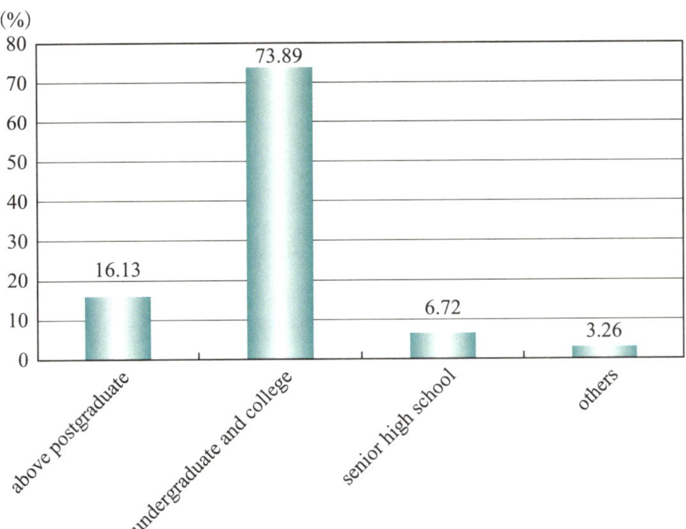

Figure 3.5 Distribution of Respondents by Educational Background

3.1.5 Distribution of Respondents by Family Assets

In this survey, there were 1283 respondents whose family assets were between 1 million and 5 million Yuan, accounting for 38.33% of the total and mad the largest group first. In the second place, there were 1038 respondents had assets under 1 million, accounting for 31.01% of the total. 680 respondents' assets were between 5 million and 10milllion, accounting for 20.32% of the total and 346 respondents had assets over 10 million,

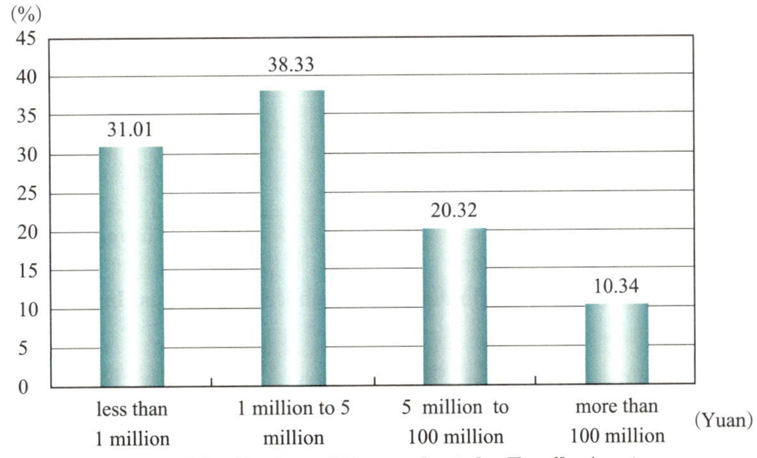

Figure 3.6 Distribution of Respondents by Family Assets

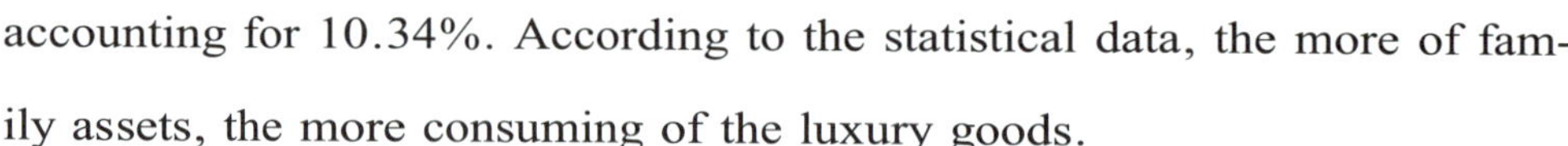

accounting for 10.34%. According to the statistical data, the more of family assets, the more consuming of the luxury goods.

3.1.6 Distribution of Respondents by Annual Income

In the report of 2015, the income stratification was adjusted and the standard of annual income changed to 0.12 thousand Yuan as the tax starting point. 1310 respondents' annual income were between 0.12 million and 1 million Yuan, accounting for 39.14% and made the largest group first. In the second place, 1008 respondents' annual income were under 0.12 million Yuan, accounting for 30.12%. 425 respondents' annual income were between 1 million and 5 million Yuan, accounting for 12.7% and 369 respondents' annual income were between 5 million and 10 million Yuan, accounting for 11.02%. Obviously, 70% of the respondents have annual income under 1 million Yuan.

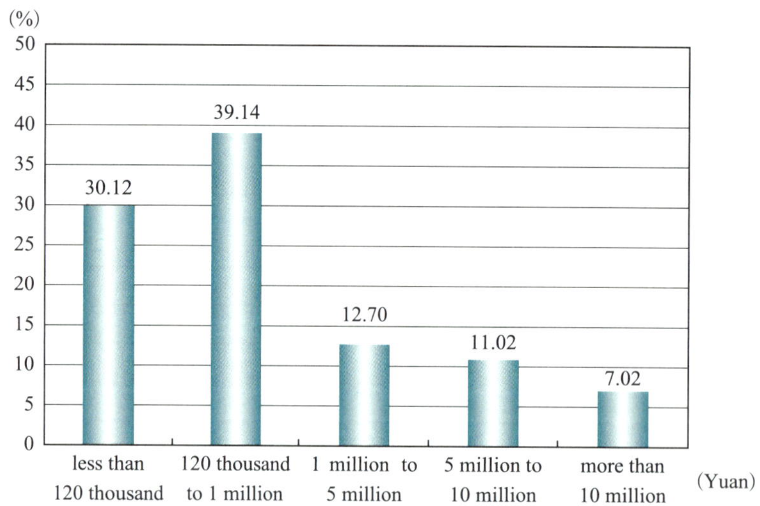

Figure 3.7 Distribution of Respondents by Annual Income

3.1.7 Distribution of Respondents by Their Residential Cities

This investigation covered cities including Beijing, Shanghai, Shenzhen, Guangzhou, Chengdu and Suzhou. The sample proportion was determined by principle of quota sample and the proportion of simple size were 20.05%, 18.79%, 16.82%, 16.82%, 13.77% and 13.74%. According to the year of 2015 report disclosure of State Statistics Bureau, Suzhou had outstanding performance in luxury goods consuming as a typical second-tier city, which reflected distribution adjustment and market result of international luxury brands.

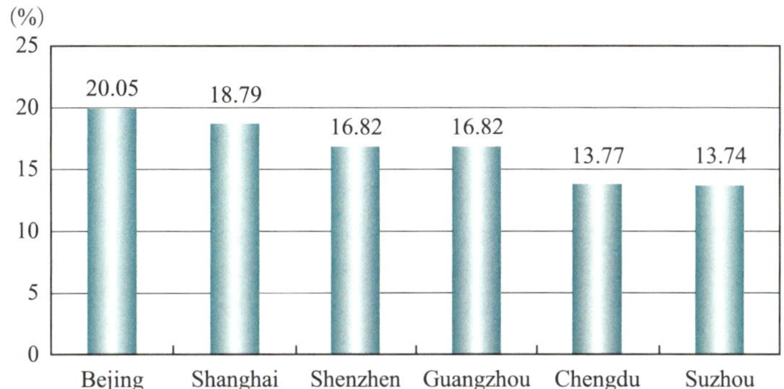

Figure 3.8 Distribution of Respondents by Their Residential Cities

3.1.8 The Share of Luxuries Expenditure of Income

It is showed in Figure 3.9 that 66.23% of respondents' expenditure of luxuries consuming was no more than 20% of their income budget. 26.69% of consumers' personal budget of luxuries were between 20% and 40% and 6.48% of consumers' personal budget of luxuries were between 40% and 60%. The percentage of consumers whose buying budget of luxuries were over 60% is 0.17%. In addition, the percentage of consumers who didn't want to buy luxuries was only 0.44%, which showed that most respondents had the budget to buy luxuries. It provided strong personal fiscal expenditure security to the development of luxuries market.

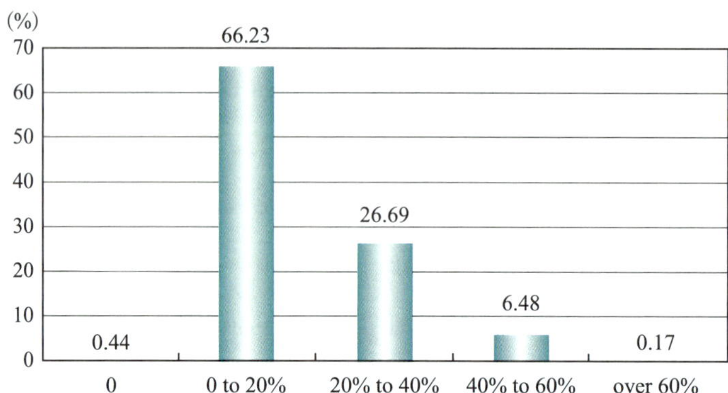

Figure 3.9 Proportion of Luxuries Consumption in Personal Income

3.1.9 Expectation of Luxuries' Purchase Frequency in the Next Year

The Figure 3.10 shows that 53.07% of respondents would buy luxuries at one to two times in the next year and 34.04% of respondents would buy luxuries at 3 to 5 times. The percentage of consumers who bought luxuries at 6 to 7 times in the next year is 9.37%. Others make up 10%. We could see obviously that most respondents had buying plans in the next year, which showed that the maintenance and development of luxuries market had steady demand basis.

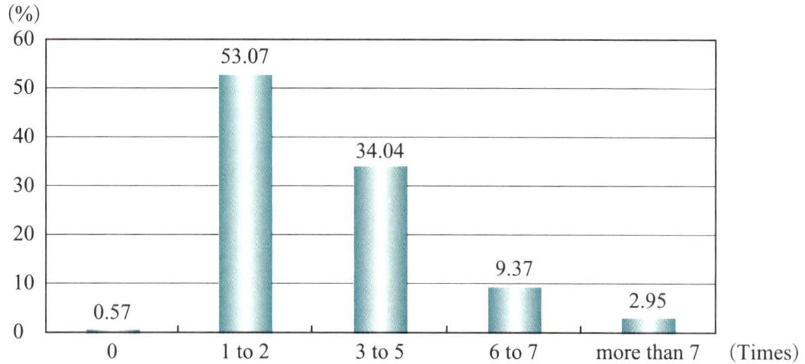

Figure 3.10 Anticipation of Frequency of Annual Buying Luxuries Annual

3.2 The Basic Information of Questionnaire

3.2.1 Meeting Self-temperament

As shown in Figure 3.11, 78.73% (2635 persons) of the participants thought luxuries should meet their own temperament; 14.04% (470 persons) of them held a neutral attitude and 7.23% (242 persons) of them opposed. At the early stage when luxury brands entered into China market, many Chinese people bought them to cater for others' preference, blindly followed the trend, neglected their own needs and did not focus on the right luxury brands fitting theirs self-temperament and image. This year's research showed that Chinese consumers today were much concerned whether luxury goods met their personal temperament, which derived from consumers' self-judgment, so its deeper connotation was the combination of luxury brands consumption and self-concept, which reflected that Chinese people's luxury consumption was gradually becoming individualistic.

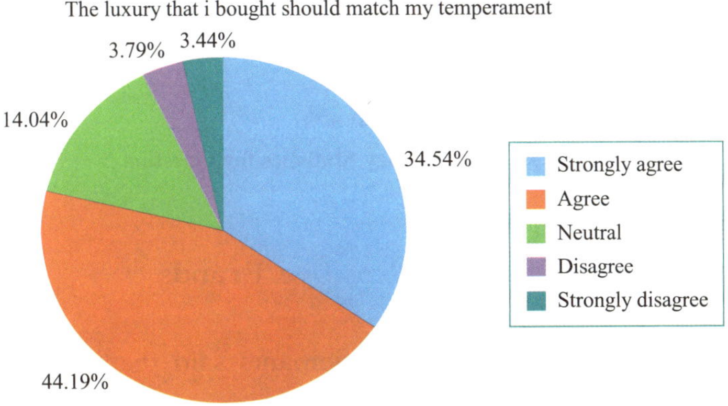

Figure 3.11 Frequency Statistics for Question 1

3.2.2 Minding the Country-of-origin of Brands

As shown in Figure 3.12, 2176 participants minded country of brand, accounting for 65.01%, i.e. over six and a half of ten consumers were concerned about the country information of the luxury brands during purchasing. While the number of participants who did not care or mind country of brand accounted only 25.58%, and only 9.41% (315 persons) did not pay any attention to country of brand. Compared with 2014, the data of 2015 showed that the proponents of this option increased 8.81% and the neutral dropped 9.60%. The above data showed more and more Chinese consumers attached importance to "country of brand", in other words, Chinese consumers were paying more attention to the brand heritage and its historical evolution. Evidently, country of origin information played significant role in improving brand value.

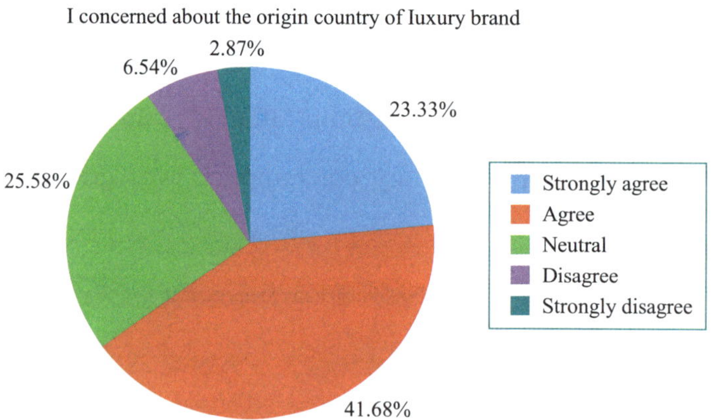

Figure 3.12 Frequency Statistics for Question 2

3.2.3 The Popularity of Sensitive Brands

As Figure 3.13 shows, 2287 participants said that the luxury brands with high recognition prioritized their choice, accounting for 68.33%.

Those who refused to consider this were 316 people(9.50%). Compared with 2014, the 2015 data showed that the proponents of this option increased by 18.41%, the neutral dropped by 14.52% and the opposed decreased by 3.89%,which again confirmed that brand recognition was the core factor of brand assets. Brand recognition was the recognition level of a given brand among consumers compared with other similar rivalry brands. The higher the brand recognition was, the deeper its impression lived on consumers' memory, and the more powerfully it affeced consumers' purchasing behavior.

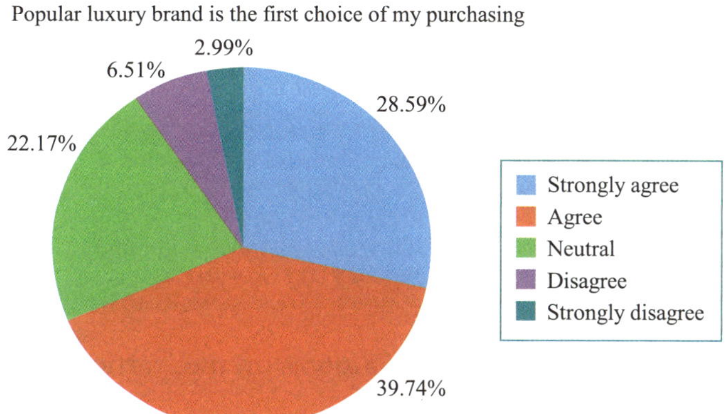

Figure 3.13 Frequency Statistics for Question 3

3.2.4 Focusing on Cost-effectiveness

When asked whether luxury goods' favorable price, such as outbound buying, duty-free shopping or discount promotion, stimulated their buying inclination, as it shows in Figure 3.14, nearly seven in ten participants (2389) said yes, which showed price factor greatly influenced Chinese consumers' luxury goods purchasing. However, compared with 2014, the 2015 data showed that the proponents of this option decreased by 5.02%, which means Chinese consumers' sensitivity to price decreased. In fact, price was a complicated concept to Chinese consumers. On one hand, it

was universally acknowledged that you got what you paid for; on the other hand, the high price of international brands in China market drove more and more Chinese consumers to take various chances to avoid unnecessary money loss, which was the result of equality principle of trade.

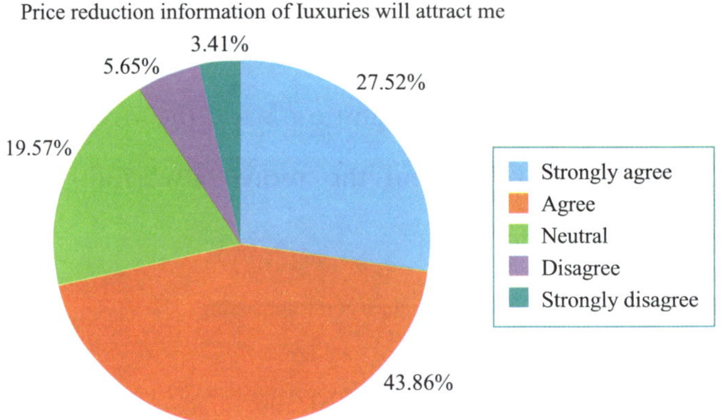

Figure 3.14　Frequency Statistics for Question 4

3.2.5　Listening to Accompanying Friends

As it shows in Figure 3.15, 53.66% of the participants (1796 persons) would listen to their accompanying friends' suggestions when buying luxury goods, the neutral (1045 persons) accounted for 31.22% and the opposed (506 persons) 15.12 %. There had always been the tradition of listening to experts' or teachers' advice, the accompanying friends or opinion leaders' effect in Chinese consumers' luxury goods purchasing behavior lied in that individuals could act without resistance from the collective or the circle. Luxury goods consumption or buying was no exception, which also reflected that the collectivism in Chinese traditional culture and value come into play. Compared with 2014, the 2015 data did not show significant change: the proponents increased by 1.92%, the neutral increased by 1.19% and the opponents decreased by 3.11%.

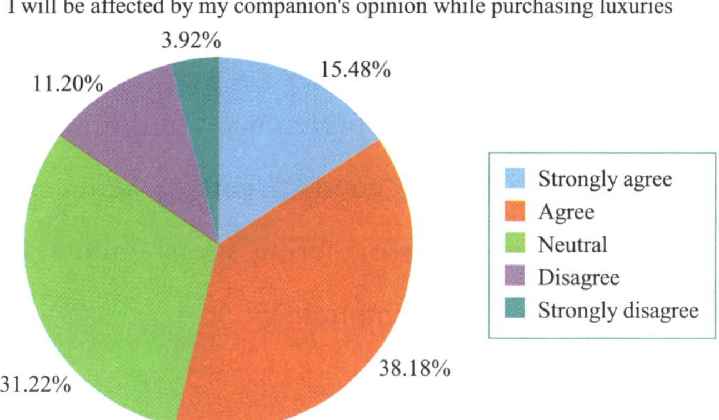

Figure 3.15 Frequency Statistics for Question 5

3.2.6 Preferring Limited Edition

As it shows in Figure 3.16, among all the participants, the number of those who preferring limited edition ware 1793 persons, accounting for 53.57%, 29.64% (992 persons) held neutral attitude, and 16.79% (562 persons) opposed. Compared with 2014, the 2015 data showed that the proponents of this option increased by 13.63%. The above data hinted that the stratification of luxury goods customized demands should attract special attention, which meaned a signal that high-end consumption is strengthening, which also showed that consumers' demands for luxury

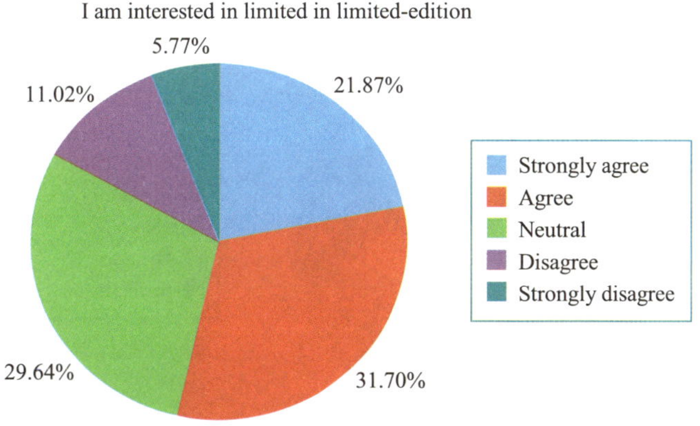

Figure 3.16 Frequency Statistics for Question 6

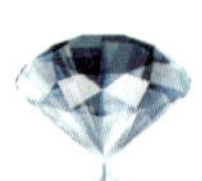

goods customization had grown. Limited edition represented unique individuality of its designer or owner; they were in the minority. Chinese luxury goods consumers had obvious preference for limited edition's mass customization. They hoped luxury goods' "scarcity, uniqueness and limit" features perfectly fitted the value of "bring users unique enjoyment and elite status" by luxury goods consumption.

3.2.7 Reverence for Nature

"Reverence for nature" is the expression of "Simplicity is profound in philosophy govern by non-action" in Chinese Taoism culture and values. As Figure 3.17 shows, seven in ten participants (2459 persons) said they "reverence nature", the neutral (656 persons)was 19.60%, and the opponent (232 persons) was 6.93%. Apparently, Taoism influences Chinese consumers' luxury goods purchasing behavior. It is worth noting that compared with 2014, 2015 data showed that the proponents of this option decreased by 7.70%, the neutral increased by 4.62% and the opponent increased by 3.07%. The comparative data also reflected the complexity of China's luxury goods consumption behavior, so how to realize the harmo-

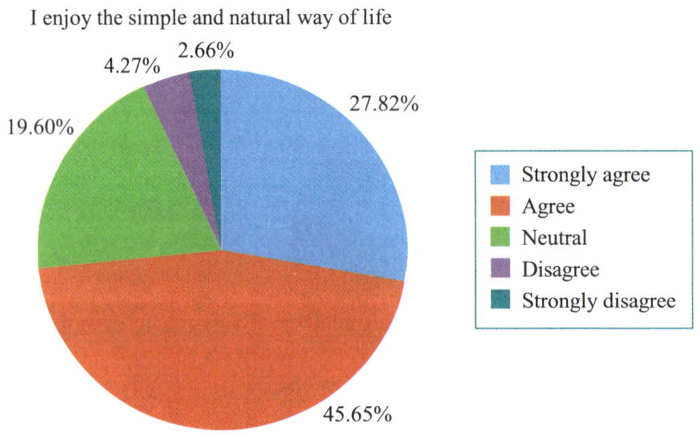

Figure 3.17 Frequency Statistics for Question 7

nious unity of "seeking something new and original" and "reverencing nature" was a problem in China market facing luxury brands.

3.2.8 Self-gift Giving

This option was used to measure self-gift giving motive in luxury goods consumption. As Figure 3.18 shows that 59.73% (1999 persons) participants bought luxury goods to treat themselves, the neutral (892 persons) was 26.65% and the opponent (456 persons)was 13.62%. This showed that western individualism values had pretreated into Chinese people's value system and influenceed Chinese people's luxury goods buying behavior. Compared with 2014, 2015 data showed that this option's proponents increased by 7.00%, the neutral decreased by 7.39% and the opposed increased by 0.39%. This data reflected that China's luxury goods self-consumption level kept rising and luxury market connected with international market was more and more routinized.

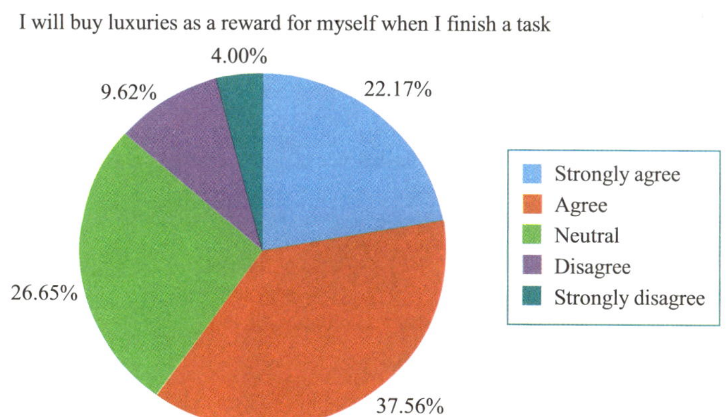

Figure 3.18 Frequency Statistics for Question 8

This was also agrees with the report result released by French Reuters. In October 2015, French Reuters released a large-scale survey result concerning the luxury goods retailers in the United States, Asia and

Europe and disclosed that Chinese consumers bought luxury goods mainly for self-use or giving to their friends, rather than giving to their superior or officials as gift.

3.2.9 Concerned about Price-budget Ratio

This question was used to test whether participants were impulsive buyers. The impulsive buyers are those who have no shopping plan and have no budget based on their income and would not compare prices in different shops. In contrast, rational buyers would make perfect choice be tween private budget, commodity quality and different prices offered by different channels. As Figure 3.19 shows that 75.56% (2529 persons) par ticipants would make rational choice. 16.97% (568 persons) held neutral attitude and 7.47% (250 persons) were opposed. It could be seen that in China's luxury goods consumption group, rational consumers were the ma - jority. Compared with 2014, the 2015 data showed that this option's proponents decreased by 4.62%, the neutral increased by 1.39% and the opposed increased by 3.23%. The general change was small.

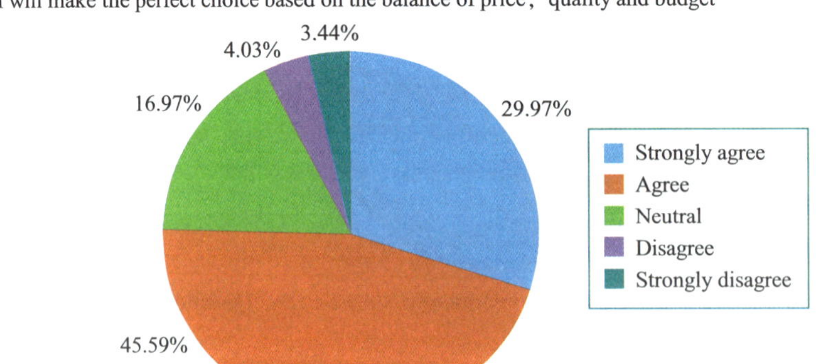

Figure 3.19 Frequency Statistics for Question 9

3.2.10 Buying Familiar Luxury Brands

As Figure 3.20 shows that 73.80% (2470 persons) participants would buy familiar luxury brands, the neutral was 18.64% (624 persons) and the opponent proportion was 7.56% (253 persons). Over seven in ten consumers would buy their familiar luxury brands, which meaned that the higher the brand familiarity was, the higher the brand's recognition.

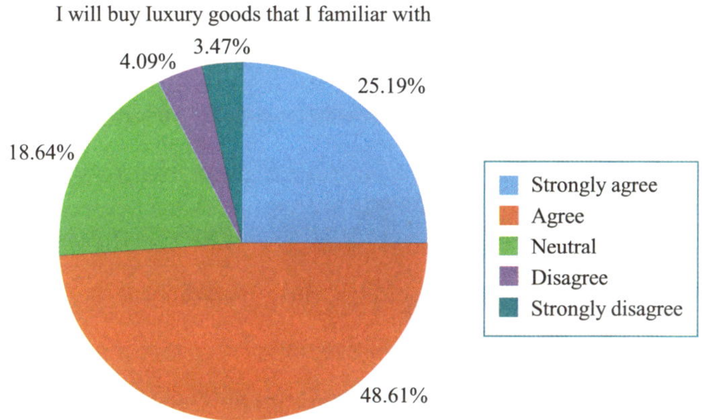

Figure 3.20 Frequency Statistics for Question 10

3.2.11 Emphasizing Shopping Environment

The question "the comfort level that I am concern about when buying luxury goods (place, shop, and staff" was used to research luxury goods consumers' concern on shopping environment, especially the comfort level when shopping. Generally, shopping environment factors include shopping places' architecture style, exterior environment, window design, and sales persons' service quality. As Figure 3.21 shows, 72.06% (2412 persons) participants were concerned about shopping environment and shopping experience, 19.90% (666 persons) held neutral attitude and 8.04% (269 persons) opposed. Compared with 2014, the 2015 data showed that this op-

tion's proponents increased by 2.75%, the neutral decreased by 1.58% and the opponent increased by 4.33%. The overall change was no big. Obviously, shopping environment and atmosphere were very important to most luxury goods buyers. Sales team with high-quality, positive and comfortable shopping experience and feeling would effectively promote luxury goods buying behavior.

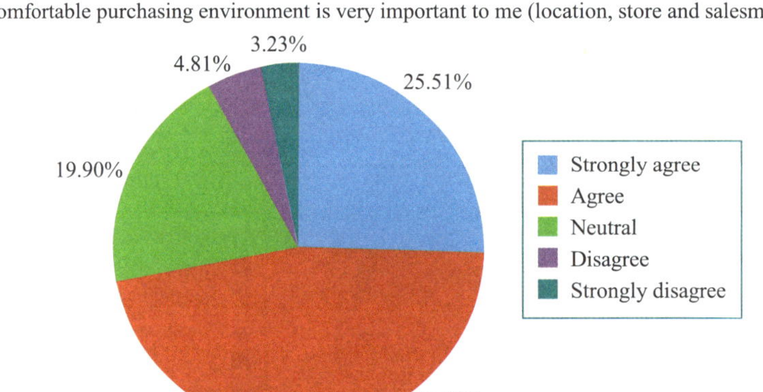

Figure 3.21 Frequency Statistics for Question 11

3.2.12 Matching Behavior and Role

The question "one's speech and behavior should match his or her role" was used to measure the effect of Confucian culture and values on Chinese consumers' luxury goods buying. Document research had shown that Confucian culture in China's traditional culture and values emphasized that when dealing with the relationship between individuals and society one should scrupulously abide by his or her duty, and self-consciously maintain social order. Because the exterior social mark of luxury goods had distinct features, Confucian culture dominating Chinese people in dealing with the relationship between individuals and society exerted driving effect on luxury goods purchasing. As Figure 3.22 shows, 78.67%

(2633 persons) participants agreed that Confucian culture and values of "one's speech and behavior should fit his or her social role", 14.73% (493 persons) held neutral attitude and 6.60% (221 persons)were against. It Could be seen that social role concept in Confucian culture or social hierarchy thinking still rooted in Chinese consumers' values and was significantly universal.

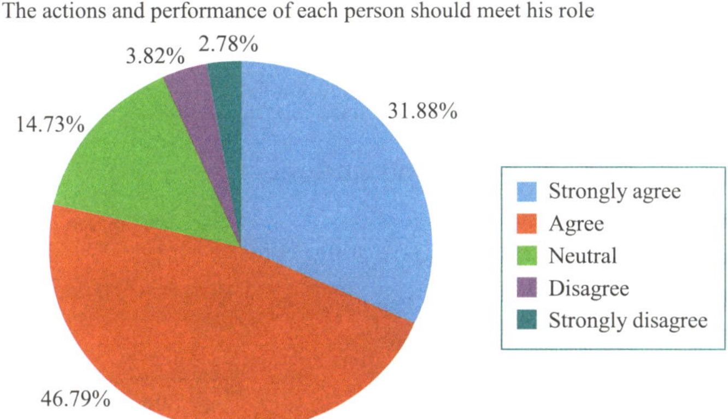

Figure 3.22 Frequency Statistics for Question 12

3.2.13 Uneasiness Brought by High-price

As Figure 3.23 shows that 41.29% （1382 persons） participants felt uneasy after buying expensive luxury goods and this would form hindrance to future luxury goods buying; 33.55% (1123 persons) participants had neutral attitude and there were 842 or 25.16% opponents. This statistics showed that only forty percent of Chinese consumers felt uneasy after buying luxury goods and sixty percent did not, which reflected that most Chinese consumers' luxury goods buying behaviors were rational, not impulsive. But it cannot be neglected that 40% of the buyers felt uneasy after buying, because they accounted for onethirds of the total group. In fact, since high expenditure behavior of buying luxury goods went against

Chinese traditional value of "being thrift is a virtue and the cultivation of a gentleman", which caused some consumers to feel guilty after buying expensive luxury goods and restrained their future buying. To analyze from this point, the weakening buying behavior of some consumers might not be caused by small purchasing power, but the guilty arisen from luxury goods consumption under traditional thinking's influence. Compared with 2014, 2015 data showed that this option's proponents increased by 4.91%, the neutral decreased by 7.75% and the opponents increased by 2.84%. The neutral consumers were reducing, signifying that participants had more specific understanding and attitude.

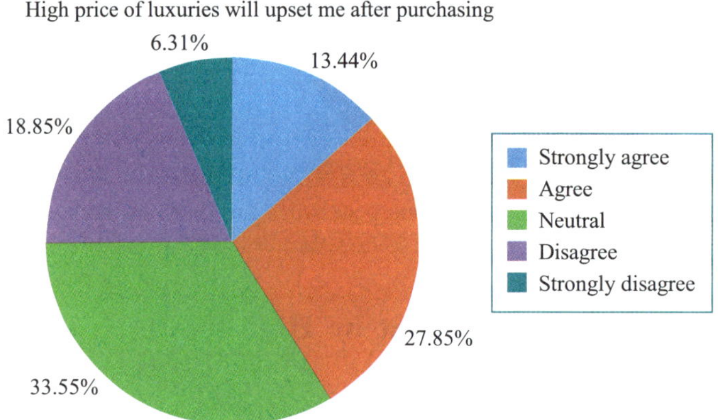

Figure 3.23 Frequency Statistics for Question 13

3.2.14 Preferring the Classic

Generally, luxury goods' classic ones have stood the test from time and market, and have greatly reduced consumers' buying risks, thus favored by most consumers. In contrast, the new arrivals exist in the market for a short time and can only win the favor of some pioneering buyers who seek something new and original and cannot be accepted by the mass. In this research, as the Figure 3.24 shows that 62.89% (2105 persons) of the participants said they found classic goods more attractive to them than new ones, 28.35% (949 persons) of them chose to be neutral and 8.76% (293 persons) were opposed. This data show the potential three-tiered market structure of China luxury goods consumer market, which meaned 62.89% of the consumers formed conservative market, 8.75% of the consumers formed pioneering market and 28.35% of them formed waiting-and-seeing market. The market scale ratio was 6 : 1 : 3. Compared with 2014, the 2015 data show that this option's proponents increased by 1.24%, the neutral decreased by 2.89%, and the opposed increased by 1.64%. There was no significant change. The comparison and analysis of the two years further explained that the tree-tiered market structure put forward in this study had stable features.In future research, we will pay full attention.

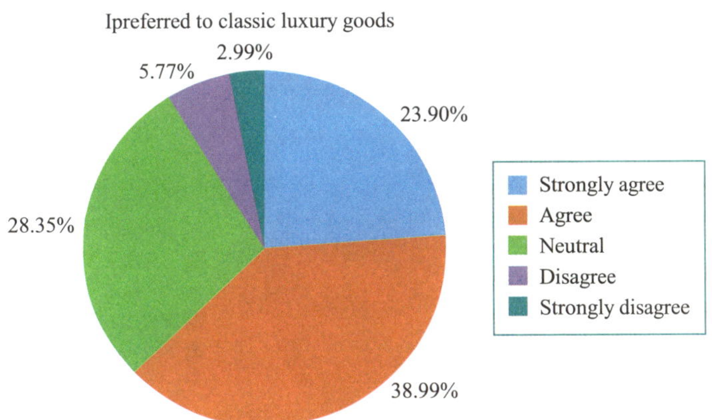

Figure 3.24 Frequency Statistics for Question 14

3.2.15 Focusing on the Maintenance and Appreciation of Value

The real connotation of luxury goods is not always the expression of money, but a cultural symptom, which reflects the accumulation of time

and the sedimentation of culture. Therefore, some luxury goods are also regarded as anti-inflation commodity and have the function of investment and appreciation of value. As Figure 3.25 shows, 61.88% (2027 persons) participants considered about their future appreciation when buying them, 26.41% (884 persons) of the surveyed stayed neutral and 11.71% (200 persons) said they did not take this into consideration. Compared with 2014, the 2015 data showed that this option's proponents increased by 9.83%, the neutral decreased by 6.42% and the opposed ones decreased by 3.42%. The above data demonstrated that Chinese consumers were becoming more concerned about luxury goods' function of maintaining and appreciating value; they showed increasing interest in those luxury ones which had collecting value. This trend certainly provided new idea and passageway for luxury brands to extend upward.

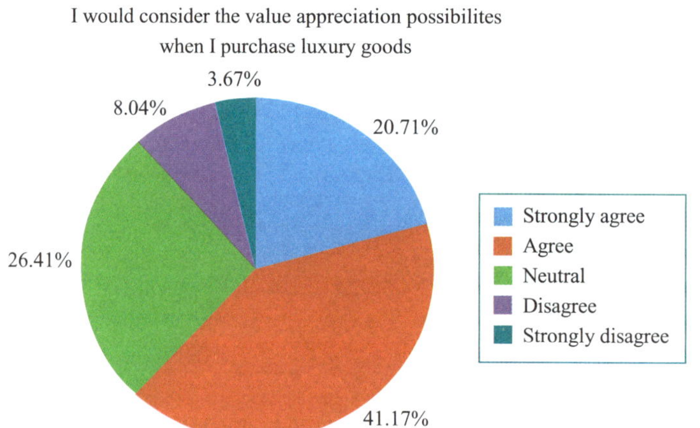

Figure 3.25 Frequency Statistics for Question 15

3.2.16 Lifting Self-confidence

As Figure 3.26 shows that 62.00% (2075 persons) of the participants hoped to lift self-confidence through consuming luxury goods, 25.90% (867 persons) stayed neutral and 12.10% (405 persons)were against. This

statistics hinted that luxury brands had double attributes, i.e. consumer could satisfy both their material and spiritual demands by consuming luxury goods, while lifting self-confidence was a manifestation of spiritual demand satisfaction.

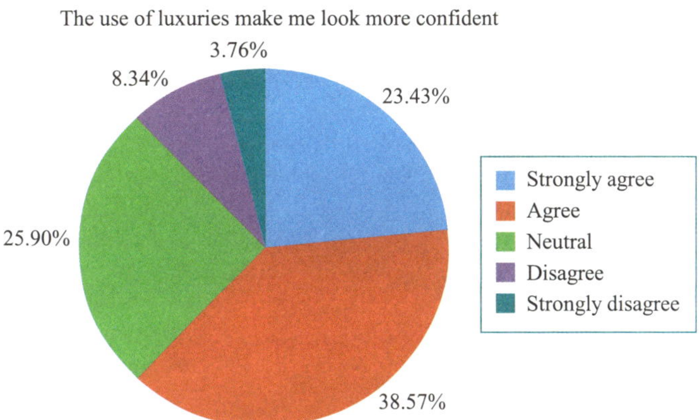

Figure 3.26 Frequency Statistics for Question 16

3.2.17 Expressing Dignity

As Figure 3.27 shows, 58.17% (1947 persons) of the participants thought luxury goods symbolize dignity, 28.83% (965 persons) remained neutral and 13.00% (435 persons) were against. Since luxury goods have the characteristics of high-quality, high-price and scarcity, luxury brands have the mark value of exclusiveness, thus becoming the symbol of one's distinguished identity. This research showsed that nearly six in ten Chinese consumers agreed with this, and only 13% disagree, which explained the show-off consumption in some Chinese consumers' luxury goods consuming behaviors.

Comparing the average value of those in Figure 3.26 and Figure 3.27 with 2014, we find in the 2015 data that the proponents increased by 9.485%, the neutral decreased by 10.53% and the opposed increased by

only 1.05%. This data showed that on one hand Chinese consumers thought luxury goods could lift self-confidence and express dignity and on the other hand Chinese consumers' luxury goods buying had two important motive—to lift self-confidence and express dignity, and these two motives were becoming more universal.

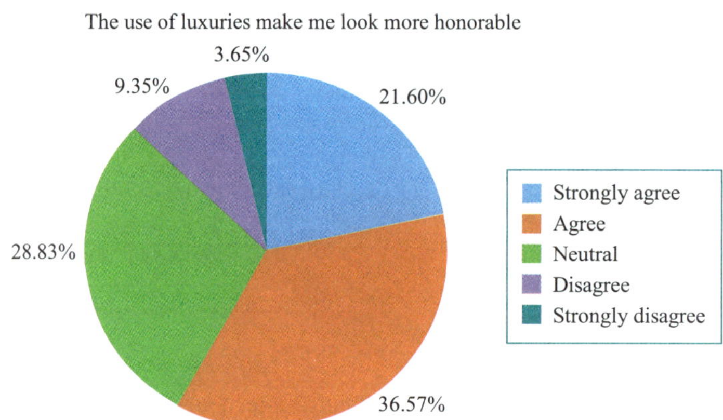

Figure 3.27 Frequency Statistics for Question 17

3.2.18 High Price and Premium Quality

As it shows in Figure 3.28, 70.12% (2347 persons) of the surveyed agreed that luxury goods' high price arose from their high quality and outstanding craft, 21.30% (713 persons) were neutral and 8.57% (287 persons) were against. We could see that the majority of Chinese consumers recognized luxury goods' high quality and high price. Compared with 2014, the 2015 data showed that this question's proponents increased by 0.68%, the neutral reduced by 1.62% and the opposed increased by 0.93%. There was no obvious change, which reflected that high price and fine quality were essential factors of luxury goods.

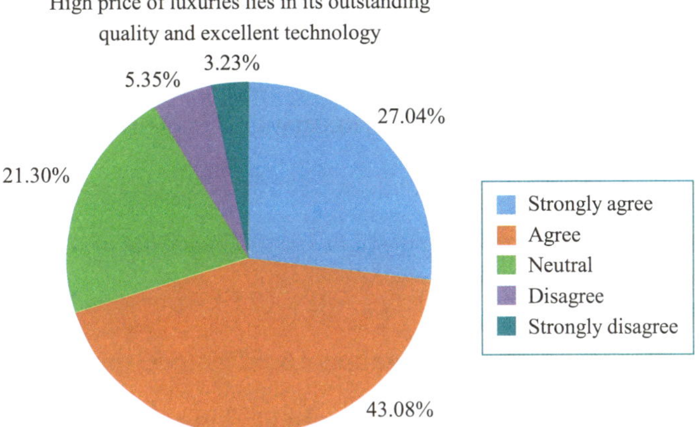

Figure 3.28 Frequency Statistics for Question 18

3.2.19 Influence of Shopping Guide

This question was used to survey whether Chinese consumers' luxury goods buying was influenced by shopping guides. As it shows in Figure 3.29, 59.30% (1985 persons) of the surveyed said they considered about sales person's suggestions, 30.06% (1006 persons) said they don't and 10.64% (356 persons) said they refused shopping guides. Compared with 2014, in 2015 data, the proponents increased by 16.19%, the neutral decreased by 10.75% and the opposed decreased by 5.40%. The above

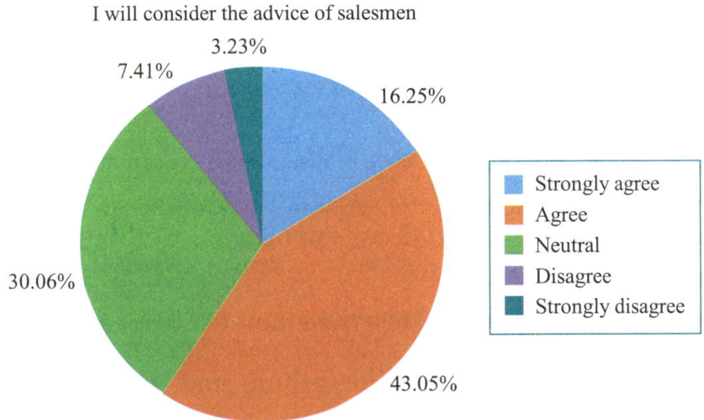

Figure 3.29 Frequency Statistics for Question 19

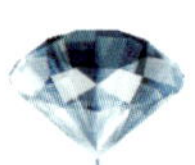

statistics showed that shopping guides played a very important role in consumers' buying decision. In store sales, would-trained shopping guides wowld actively advance the sales at luxury goods stores.

3.2.20 Selecting Good-bargain

As it shows in Figure 3.30, 75.74% (2535 persons) of the surveyed would patiently select relative bargains, 16.52% (553 persons) stayed neutral and 7.74% (259 persons)were against. This data showed that most Chinese people's luxury goods consumption was rational. They compared and analyzed, then judged whether it was a bargain before they acted. Compared with 2014, the proponents in 2015 data increased by 2.44%, the neutral decreased by 2.44% and the opposed increased by 1.84%. There was no big difference, which meaned that this behavioral habit was relatively stable.

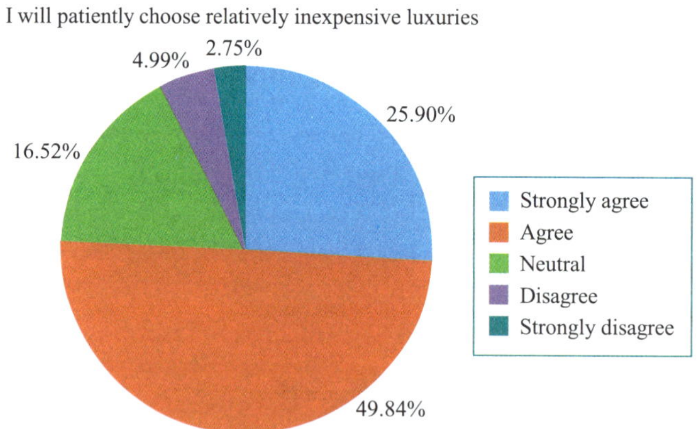

Figure 3.30 Frequency Statistics for Question 20

3.2.21 Moderation and Low-profile

This question was used to test whether Chinese luxury goods consumers were influenced by Confucian culture and values of "the doctrine of mean" in daily life. As it shown in Figure 3.31, 62.27% (2084 per-

sons) of the participants observed the doctrine of mean, kept low key, and did not want to lose justice and serenity, 25.87% (866 persons) stayed neutral and 11.86% (397 persons) of them were opposed. We could see that the majority of Chinese luxury goods consumers were deeply influenced by Confucian culture and values. Compared with 2014, the proponents in the 2015 data decreased by 10.43%, the neutral increased by 5.37%, and the proponents increased by 5.05%, which meaned that people were becoming more high-profiled. Luxury goods consumption itself was a high-profile behavior.

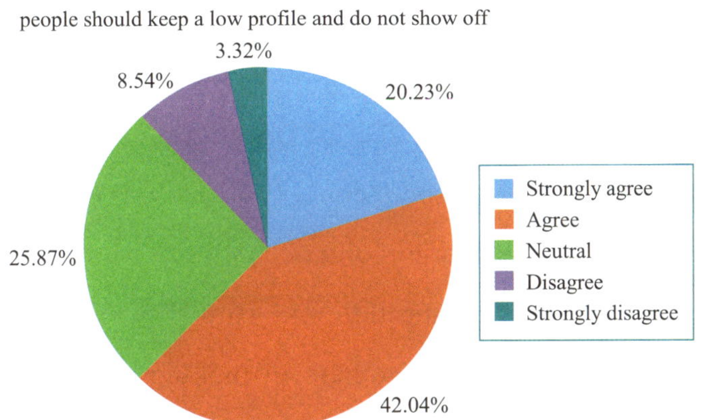

Figure 3.31 Frequency Statistics for Question 21

3.2.22 One's Action Meet His Status

This was a new added question of the report of 2015, which used to test whether Confucian culture influences Chinese luxuries consumers or not in daily life. Figure 3.32 shows that 75.92% of respondents (2541 persons) considered that one's action should accord with his /her status. 16.94% of respondents (567 persons) were neutral and others (7.14%) were oppose in this question. This suggested that most consumers thought that one's action should meet his/her action in the guidance of Confucian culture.

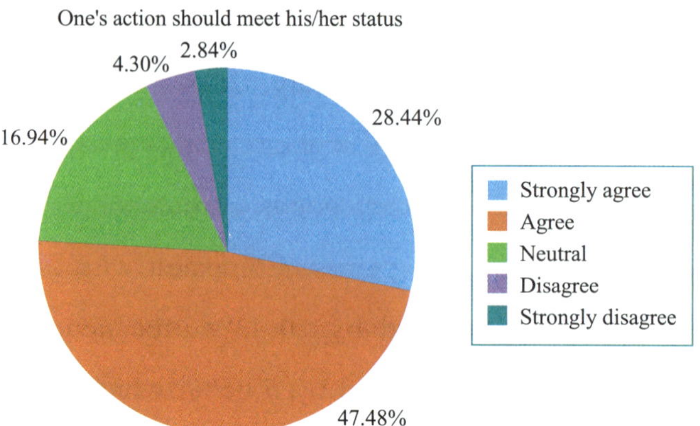

Figure 3.32 Frequency Statistics for Question 22

3.2.23 Effect of Meeting Group

This question was used to survey whether Chinese luxury goods consuming have conformity or the effect of meeting group. We can see from Figure 3.33 that 50.80% of respondents (1700 persons) thought their buying decisions were influenced by others. 33.13% of respondents (1109 persons) were neutral on this question and 16.07% (538 persons) thought that they were not influenced by others in making buying luxury goods. The supporters increased 14.18% in this question and opponents decreased 11.31%. This showsed that Chinese luxury goods consuming were increasingly influenced by others and the effect of opinion leader were im-

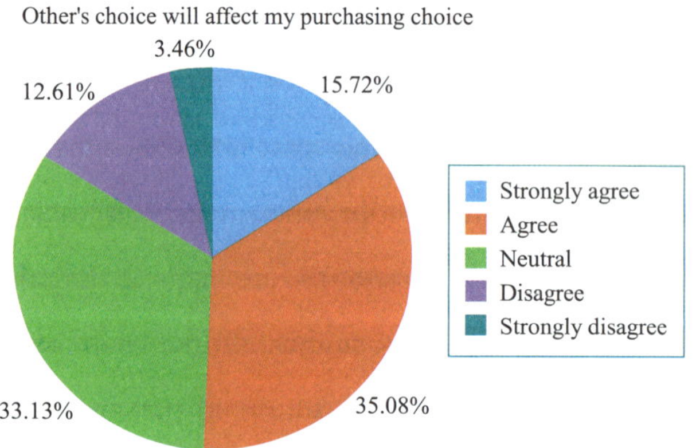

Figure 3.33 Frequency Statistics for Question 23

portant.

The unique design style and high price decide that luxury goods are not mass consumer products and only a few consumers knowing the connotation of luxuries would pay for their high prices. The luxuries that possessed by minority are considered as sign or symbol of their group. People who want enter into this group should have this symbol. It is said that Reuters conducted a large-scale survey regarding the retailers in United States, Asia and Europe on October, 2015. The result showed that the consumption habits and tastes of Chinese luxuries consumers were changing tremendously. Although traditional luxury brands were popular, many newly light luxury brands were developing prosperously under the influence of opinion leaders such as super stars.

3.2.24 Social Relation

This question aimed to find out whether sending gifts was a big motivation for people to purchase luxuries. From the results, 60.27% respondents (2017 persons) thought that buying a gift for others is necessary. 977 respondents(29.19%)chose neutral and 353 respondents 10.54% were against the view. We could see from the result that the idea of buying luxury goods as gifts was very common and well-accepted in luxury goods consuming. More than 60% respondents were willing to buy luxury goods as a gifts to others to improve their social relationship. Obviously, the attributive characters of luxury goods made great effects in becoming gifts and the values of advocating etiquette and courtesy demands reciprocity in Confucian culture influenced Chinese luxury goods buying actions.

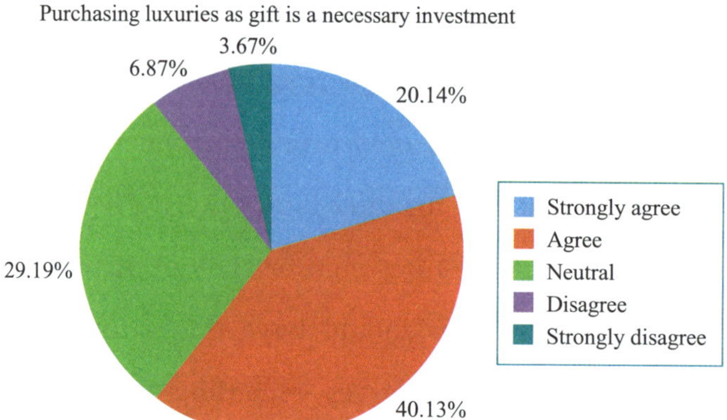

Figure 3.34　Frequency Statistics for Question 24

3.2.25　Integrating into the Circle

This question was set to investigate whether Chinese luxury consumers pay much attention to their appearance and image in the eyes of others. The results showed that 72.30% respondents (2420 persons) thought that suitable usage of luxury goods could help them integrate into certain occasions or at least not to be embarrassed on certain occasions. In addition, 657 respondents (19.63%)held neutral view and 270 respondents (8.07%)were against it. From the result, we fould that for Chinese luxury consumers, buying luxury goods was an obligation of being a member of

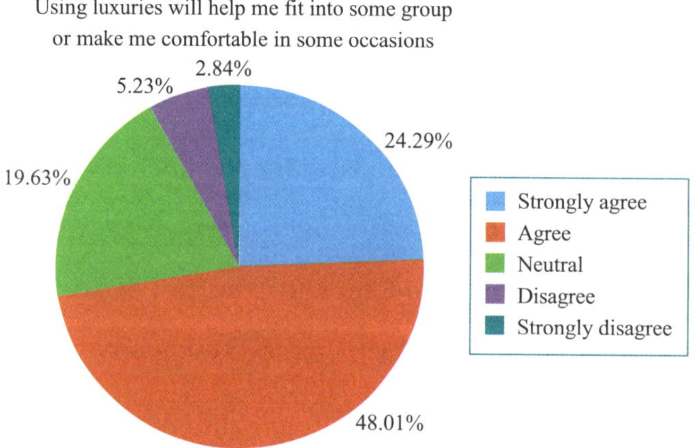

Figure 3.35　Frequency Statistics for Question 25

a certain distinguished group. Being compatible with the social status and social image of the groups they belong to was a very important motivation for them to buy luxuries. Compared with 2014, the proponents in the 2015 data increased by 13.38%, the neutral decreased by 11.23%, and the proponents decreased by 2.14%, which meaned that cumulative effect of luxury goods strengthened hugely.

3.2.26 Believing in Fate

The purpose of this question was to investigate whether Chinese luxuries consumers were affected by Chinese traditional Buddhist culture or not. The survey results showed that 2521 respondents believed things and people in life we encountered come as fate, accounting for 75.32% of the total, while 598 respondents(17.87%)held neutral views. There were only 228 respondents(6.81%)who were against it. We could see that luxury consumers in China were widely influenced by traditional Buddhist culture. Compared with 2014, the proponents in the 2015 data decreased by 2.44%, the neutral increased by 0.02%, and the proponents increased by 2.42%.

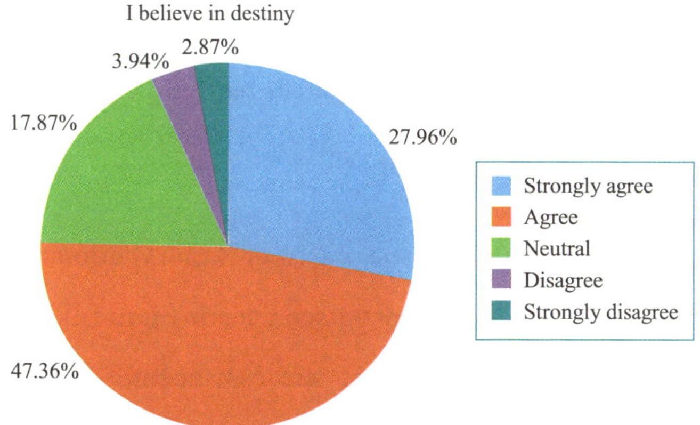

Figure 3.36 Frequency Statistics for Question 26

3.2.27 Following the Etiquettes

This question was used to investigate to what extent Chinese luxuries consumers were affected by the traditional culture's demand to "follow the etiquette". 2644 respondents thought that we should follow conventional protocol of doing things, accounting of 79% of the total. 495 respondents (14.79%)held neutral view and 208 respondents(6.21%)were against it. It could be seen that the culture of etiquettes had taken root in the value system of Chinese consumers. In addition, Compared with 2014, the 2015 data showed that this question's proponents decreased by 9.2%, the neutral increased by 5.33% and the opposed increased by 3.87%. In modern life, the influence of traditional etiquettes had the decreasing trend.

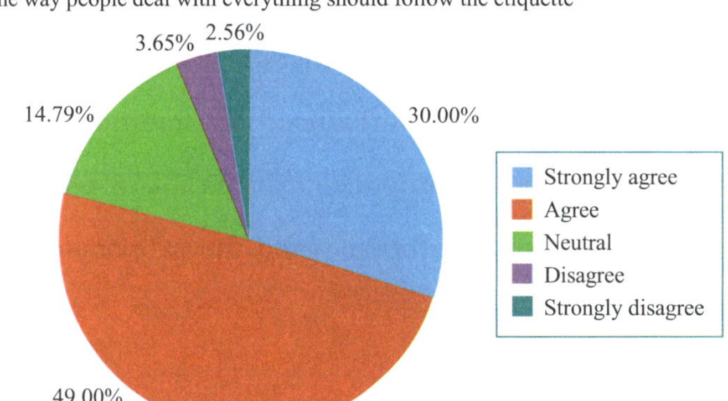

Figure 3.37 Frequency Statistics for Question 27

3.2.28 Symbol of Success

This question was used to test whether luxury goods could present success and its wideness. As it can be seen from Figure 3.38,1853 respondents regarded luxuries as symbol of success, accounting for 55.36% of the total. 977 respondents(29.19%)held neutral view, while there were 517 respondents(15.45%)who disagreed with it. Thus, we could conclude

that more than half of consumers took luxuries as the symbol of success.

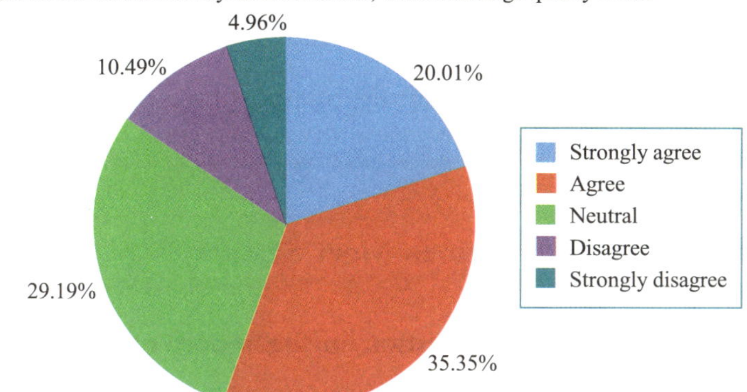

Figure 3.38 Frequency Statistics for Question 28

3.2.29 Improving Quality

As we can see from Figure 3.39, 2130 respondents thought that buy ing luxury goods could improve the quality of life, accounting of 63.64% of the total. 821 respondents(24.53%)held neutral view and 396 respondents(11.83%)were against it. The data showed that most Chinese consumers considered luxury goods as a life style and consumptive attitude of high quality.

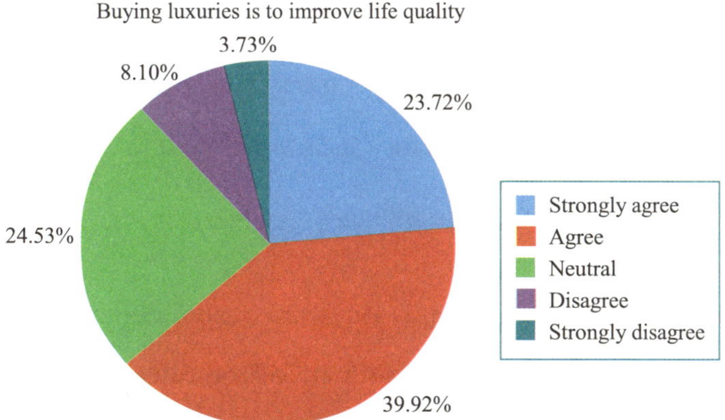

Figure 3.39 Frequency Statistics for Question 29

Compared with 2014, the 2015 data showed that this question's proponents increased by 13.43%, the neutral increased by 11.11% and the opposed reduced by 3.32%. It said that more and more consumers payed high attention to the symbolic meaning of luxury goods and the effects to improve life quality.

3.2.30 Consuming Actions Meet Status

This was a newly added question in the report of 2015. Figure 3.40 shows that 2496 respondents thought that one's consumptive actions should fit to his/her social status, accounting of 74.57% of the total. 604 respondents(18.05%)held neutral view and 247 respondents(7.38%)were against it. The data said that respondents' consumptive actions had been influence by sense of hierarchy of Confusion culture.

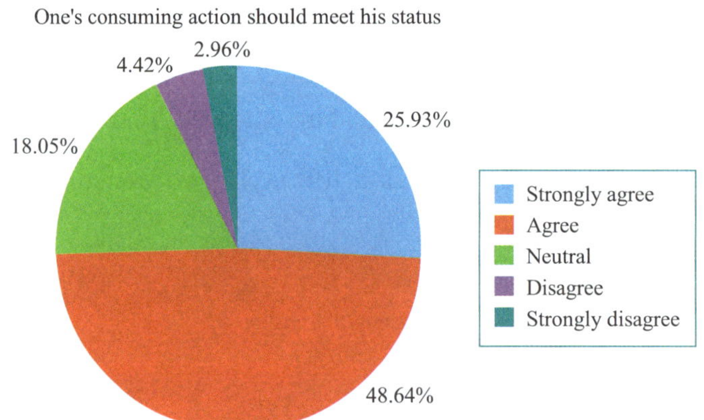

Figure 3.40 Frequency Statistics for Question 30

3.2.31 Soothing Mood

As we can see from Figure 3.41, 1823 respondents thought that they bought luxury goods in order to sooth mood or release feelings, accounting of 54.47% of the total. 941 respondents(28.11%)held neutral view and 583 respondents(17.42%)were against it. This data revealed that more

than half of Chinese consumers bought luxury goods in order to release feelings. Compared with 2014, the 2015 data showed that this question's proponents increased by 14.22%, the neutral decreased by 0.86% and the opposed reduced by 13.3%. It said that there were more and more Chinese consumers buying luxury goods in order to sooth mood.

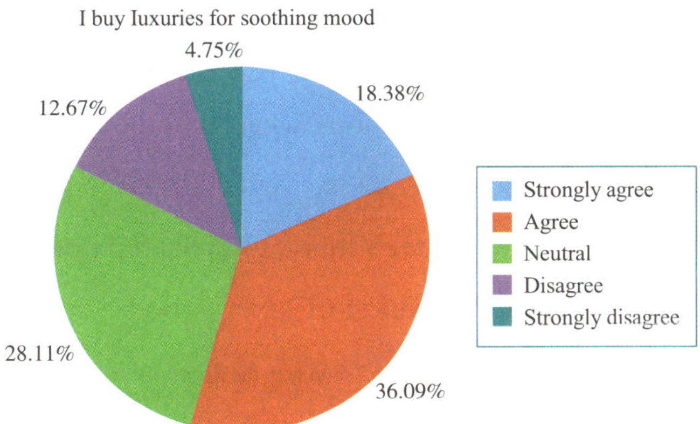

Figure 3.41 Frequency Statistics for Question 31

3.2.32 Listening to Others

This question was a newly added item of the report of 2015. It is can been seen from Figure 3.42, 69.76% (2335 persons) considered that elders and teachers' words were important to them. 794 respondents

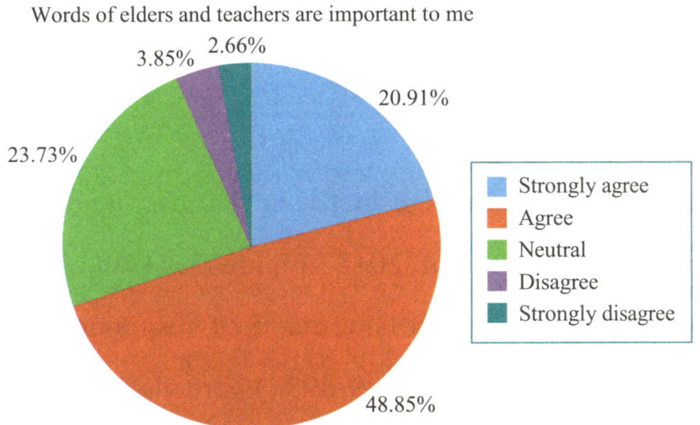

Figure 3.42 Frequency Statistics for Question 32

(23.73%)held neutral view and 218 respondents （6.51%） were against it. The data said that nearly seventy percent Chinese consumers had the habit of listening to others. They enriched their knowledge and made smart motions by learning from others.

3.2.33 Face-culture

As Figure 3.43 shows, 50.37% (1368 persons) participants considered that they tended to high-end shops when they bought things with the riches, 35.08% (1174 persons) of the surveyed stayed neutral and 14.55% (487 persons) said they did not take this into consideration. This data said that there existed vanity in the market of luxury goods.

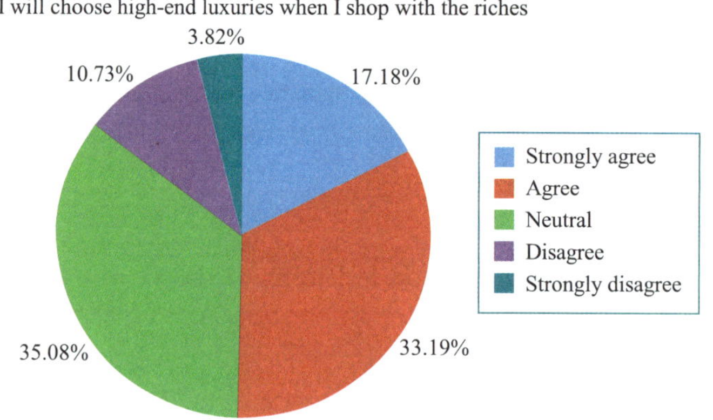

Figure 3.43 Frequency Statistics for Question 33

3.2.34 Karma

This question was used to test the influence of Buddhist culture on Chinese consumers by believing ideas of karma, which was a newly added question in the report of 2015. Figure 3.44 showed that 65.94% (2207 persons) believeed ideas of karma. 829 respondents(24.77%)held neutral view and 311 respondents(9.29%)were against it. The data revealed that no more than 10% respondents did not believe ideas of karma and most respondents believed it, which reflected that the binding of Buddhist value influenced Chinese consumers in buying luxury goods.

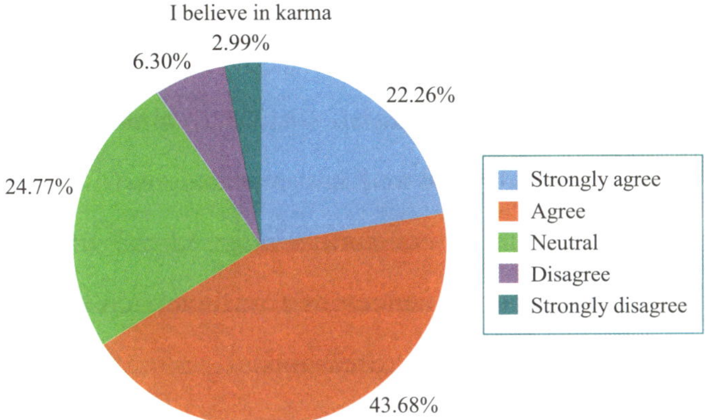

Figure 3.44 Frequency Statistics for Question 34

3.2.35 Consciousness and Self-discipline

This was a newly added question in 2015's report. It can been seen from Figure 3.45, 74.82% (2504 persons) respondents considered that they were delighted with their self-discipline. 636 respondents (19.00%) held neutral view and 207 respondents (6.18%) were against it. This question showed that Chinese consumers hoped to present the virtue of consciousness under the effects of Confucian culture values.

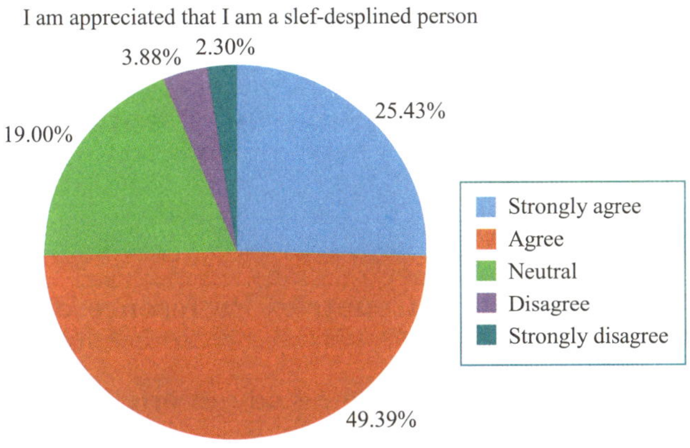

Figure 3.45 Frequency Statistics for Question 35

3.2.36 Dressings Meet Status

This was a newly added question in 2015's report. As we can see from Figure 3.46, 2489 respondents thoughts that one's dressing should fit to his/her social status, accounting of 74.37% of the total. 628 respondents(18.76%)held neutral view and 230 respondents(6.87%)were against it. This reflected that Chinese consumers pursued the fitness of dressings and social status under the influences of Confucian culture values. It was important to pay attention to one's dressings.

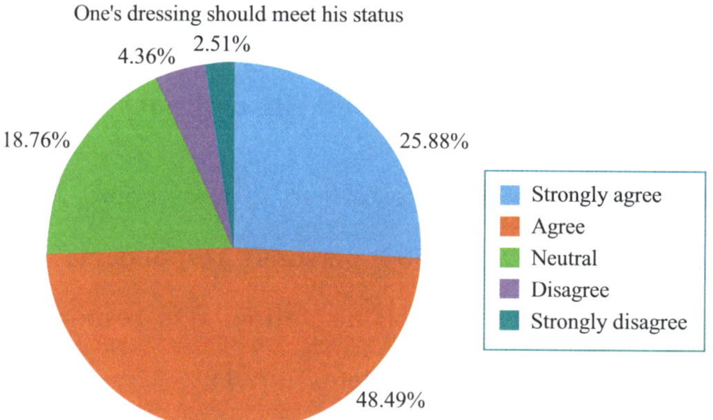

Figure 3.46 Frequency Statistics for Question 36

3.3 The Originating Countries Preference of Brands and Choice of Channels

3.3.1 The Originating Countries Preference of Brands

As we can see in Figure 3.47, the study of originating countries preference of brands was intended to know which countries' luxury goods were known by Chinese. Countries listed in questionnaire includes U.S.A, Switzerland, German, Italy, Japan, France, Span and U.K. More than 90% luxury brands come from these countries. The statistics result showed that the top3 were France, U.S.A and Italy. 59.93% people chose France, which decreased 10% compared to 2014. U.S.A come in the second place and Italy was the third place. The rank of last year was France (71.6%), Italy (68.2%), Switzerland (47.0%), U.S.A (28.5%), German (28.4%), U.K.(25.0%), Japan(13.1%) and Span(7.1%).

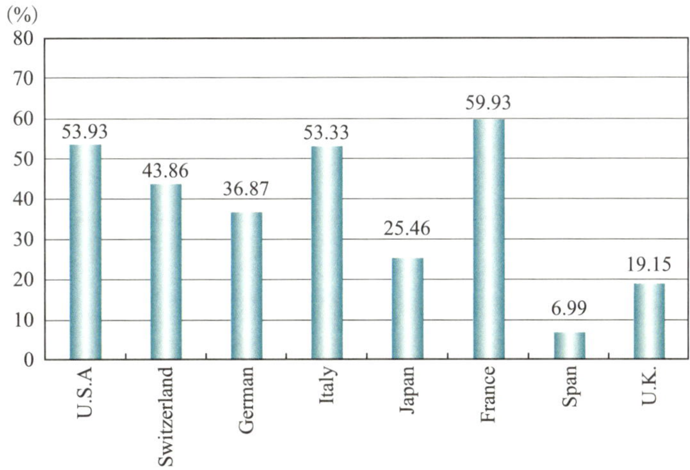

Figure 3.47 Frequency Statistics of Originating Countries of Brands

3.3.2 The Determinants of Preference of Originating Countries of Brands

As it is can be seen from Figure 3.48, when asking the question of dominants influencing preference of originating countries, 86.17% respondents chose excellent quality. 79.00% respondents chose inheritance of technique and 76.70% chose design aesthetics. We can see from the result that views of most respondents were same. In the view of Chinese consumers, luxury goods equaled to excellent quality, the inheritance of clas-

sic technique and specific design aesthetics. The three nature of luxuries built marvelous word of mouth and reputation in Chinese consumers.

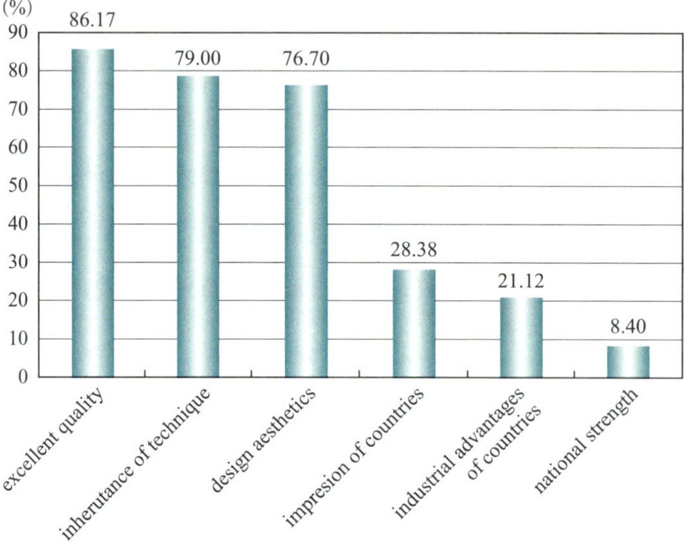

Figure 3.48 Frequency Statistics for Dominants of Preference of Originating Countries

3.3.3 Channel of Buying Luxuries Goods

This was a newly added question in 2015's report. When it comes to the question of buying channels of luxuries, the options includes franchised stores, discount stores, purchasing agents, internet and so on. Figure 3.49 shows that 64.48% respondents chose franchised stores, 53.78%

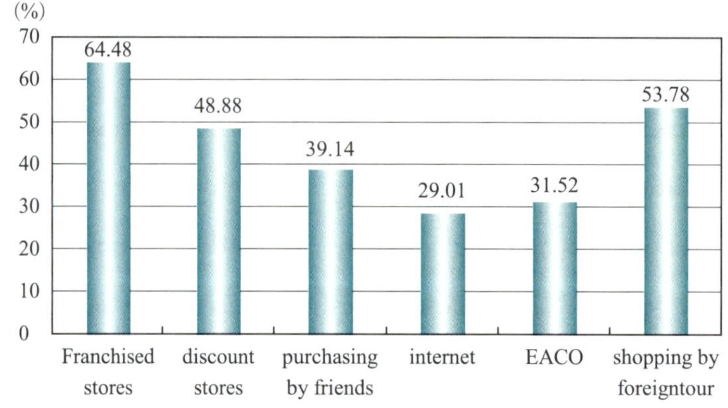

Figure 3.49 Frequency Statistics for Buying Channels of Luxury Goods

respondents chose shopping by foreign tour and 48.88% chose discount stores. The first choice of consumers was franchised. And with the rising of foreign tour, more and more consumers would buy luxury goods by foreign travel.

3.4 Chinese Luxury Goods Consumption and Luxuries in Chinese Views

Based on the results of the statistical analysis of sample data, the following is a summary report of Chinese luxury consumption and the Chinese people's understanding of luxury goods.

3.4.1 Chinese Luxury Goods Consumption

(1) Apparent Collectivism.

Influenced by the Chinese traditional culture, the sense of group identity and belongings of Chinese consumers was very intense, which had made their purchasing behaviors happened by groups, especially for upmarket products such as luxuries. Chinese luxuries purchasing behaviors were easily affected by surroundings, which could be seen from the characteristics of "preference for classics", "insinuating into groups", "bandwagon effect" and so on.

(2) Coexistence of Rationality and Impulse.

Seeing from the ups and downs of the world's luxury consumption, luxury consumption has a process from irrational growth to rational regression and a stage from conspicuous consumption into the scientific consumption. Because of the asymmetric information, luxury consumption

behavior is complex with the coexistence of rationality and impulse. For example, characteristics such as "concern on price-quality budget", "perceived good deal", "self-discipline", "gift for self "and "preference for classical and limited items" showed consumers' rational choice for luxuries. And consumers were gradually using luxuries to meet their deeper level demands, such as "to enhance the confidence". Because consumers were gaining increasing income and becoming more educated, they were more and more concerned about their own needs. Although the phenomenon of conspicuous consumption in China still exists, but it has improved a little bit, such as "expression of honor", "symbol of success", and "face culture". Showing wealth had become the past, while the mainstream of the consumption culture would be "low key", "cultural background" and "connotative meaning". In addition, as for the constant pursuit of personality, there were increasing personalized activities and luxury consumption. Luxuries would return to affordable prices and consumers' behaviors would be gradually based on brand cultural identity.

As shown in Figure 3.48, more than 70% of the respondents would take "good quality", "crafts heritage" and "design aesthetic" into consideration when they bought luxuries. Consumers used to measure luxury goods with price when luxury goods began to enter China's market, which manifested they were not mature and rational enough. This survey found that the current Chinese consumers not only paid attention to the price of luxury goods, but also took notice of their brand culture and design style, such as "national impression", "national industrial advantage", and "national political and economic strength". This showed that China's luxury consumers started to enter a mature stage to appreciate the inner beauty of luxuries from a naive stage of low level involvement and awareness.

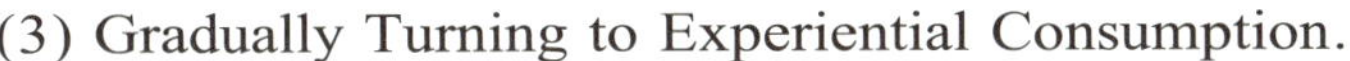

(3) Gradually Turning to Experiential Consumption.

Traditional luxury consumption is characterized by a typical conspicuous consumption while the new emerging luxury consumption focuses on consumers' experimenting. When a simple high quality service could not meet the needs of high-end customers, experiential consumption becomes very important. "Pay attention to the shopping environment" showed that creating a comfortable and delicate space was a way to please customers.

(4) Preference Traditional Shopping Channel and Trying E-business.

As shown in Figure 3.49, consumers could buy luxury goods from franchised stores, discount stores, friends purchasing, global online shopping, abroad travel shopping, etc. The first choice was the franchised store, followed by online shopping. This could be referred to as the transition of the full channel mode. Full channel retail is the advanced stage of the retail channels from a single channel, to multi-channel, and to cross-channels. As consumers are faced with multiple types of purchasing channels in every stage, Full channel retail centered on consumers can better fit the new consumer behaviors, and bring higher experiential value to them.

3.4.2 Luxuries in Chinese Opinion

Compared with the corresponding index of 2014, it could be seen from the statistical analysis result of the sample data this year that the luxuries in Chinese opinion were featured with "high price and high quality, appreciation and symbolic mark". According to literature study, culture is the expression and result of historical accumulation, so the "profound culture and historical accumulation" in the report of 2014 were combined to be "cultural inheritance". Furthermore, three new features were reveled

from the statistical result of the investigation: "scarcity, coexistence of classics and creativity and cognition of opinion leader".

(1) High Price and High Quality.

High price and high quality is the primary feature of luxuries. Excellent product design, superior raw material and exquisite workmanship must be adopted by luxuries to guarantee the stable high quality. Superior quality was taken as the primary reason of preferring luxuries by more than 80% of the respondents, followed by the inheritance of craft and aesthetic design.

(2) Scarcity.

For more than half of the respondents, the limited quantity and scarcity were important reasons of preferring and purchasing luxuries. In fact, through analysis from the aspect of luxuries manufacturers, they would strictly control the product quantity and time of accessing to market to highlight the symbolic significance of their products in terms of wealth, status and right so as to make people feel the scarcity of the products. Obviously, if luxuries are featured with excellent design, superior raw material and exquisite workmanship, they are not easily to be produced massive ly. The scarcity of luxuries was accepted by more than half of Chinese consumers and only a few people owned luxuries because of scarcity.

(3) Cultural Inheritance.

Most luxuries are operated by family businesses to serve the noble and many luxuries were even used by the imperial household. Luxuries have a long history through inheritance of several generations. The main feature of luxuries is the unique glorious history. The value of luxuries is not only shown from the physical product but also from the brand concept, spiritual pursuit and humanistic connotation. The consumption of luxuries is consumption of brand culture and identification of the history, background and culture of the brand. Brand history, founder, original country and craft inheritance are the four major supporting elements of the luxury. Chinese consumers paid attention to the culture in the original country of the brand as well as the special cultural deposits and connota tion the original country given to the brand.

(4) Coexistence of Classics and Creativity.

Luxury is the product of the age or the product under certain social and economic condition. As time goes on, there will be no changeless boundary between the necessities of life and luxuries. The necessities in the past may become luxuries because of non-renewable raw materials, rare quantity, time accumulation and other elements, so the objective cognition of the luxury reflects the mature consumption. The identification for the creativity of the luxury is highlighted through the further understanding of design and the transition from showy luxury consumption to personalized consumption of design. More than 60% of the consumers preferred classic style of the luxury for its unique design and outstanding func tion. Besides, the stable three-part structure in Chinese luxury market revealed from the investigation result reflects that consumers' choice of luxury is the result of integration of personality and classic type.

(5) Appreciation.

Luxuries, especially the limited or customized ones are featured with use value and collection value. Compared with ordinary consumer goods, some special commodities such as jewelry and watch are featured with special value of appreciation because of time accumulation, rare raw material, lost craft and the like. More than 60% of Chinese consumers might consider the appreciation of the luxury while purchasing it. For people

who collect luxuries for appreciation or conduct financial management through luxuries in use of financial investment methods, the investment in use of luxuries was a new channel for investors.

(6) Symbol Mark.

The symbolic mark of luxuries refers to the symbolic meaning of satisfying the consumers' need of showing off wealth, status and lifestyle. In the immature stage of consumption, people prefer luxuries because they want to show off their economic strength and social status or create, maintain and extend the space of individual survival and career development through luxuries. Chinese consumers paid more attention to the symbolic value of the luxury because they wanted to pursue self-esteem, high end, confidence, success, wealth, status, acceptance of the circle and other expressions. Besides, consuming luxuries of the same symbol system could obtain the sense of identity and belonging inside of the group, so the symbolic value of the luxury was obvious.

(7) Cognition of Opinion Leader.

Chinese people were in the habit of listening to suggestions of partners and experts, so the "opinion leader" was the important carrier of the interpersonal communication network. The effect of "opinion leader" had promoted the development of many newly-developing luxury brands because the consumption habit and taste of luxury consumers had changed a lot, which showed the symbolic feature of the luxury as the group mark. In order to be accepted by the group, people had to get the symbol, so the guiding function of the opinion leader in luxury consumption played an important role.

Chapter 4 The Generality and Particularity of Chinese Consumers' Buying Decision

Chapter 4 is based on the statistical analysis result of Chapter 3 and makes a conclusion of the generality and particularity rule in the characteristics of Chinese consumers' purchase decision regarding luxury goods. The following fifteen factors have been discovered, including giving vent to emotion, self-worth, scarcity or limited quantity, self-gift giving, good life, excellent quality, shopping situation, social relation, doing one's duty, opinion leadership, integrating into the circle, preference for classical styles, brand awareness, price sensitivity, country-of-origin of brands. These factors are the universal or fundamental characteristics of Chinese consumers' purchase decision regarding luxury goods. We have also found that those fifteen factors mentioned above vary from the differences in demographic characteristics of consumers. That is to say, these factors are special due to the difference in market segmentation, or so called particularity. Specific report is given as follows.

Figure 4.1 is regression analysis result of partial correlation between Chinese consumers' purchase predisposition and their decision-making characteristics. In the chart, decision-making characteristics indicators were ranked from highest to lowest. Figure 4.2 is a bar chart concerning

mean value of these characteristics and mean value was sorted from highest to lowest.

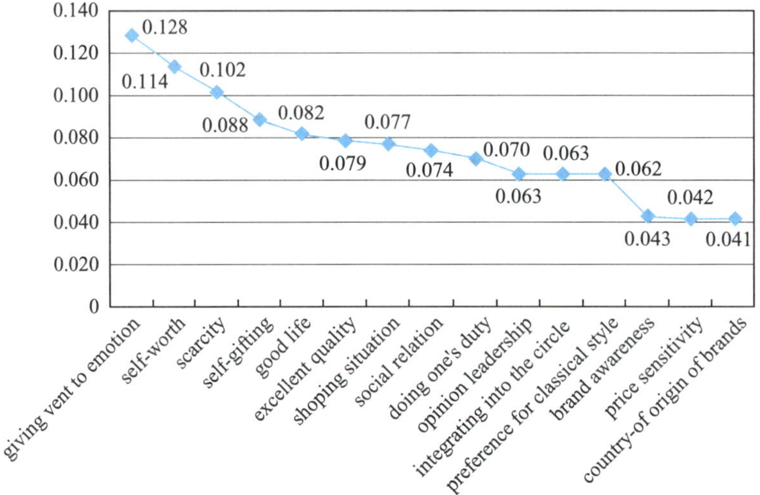

Figure 4.1 The Partial Correlation of Regression about Buying Tendency and Decision Characteristics

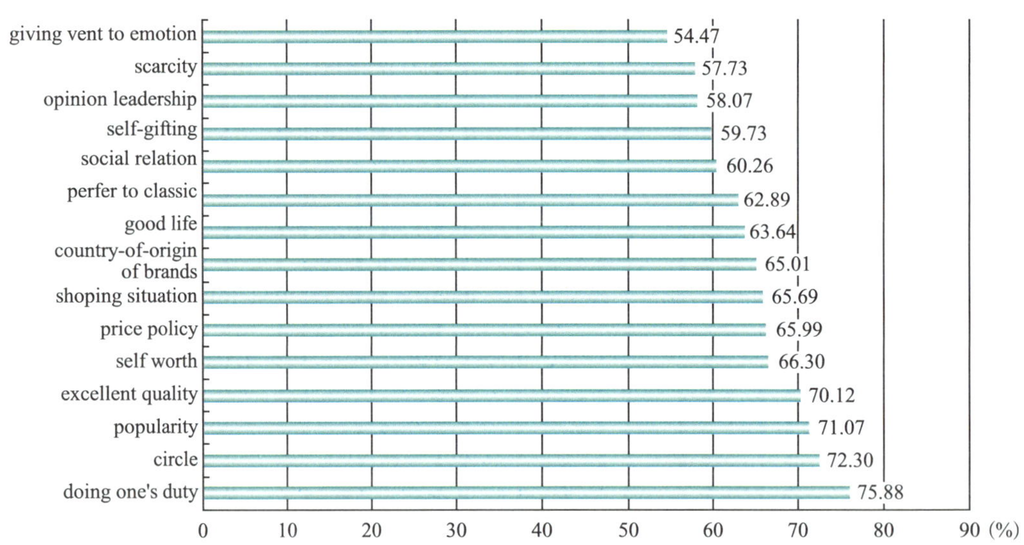

Figure 4.2 The Bar of Mean Value about Buying Decision Characteristics of Luxuries

4.1 Giving Vent to Emotion

Emotion is strong feelings which cannot be controlled easily and exert influence on behaviors and generally refers to a certain feeling that can be recognized. Some document reveals that emotion affects consumers' shopping behaviors. For example, impulse purchasing behaviors is a behavioral reflection of emotionalization. Of course, luxury goods purchasing behaviors are also without exception, even more obvious. In this survey, the item "I will purchase luxury goods for relieving my feelings" was designed to measure the influence that giving vent to emotion exerted on Chinese consumers' purchase behaviors regarding luxury goods.

Figure 4.3 is a bar chart concerning the difference in gender and age of consumers giving vent to emotion. The chart shows that among the group of people with age from 18 to 55, the ratio of people thinking that luxury goods purchasing behaviors had something to do with giving vent

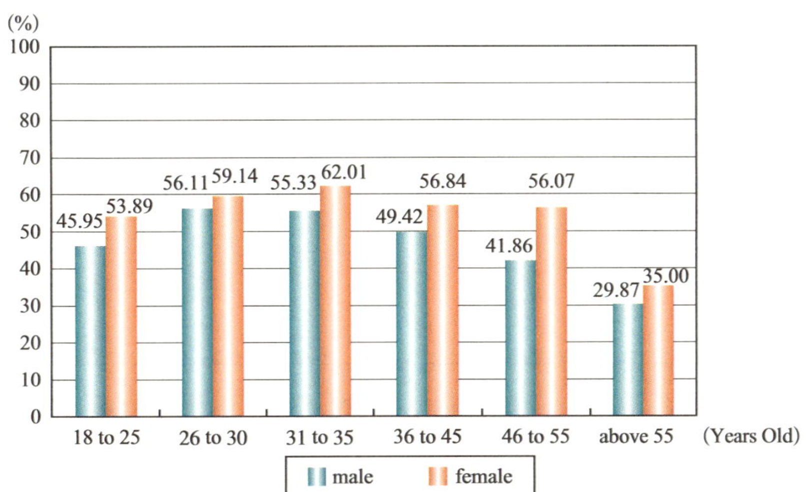

Figure 4.3 The Bar of the Differences in Gender and Age of Giving Vent to Emotion

to emotion was 41% to 62%, and as for people with every group of ages, it was easier for women to be emotional compared with men.

Generally speaking, as for the respondents with every group of ages, women consumers are more likely to give vent to emotion through purchasing luxury goods when compared with men consumers.

Given that occupational pressure has something to do with giving vent to emotion, the statistical result of occupational difference in "giving vent to emotion" was presented in Figure 4.4. The Figure shows that white-collars work in foreign-invested enterprises were major group of people who gave vent to emotion through purchasing luxury goods, accounting for 62.83%, the highest ratio. This ratio was higher than that of other group of people by 5% to 10%. Then as sorted from highest to lowest, they were in sequence professionals, white-collar workers in domestic enterprises, enterpreneurs, family, enterpreneurs freelances and students. Because of high work pressure and relatively high living costs, white-collars work in foreign-invested enterprises consequently would choose to re-

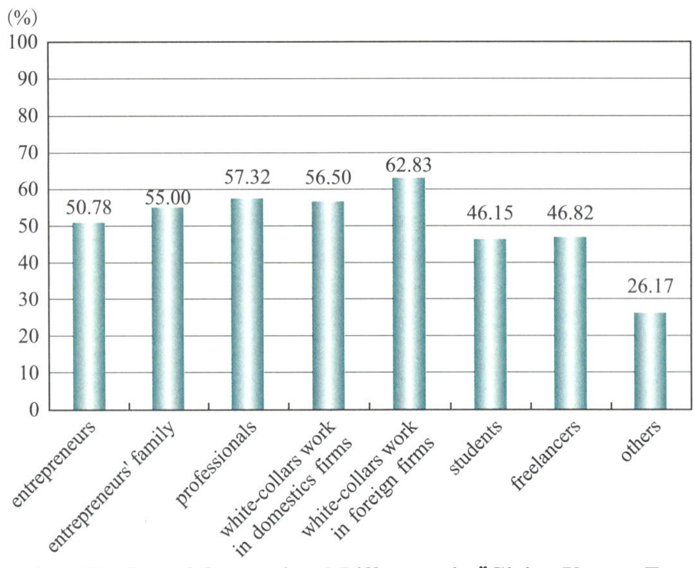

Figure 4.4 The Bar of Occupational Difference in "Giving Vent to Emotion"

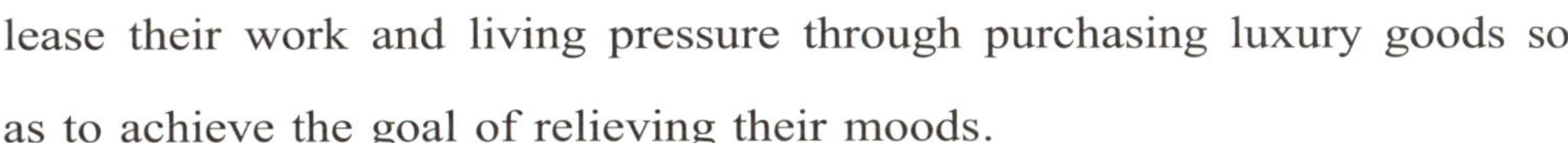

lease their work and living pressure through purchasing luxury goods so as to achieve the goal of relieving their moods.

4.2 Self-worth

Self-worth is a subjective cognition that individuals make of their importance in individual, family and the society. Enduring self-worth cognition is a relatively stable expression of personality and is likely to exert influence on consuming behaviors and purchasing behaviors of individuals. This survey adopted the following three items to measure the influence that "self-worth" exerted on Chinese consumers' luxury goods purchase. Item 1: using luxury goods can make me appear to be more distinguished; item 2: using luxury goods can make me feel more confident; item 3: the luxury goods that I purchase should match my temperament.

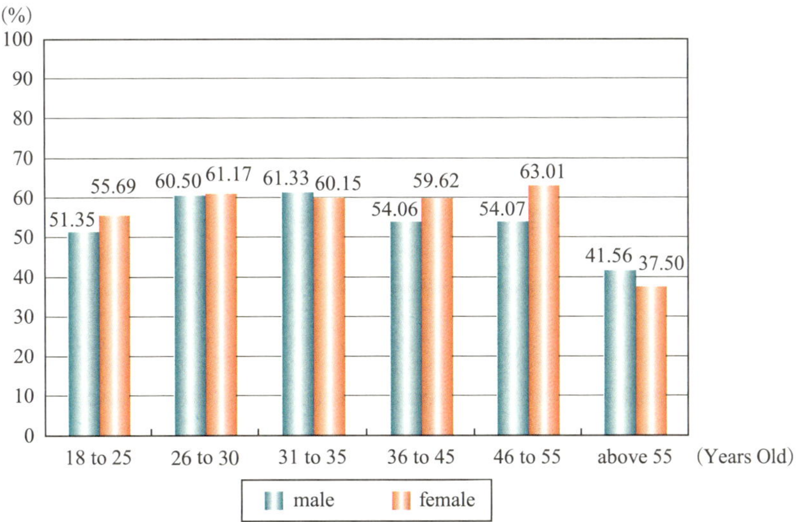

Figure 4.5 The Bar of Difference in Gender and Age in Favor of Self-worth

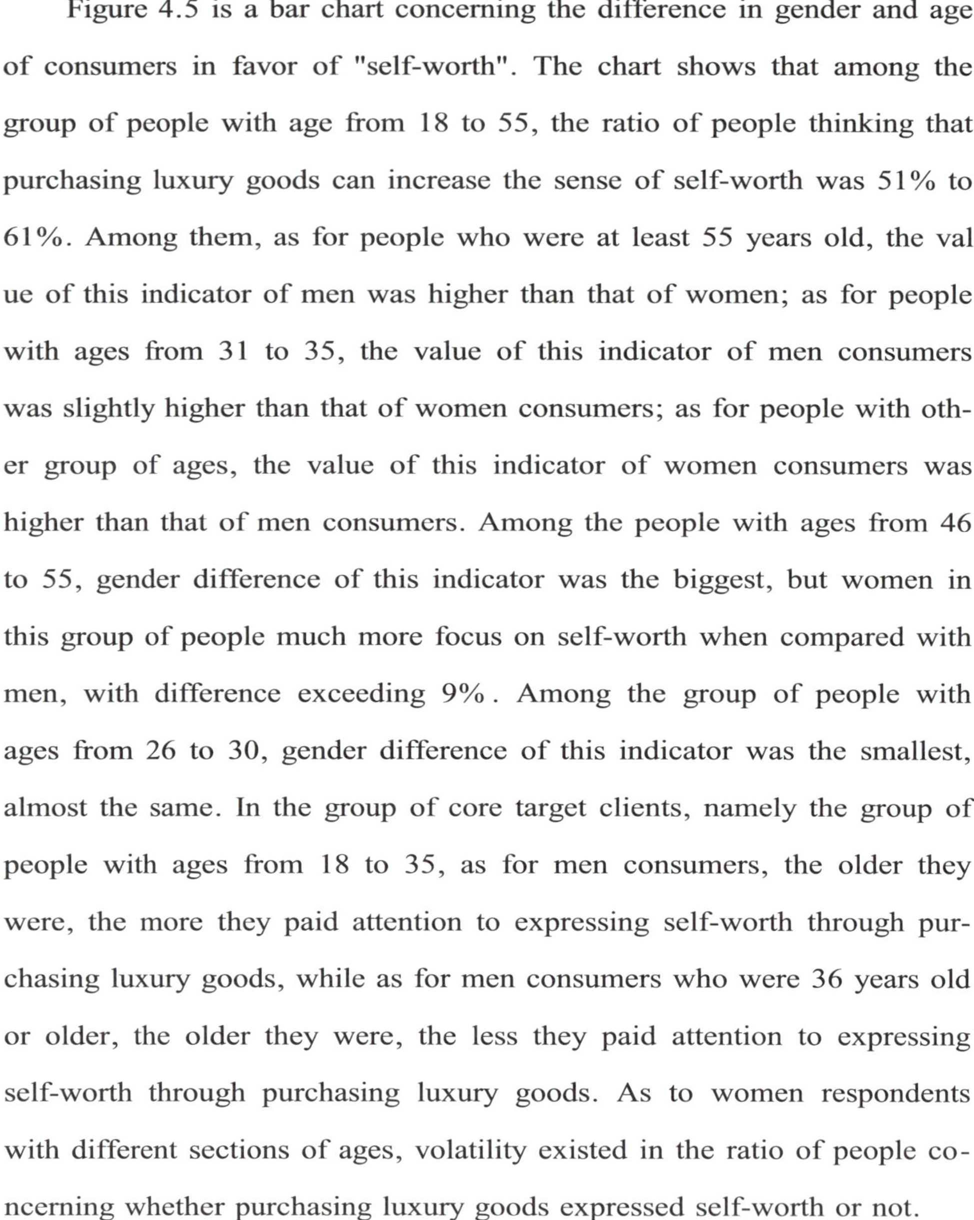

Figure 4.5 is a bar chart concerning the difference in gender and age of consumers in favor of "self-worth". The chart shows that among the group of people with age from 18 to 55, the ratio of people thinking that purchasing luxury goods can increase the sense of self-worth was 51% to 61%. Among them, as for people who were at least 55 years old, the value of this indicator of men was higher than that of women; as for people with ages from 31 to 35, the value of this indicator of men consumers was slightly higher than that of women consumers; as for people with other group of ages, the value of this indicator of women consumers was higher than that of men consumers. Among the people with ages from 46 to 55, gender difference of this indicator was the biggest, but women in this group of people much more focus on self-worth when compared with men, with difference exceeding 9%. Among the group of people with ages from 26 to 30, gender difference of this indicator was the smallest, almost the same. In the group of core target clients, namely the group of people with ages from 18 to 35, as for men consumers, the older they were, the more they paid attention to expressing self-worth through purchasing luxury goods, while as for men consumers who were 36 years old or older, the older they were, the less they paid attention to expressing self-worth through purchasing luxury goods. As to women respondents with different sections of ages, volatility existed in the ratio of people concerning whether purchasing luxury goods expressed self-worth or not.

Generally speaking, for the respondents with every section of ages, except for the fact that among the group of luxury goods purchasers with ages from 31 to 35 and of 55 or older, men paid much more attention to self-worth when compared with women, in other groups of ages, women consumers were more likely to use luxury goods to express "self-worth"

when compared with men consumers.

Given that occupational difference had something to do with self-worth cognition, the statistical result of occupational difference in "self-worth" was presented in Figure 4.6. The chart shows, white-collars work in foreign-invested enterprises were major group of people who improved their self-worth through purchasing luxury goods, accounting for 63.94%, the highest ratio. The value of this indicator for white-collars work in domestic enterprises, professionals, entrepreneurs and entrepreneurs' family ranged from about 57% to 60%, no obvious difference; the value of this indicator for freelances and students was relatively low, almost less than 52%. Due to the fact that educational levels of white-collars were generally high and they were generally open-minded, their luxury goods consuming behaviors relatively focused on self-worth and psychological pleasure, thus white-collars were supposed to highlight their high-quality life and fashion taste and showed their temperament, confidence and dignity through purchasing luxury goods.

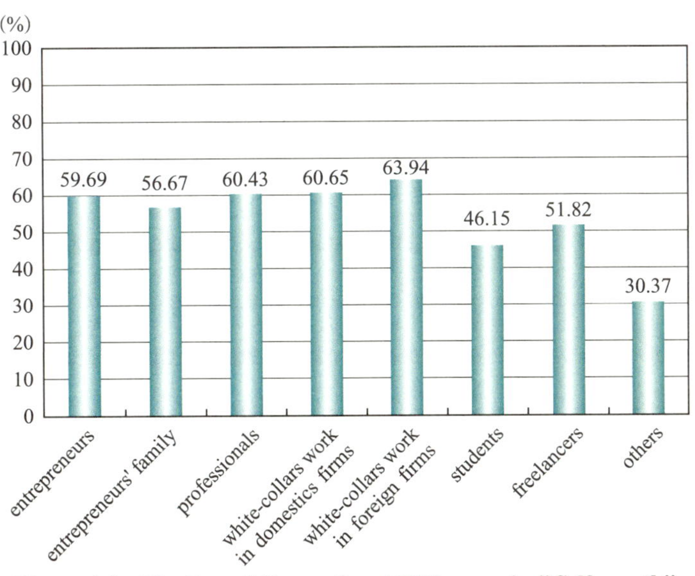

Figure 4.6 The Bar of Occupational Difference in "Self-worth"

4.3 Scarcity or Limited Quantity

One of the core contents of economics is tapping the premium effect of all "scarce resources" to create social fortune. This survey adopts the following two items to measure the influence or function that "scarcity or limited quantity" exerts on the luxury goods purchase behaviors of Chinese consumers. Item 1: scarce luxury goods will increase my purchasing interest; item 2: when purchasing luxury goods (antique, work of art, jew elry, wine, etc.) future increase in value will be taken into account.

Figure 4.7 is a bar chart concerning the difference in gender and age of consumers in favor of "scarcity or limited quantity". The chart shows, among the group of people with ages from 18 to 55, the ratio of people thinking that purchasing luxury goods had something to do with "scarcity or limited quantity"was 43% to 57%. Among them, except for the fact that for people with ages from 31 to 35, the value of this indicator of men was slightly higher than that of women; for people with other sections of ages, the value of this indicator of women consumers was higher than that of men consumers. While as for people who were more than 55 years old, gender difference of this indicator was the biggest, and women in this group of people cared much more about the scarcity and limited quantity of luxury goods when compared with men, with difference exceeding about 20%. Among the group of people with ages from 31 to 35, gender difference of this indicator was the smallest, with difference exceeding only 1%. In the group of core target clients, namely the group of people with ages from 18 to 35, as for men consumers, the older they were, the

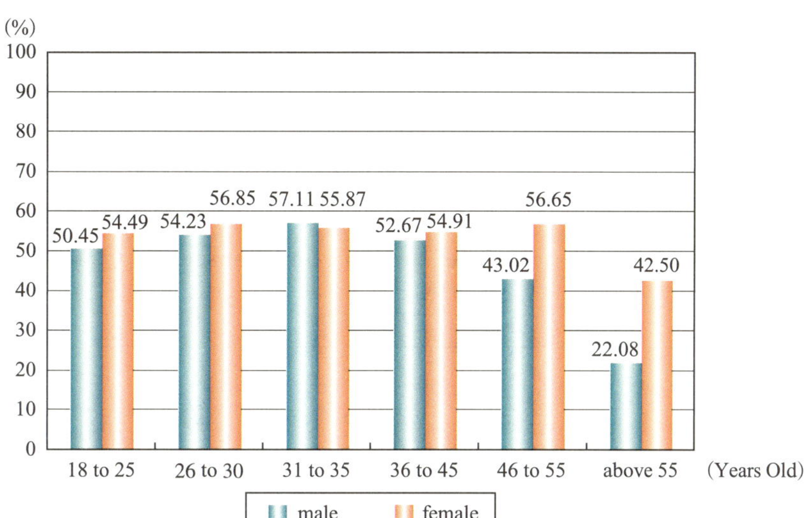

Figure 4.7 The Bar of Difference in Gender and Age of Consumers in Favor of Scarcity

more they paid attention to the scarcity and limited quantity of luxury goods, while as for consumers who were 36 years old or older, the older they were, the less they paid attention to the scarcity and limited quantity of luxury goods. As to women respondents with different sections of ages, volatility existed in the ratio of people caring about the scarcity and limited quantity of luxury goods.

Generally speaking, for the respondents with every section of ages, except for the fact that among the group of luxury goods purchasers with ages from 31 to 35, men paid a little bit more attention to the scarcity and limited quantity of luxury goods when compared with women, in other groups of ages, women consumers were more likely to the scarcity and limited quantity of luxury goods when compared with men consumers.

Given that the behaviors that consumers buy expensive luxury goods of scarcity and limited quantity are restricted by their purchasing power, thus this report further analyzes if, in the context of different income levels, there is an obvious difference in the pursuit of scarcity and limited

quantity of luxury goods. As for people pursuing the scarcity and limited quantity of luxury goods, the statistical result of their personal income difference was presented in Figure 4.8. The straight line in the chart showed the variation tendency of the attention paid by consumers to scarcity and limited quantity of luxury goods as their income increases.

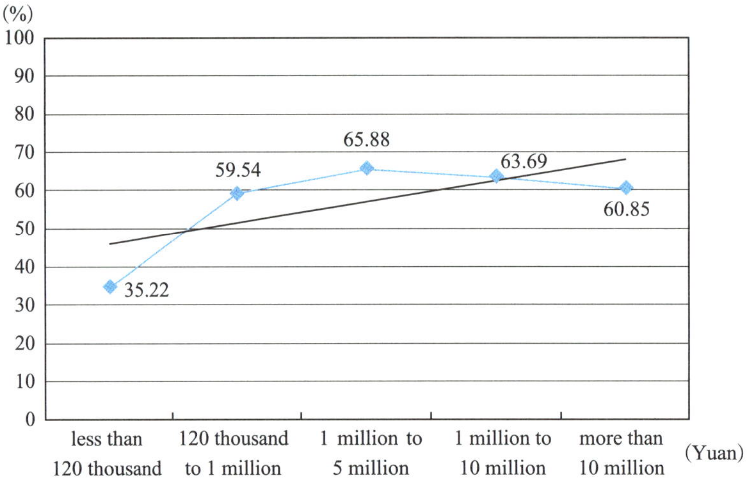

Figure 4.8 The Bar of Personal Income about Scarcity and Limited Quantity

4.4 Self-gift Giving

Purchasing luxury goods as "self-gift giving" is an outstanding variation tendency of Chinese consumers' behaviors of purchasing luxury goods. More and more Chinese consumers praise or indulge themselves through purchasing luxury goods. The practice of buying a gift for oneself so as to reward oneself is becoming more and more prevalent. In order to explore the phenomenon of self-gift giving occurring in the behaviors of consumers' purchase of luxury goods, this survey has designed the item that "when reaching the goal or completing important tasks, I will pur-

chase luxury goods to reward myself" .

Figure 4.9 is a bar chart concerning the difference in gender and age of consumers in favor of "self-gift giving". The chart shows, among the group of people with ages from 18 to 55, the ratio of people thinking that purchasing luxury goods had something to do with "self-gift giving" was 43% to 66% and for people with every section of ages, the value of this indicator of women consumers was higher than that of men consumers. While as for people with ages from 46 to 55, gender difference of this indicator was the biggest, and in this group of people, the value of this indicator of women consumers was generally higher when compared with that of men, with value reaching up to 22%. Among the group of people with ages from 18 to 30, gender difference of this indicator was little. In the group of core target clients, namely the group of people with ages from 18 to 35, as for men consumers, the older they were, the more they were likely to buy luxury goods in the name of self-gift giving; while as for consumers who were 36 years old or older, a decline tendency exised in

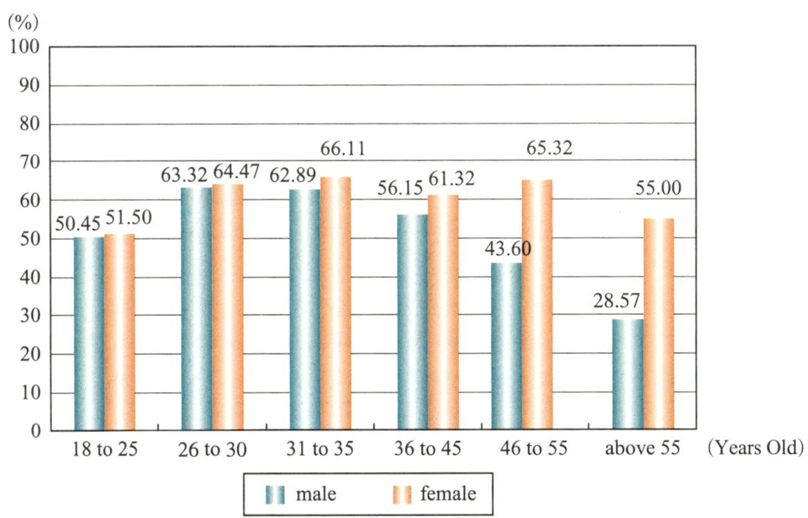

Figure 4.9 The Bar about Differences in Gender and Age of Consumers in Favor of Self-gifting

the group of men consumers, but for women consumers, volatility existed in the value of this indicator.

Generally speaking, for the respondents with every section of ages, the behaviors of purchasing luxury goods with the intention of self-gift giving were more prevalent among women consumers compared with men consumers.

Considering the relationship between different occupations and motivation of self-gift giving, the statistical result of occupational difference in "self-gift giving" was presented in Figure 4.10. The chart shows that white-collars work in foreign-invested enterprises were major group of people who chose "self-gift giving" as the motivation to purchase luxury goods, accounting for 66.73%, the highest ratio. The value of this indicator for white-collars work in domestic enterprises, professionals, entrepreneurs and entrepreneurs' family ranged from about 57% to 60%, no obvious difference, meaning that they all liked to purchase luxury goods for themselves. Thus, it revealed that there was a wide range of and high-

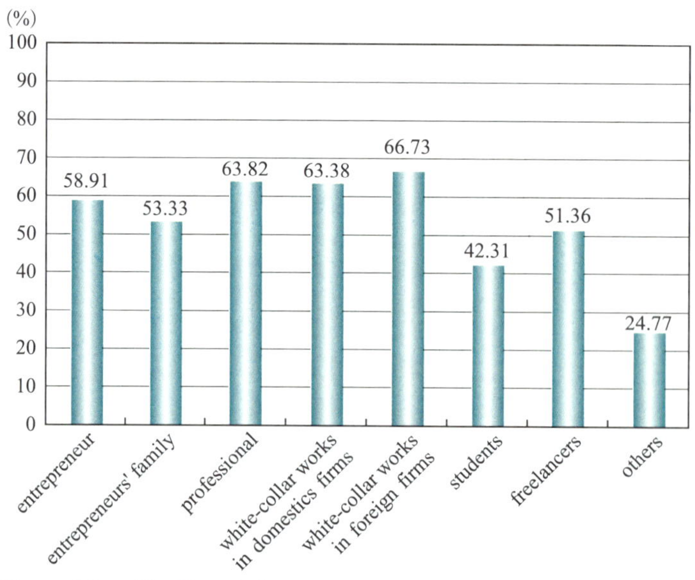

Figure 4.10 The Bar of Occupational Difference in Self-gift Giving

level group of people who purchasing gifts for themselves. Document research shows that the behavior of self-gift giving has a feature of not being sensitive to price, consequently bringing huge business value to luxury brands owners. Certain attention should be paid to that.

4.5 Good Life

High-quality life is often achieved through high-level spiritual and material consumption, and based on their prominent quality, human values and historical value, luxury goods can provide people with high-quality life. This survey has designed an item "The purpose of purchasing luxury goods is increasing life quality" to measure the motivation of Chinese consumers' purchase of luxury goods.

Figure 4.11 is a bar chart concerning the difference in gender and age of consumers in favor of "purchasing luxury goods for a good life". The chart shows, among the group of people with ages from 18 to 55, the ratio of people thinking that purchasing luxury goods served for the pursuit of a good life accounted for 48% to 68% and for people with every section of ages, women consumers cared much more about the high-quality life brought by luxury goods compared with men consumers. While as for people with ages from 18 to 25, gender difference of this indicator was the biggest, with value reaching up to almost 14%. This means that women consumers in this group were more likely to reach the goal of living a good life through purchasing luxury goods compared with men consumers in this group. Among the group of people with ages from 31 to 35, gender difference of this indicator was little. In the group of core tar-

get clients, namely the group of people with ages from 18 to 35, the older they were, the more they were likely to enjoy a good life through buying luxury goods; while as for consumers who were 36 years old or older, a decline tendency existed in the group of men consumers, but for women consumers, volatility existed in the value of this indicator.

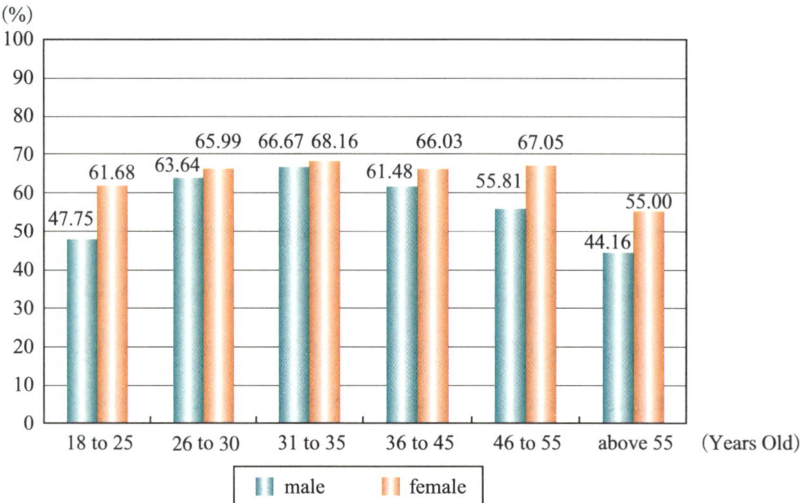

Figure 4.11 The Bar of the Differences in Gender and Age of Consumers in Favor of Good Life

Generally speaking, for the respondents with every section of ages, women consumers were more likely to reach the goal of living a good life through purchasing luxury goods compared with men consumers.

Considering the relationship between different occupations and motivation of living a good life, the statistical result of occupational difference in "living a good life" was presented in Figure 4.12. The chart shows that white-collars work in foreign-invested enterprises best liked enjoying a good life through purchasing luxury goods, accounting for 70.45%, the highest ratio. The value of this indicator for white-collars worker in domestic enterprises, professionals, entrepreneurs and entrepreneurs' family ranged from about 60% to 68%, no obvious difference. However, the value of this indicator of freelancers, students and entrepreneurs' family was relatively low, among which the situation of freelance was relatively complicated and further research remained to be conducted. But after further analysis of the statistical result of students and entrepreneurs'family, we think that it reflected the feature of pragmatism and materialism tendency in their purchase and consumption of luxury goods, which had something to do with the fact that social autonomy of this group of people was relatively weak.

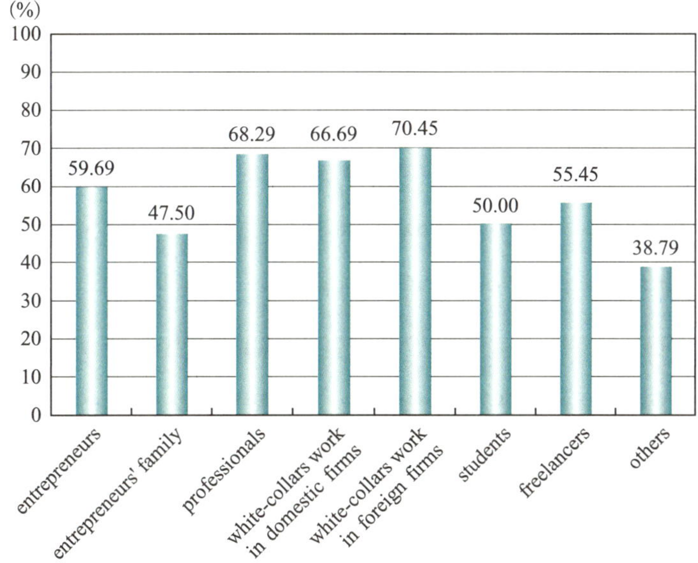

Figure 4.12 The Bar of Occupational Differences in Living a Good Life

4.6 Excellent Quality

Excellent quality of luxury goods refers to fact that quality of luxury goods has the characteristics of continuity, stability and uniqueness, thus making luxury goods having perfect product function value. Excellent quality is the essential attribute and condition for luxury goods. This sur-

vey has designed an item "The purpose of purchasing luxury goods is improving life quality" to get to know Chinese consumers' attitude towards the quality of luxury goods.

Figure 4.13 is a bar chart concerning the difference in gender and age of consumers in favor of "pursuing excellent quality". The chart shows, among the group of people with ages from 18 to 55, the ratio of people thinking that purchasing luxury goods was because of the pursuit of excellent quality accounted for 61% to 74%, among which except for the fact that difference in gender and age was not obvious among luxury goods purchasers with ages from 31 to 35, for people with other section of ages, women paid much more attention to excellent quality when compared with men. While as for people who were more than 55 years old, gender difference of this indicator was the biggest, with value reaching up to 4%. In the group of core target clients, namely the group of people with ages from 18 to 45, the youngest group of luxury goods purchasers were those with ages from 18 to 25. The ratio of the youngest group of luxury goods purchasers pursuing excellent quality was lower by about 10% than that of older group of luxury goods purchasers with ages from 26 to 45. Among the older group of luxury goods purchasers, there were about 70% on average who cared much if luxury goods have excellent quality. This tendency was applicable to group of luxury goods purchasers with ages from 46 to 55. Among all the respondents, only the value of group of people who were more than 55 years old was relatively low in this indicator, but still accounting for over 50% of this group.

Generally speaking, for the respondents with every section of ages, women consumers cared more about "excellent quality" of luxury goods compared with men consumers. Only for group of people with ages from

31 to 45, men and women consumers shared almost the same concern for "excellent quality" of luxury goods.

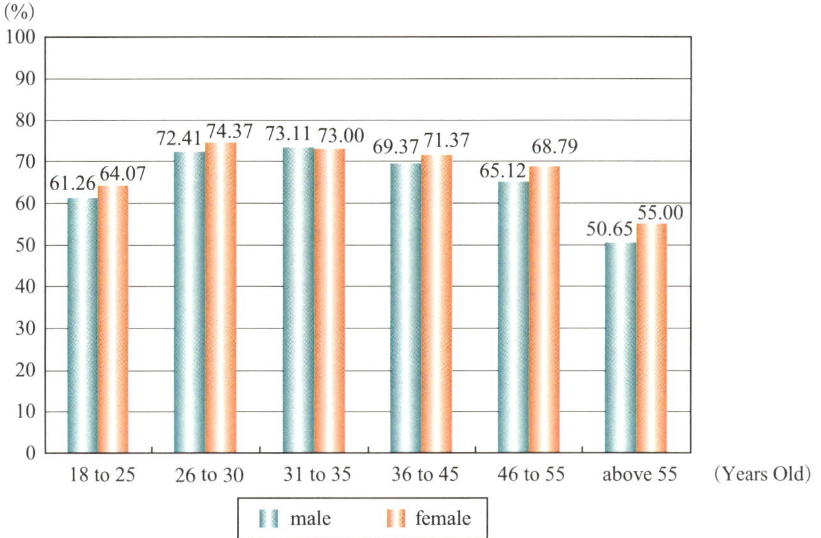

Figure 4.13 The Bar of the Difference in Gender and Age of Consumers in Favor of Excellent Quality

Does Chinese consumers' demands for "excellent quality" of luxury goods vary from the difference in cities where they live in? As Figure 4.14 shows, residents in Shenzhen, Suzhou and Shanghai had the most strict requirement in quality of luxury goods, reaching 72% on average,

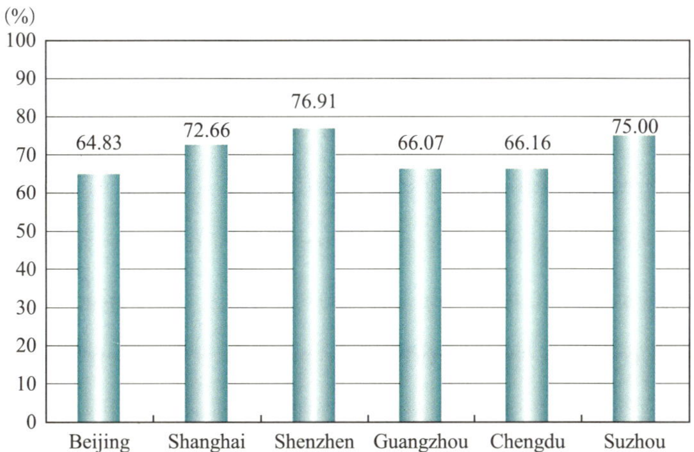

Figure 4.14 The Bar of City Differences in Excellent Quality

and for residents in Chengdu, Guangzhou and Beijing, the requirement in quality of luxury goods reached about 66%. In particular, as a second-tier city, the quality requirement for luxury goods had by consumers in Suzhou was the same with that had by consumers in such first-tier cities as Shanghai, meaning that luxury goods consumers in Suzhou were matured and wise and not supposed to blindly pursue luxury brands at the sacrifice of quality requirement for luxury goods.

4.7 Shopping Situation

Shopping situation refers to a factor relying on time and place and having nothing to do with individual or stimulant property but exerting obvious and systematic influence on the current behaviors of consumers. S-R theory in consumer behavior reveals that stimulated by the shopping situation, consumers will change decision-making at any time. This sort of stimulus mainly include: store atmosphere, on-site sales promotion, sales promotion specialists, etc. When selecting or purchasing luxury goods, consumers are supposed to show special preference for shopping atmosphere that they are quite familiar with and feel free and cozy. High-quality sales promotion specialists can be able to directly boost shopping confidence of consumers and promote or contribute to the conclusion of transactions. This survey adopts the following two items to measure the influence of shopping situation on the purchasing behaviors of consumers. Item 1: I will refer to the introduction and advice given by luxury goods sales personnel; item 2: I care about the "comfort level" (place, shopfront and personnel) when I purchase luxury goods.

Figure 4.15 is a bar chart concerning the difference in gender and age of consumers caring about "shopping situation". The chart shows, among the group of people with ages from 18 to 55, the ratio of people thinking that purchasing luxury goods has something to do with "shopping situation" was 52% to 64% and for people with every section of ages, women consumers care much more about shopping situation of luxury goods compared with men consumers. While as for people who were more than 55 years old, gender difference of this indicator was the biggest, with value reaching up to 11%, which means that women consumers in this group were much more concerned about the shopping atmosphere or shopping situation of luxury goods compared with men consumers in this group. Among the group of people with ages from 18 to 30, gender difference of this indicator was the smallest, only about 3%. In the group of core target clients, namely the group of people with ages from 18 to 35, the older they were, the more they were concerned about the shopping situation of luxury goods: while as for consumers who were

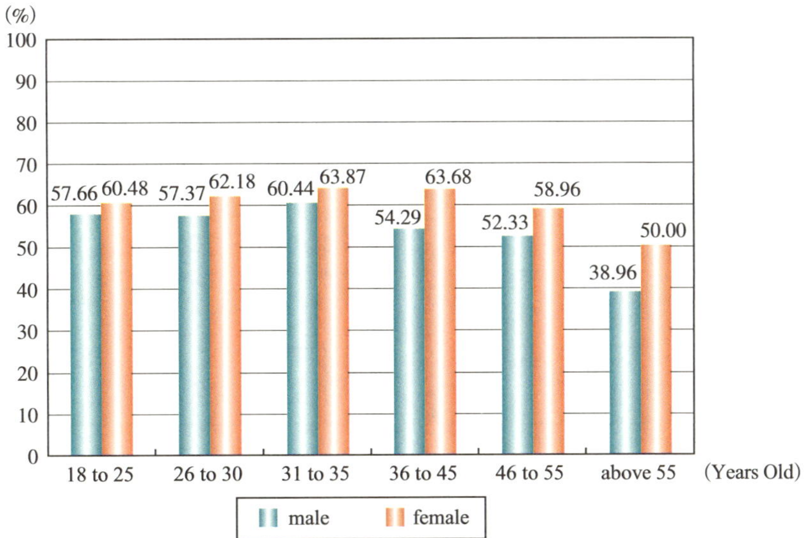

Figure 4.15 The Bar of the Differences in Gender and Age of Consumers in Favor of Shopping Situation

36 years old or older, the relationship between the ages and shopping situation was negative correlation.

Generally speaking, for the respondents with every section of ages, women consumers were much more concerned about shopping atmosphere or shopping situation of luxury goods compared with men consumers.

Does Chinese consumers' demands for "shopping situation" of luxury goods vary from the difference in their occupations? As Figure 4.16 shows, 52.33% of entrepreneurs, 50% of entrepreneurs' family members of business owners, 63.01% of professionals, 61.31% of white-collars work in domestic firm, 63.57% of white-collars work in foreign firms, 59.62% of students and 56.82% of freelances relatively cared about shopping situation of luxury goods, among which white-collar workers in foreign firm paid more attention to shopping situation of luxury goods than others do and entrepreneurs family paid less attention to shopping situation of luxury goods than others do. Due to the fact that difference in gender and age of consumers caring about "shopping situation" was not that

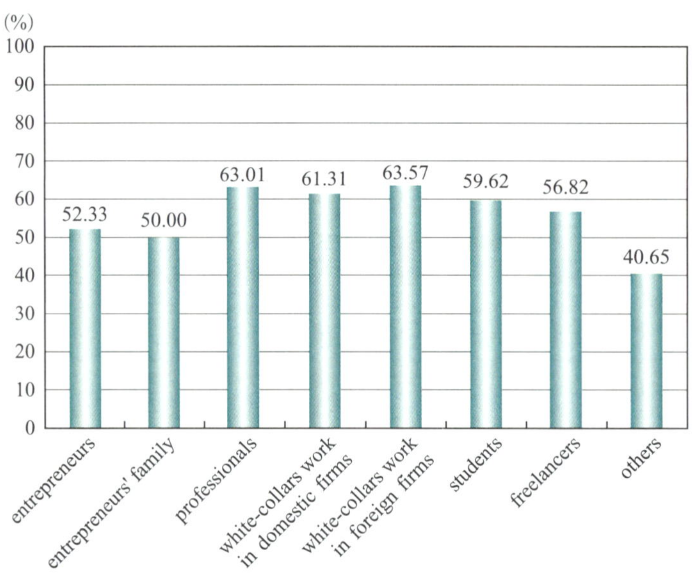

Figure 4.16 The Bar of Occupational Differences in Shopping Situation

obvious and all kept at 50% or above, we can make the conclusion that most of Chinese consumers cared about "shopping situation" when purchasing luxury goods and paid attention to luxury goods shopping experience.

4.8 Social Relation

Giving others luxury goods as a present can reflect how the gift giver get along with the recipient, or social relation value of the recipient for the gift giver. This survey has designed the following item "giving others luxury goods as a present is a necessary investment" to measure the role that luxury goods play in Chinese consumers' maintenance of "social relation".

Figure 4.17 is a bar chart concerning the difference in gender and age of consumers caring about "social relation". The chart shows, among the group of people with ages from 18 to 55, the ratio of respondents in favor of establishing social relation through sending luxury goods was 50% to 67% and among the respondents with ages from 26 to 45, men consumers care much more about establishing social relation through sending luxury goods compared with women consumers. While as for people who were more than 46 years old, the value of this indicator of women was generally higher than that of men. For the respondents with ages from 46 to 55, gender difference of this indicator was the biggest, with value reaching up to about 9%, and in this group of respondents, women consumers were more likely to give luxury goods as a present to maintain "social relation" compared with men consumers in this group.

For the respondents with other sections of ages, gender difference of this indicator was relatively small on average. In the group of core target clients, namely the group of people with ages from 18 to 35, the older they were, the more they tended to reach the goal of maintaining "social relation" luxury goods through purchasing luxury goods.

Generally speaking, men consumers with ages from 26 to 45 were more willing to use luxury goods to establish "social relation" compared with women consumers, while for consumers with other sections of ages, the ratio of women consumers caring about "social relation" was higher than that of men consumers.

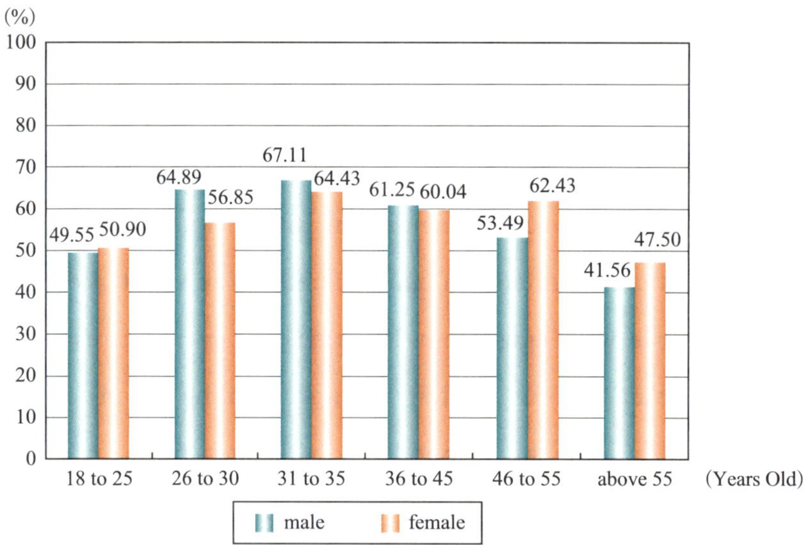

Figure 4.17 The Bar of Differences in Gender and Age of Consumers Caring about Social Relation

Since there are differences in the occupations of consumers, how they see the role that luxury goods play in the establishment of social relation is not all the same. The statistical result of difference in occupations of consumers in favor of social relation was presented in Figure 4.18. The chart shows that white-collars work in foreignfirms best like establishing

social relation through purchasing luxury goods, accounting for 67.10%, the highest ratio. The value of this indicator for white-collars work in domestic firms, professionals, entrepreneurs and entreprene-urs' family ranged from about 59% to 65%. However, the score of this indicator given by students was less than 50%, which means that generally speaking, students in the school were not supposed to maintain personal social relation through purchasing luxury goods. For the respondents taking up other occupations, about 60% of them agreed on this item. Due to the fact that the research group had not further defined the item of "other", it was very hard to tell who showed special preference for giving luxury goods as a present, which remained to be further researched in future report.

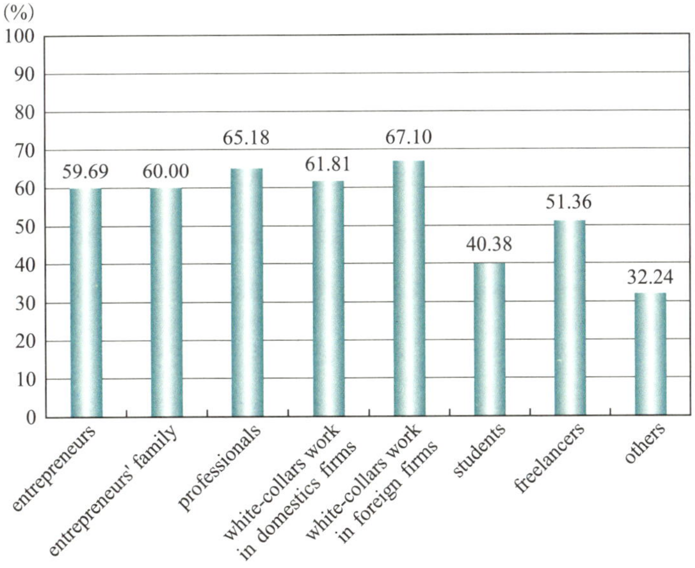

Figure 4.18 The Bar of Occupational Differences in Social Relation

4.9 Doing One's Duty

Chinese people are expected to strictly comply with the principle of

doing one's duty in their daily lives. Doing one's duty is an important part of Chinese traditional cultural values. This survey is done to get to know Chinese consumers' personal viewpoint on doing one's duty from the perspective of individual words and deeds and consuming behaviors.

Figure 4.19 is a bar chart concerning the difference in gender and age of consumers in favor of the indicator of "doing one's duty". The chart shows, among the group of people who were more than 18 years old, the ratio of respondents thinking the principle of doing one's duty should be strictly complied with in individual behaviors was 60% to 80%. Among them, except for the fact that for people with ages from 31 to 35, the value of this indicator of men consumers was relatively higher than that of women consumers, for women consumers with other sections of ages, their value of this indicator was generally higher than that of men consumers. For the respondents who were more than 55 years old, gender difference of this indicator was the biggest, with the ration of women consumers more strictly complying with the principle of doing one's duty exceeding that of men consumers by 10%. For the respondents with ages from 31 to 35, there was nearly no gender difference for this indicator. The statistical result also shows that in the group of core target clients, namely the group of people with ages from 18 to 35, the older they were, the more they tended to pay attention to the principle of doing one's duty, while for men consumers who were 36 years old or above, the older they were, the less they paid attention to the principle of doing one's duty. However, the feature of volatility existed in the ratio of women respondents who were 36 years old or above in terms of the cognition of the traditional cultural value of doing one's duty.

Generally speaking, except for the fact that for people with ages from 31 to 35, the value of this indicator of men consumers was relatively higher than that of women consumers, for women consumers with every section of ages, they generally advocated the traditional cultural value of doing one's duty when compared with men consumers.

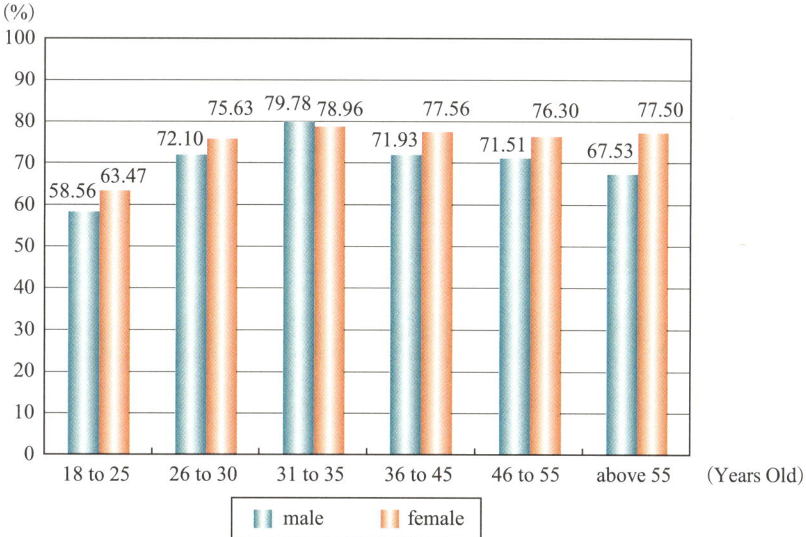

Figure 4.19 The Bar of Differences in Gender and Age of Consumers in Favor of Doing One's Duty

This survey serves to further understand whether the cultural value of doing one's duty varies from different educational degree. The statistical result of difference in educational degree of consumers in favor of doing one's duty was presented in Figure 4.20. The chart shows that the ratio of respondents with master degree or above caring the cultural value of doing one's duty was 74.26%, the ratio of respondents with bachelor or associate degree caring the cultural value of doing one's duty being 77.32%, the ratio of respondents receiving high school or technical secondary education caring the cultural value of doing one's duty being 62.22%, and others being 39.45%. Obviously, the group of respondents having bache-

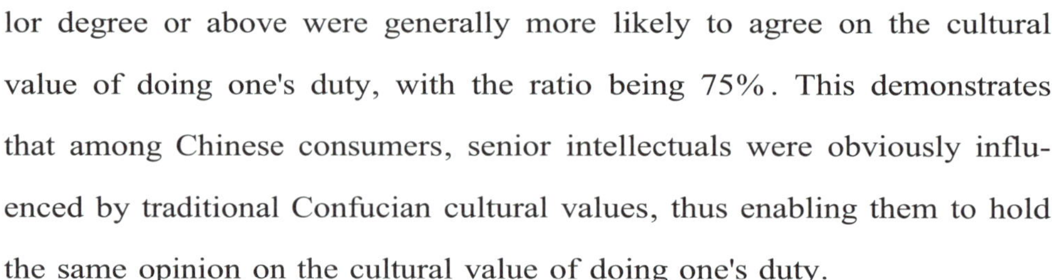

lor degree or above were generally more likely to agree on the cultural value of doing one's duty, with the ratio being 75%. This demonstrates that among Chinese consumers, senior intellectuals were obviously influenced by traditional Confucian cultural values, thus enabling them to hold the same opinion on the cultural value of doing one's duty.

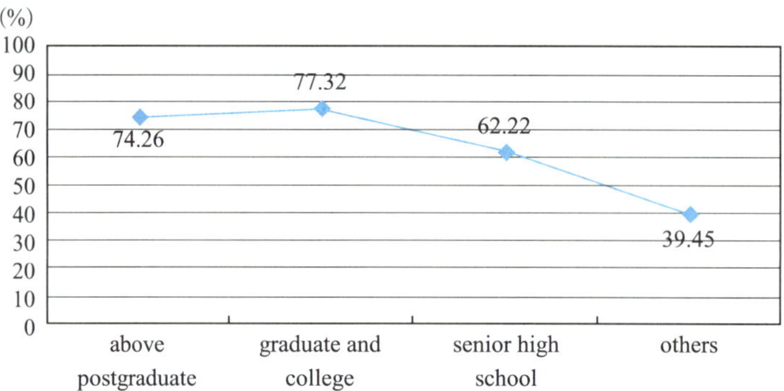

Figure 4.20 The Bar of Educational Differences in Doing One's Duty

4.10 Opinion Leadership

Compared with western consumers, Chinese consumers pay more attention to the comments given by others, since the purpose of their con suming behaviors is not only satisfying personal needs but also catering for the viewpoints held by others and gaining the recognition of the team. Here, we want to know the influence exerted by opinion leadership and the comments given by peers on Chinese luxury goods consumers. Opinion leadership is an "active factor" that often provides others with information in interpersonal communication network and meanwhile exerts influence on others, which plays a role of intermediary or filtration in the process of mass-communication. Comments from companions are summation of opinions expressed by companions from such perspectives as com-

modities' functions, styles and price when accompanying consumers in shopping. Their comments does not only include their cognitive understanding of commodities, but also reveal the tendency of their personal value, attitude, belief, mood, etc. This survey adopts the following three items to measure the impact "opinion leadership" had on Chinese consumers' behaviors of purchasing luxury goods. Item 1: The brands or styles of luxury goods bought by others will influence my purchase choice; Item 2: when going shopping, I am influenced by peer friends; Item 3: For me, the words said by teachers and predecessors are of importance.

Figure 4.21 is a bar chart concerning the difference in gender and age of consumers in favor of "opinion leadership". The chart shows, among the group of people with ages from 18 to 55, the ratio of respon dents thinking that they were influenced by "opinion leadership" when purchasing luxury goods was 50% to 67%. Among them, for the respondents with ages from 26 to 30 and from 36 to 45, the value of men consumers in the indicator of opinion leadership was slightly higher than that of women consumers, while for the respondents with other sections of ages, the situation was precisely on the contrary, showing that women consumers paid more attention to "opinion leadership" when compared with men consumers. For the group of respondents who were more than 55 years old, gender difference of this indicator was the biggest, with the ration of women consumers in favor of "opinion leadership" when purchasing luxury goods exceeding that of men consumers by 10%.

Generally speaking, for the respondents with every section of ages, women consumers in the group of people with ages from 18 to 25, from 31 to 35 and people who were 46 years old or above are more likely to be

in favor of opinion leadership when purchasing luxury goods, while for the other two groups of people, compared with women consumers, men consumers were much more desired for gaining the advice of opinion leadership when purchasing luxury goods.

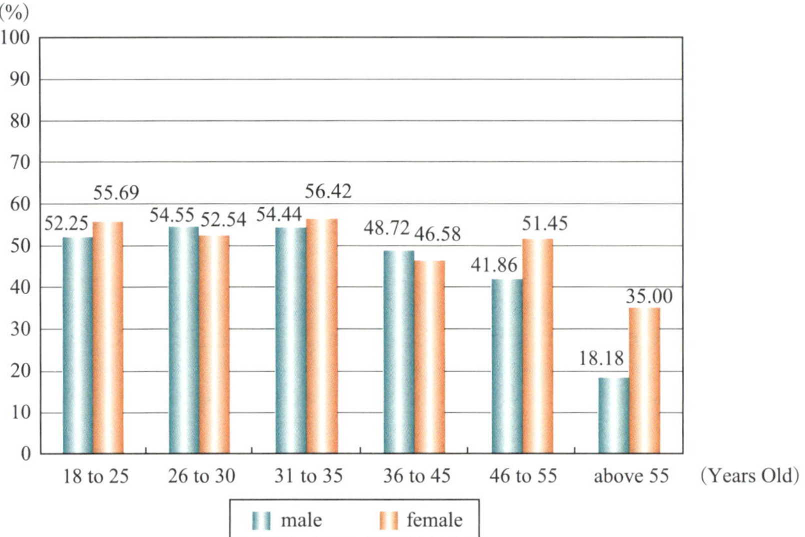

Figure 4.21 The Bar of Differences in Gender and Age of Consumers in Favor of Opinion Leadership

The following is a bar chart concerning the difference in occupations of consumers in favor of "opinion leadership". The chart shows that white-collars work in foreign firms recognized"opinion leadership" the most, accounting for 55.95%. The value of this indicator for white-collars work in domestic enterprises, professionals, entrepreneurs and entrepreneurs' family ranged from about 51% to 55%, with the difference being not obvious. This means that opinion leadership could exert influence on luxury goods purchase behaviors of most of the consumers. We had also found that freelances had the lowest demand for "opinion leadership", which was perhaps due to the nature of their job that was free and casual. They were more desired for gaining freedom and enjoying freedom com-

pared with peers, never too easy to be influenced by surrounding people and things.

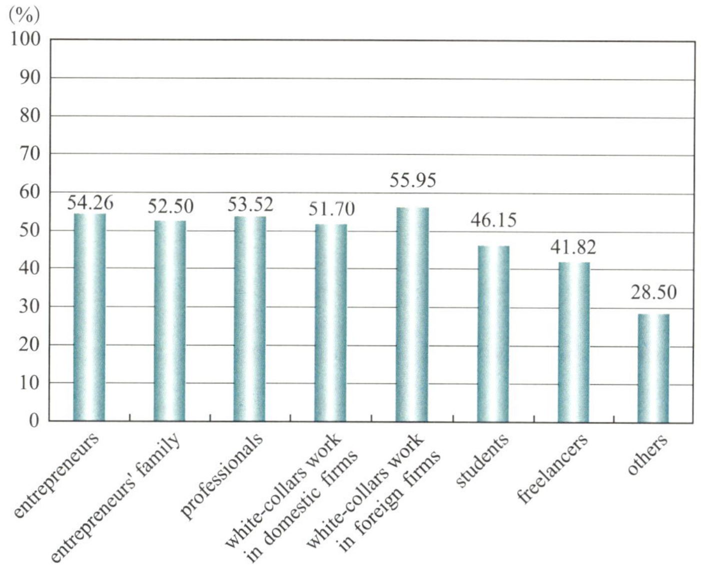

Figure 4.22 The Bar of Occupational Differences in Opinion Leadership

4.11 Integrating into the Circle

The circle refers to a group of people composed of those sharing common habits and benefits. In modern society, the trace of the circle has permeated into every walk of life, from a country and the society to a family and an office, being everywhere. The circle can not only decide a person's living space and range, but also acts as the key to his status in the circle. Document research shows that people want to reflect their high status in social circle through luxury goods consumption, and expect to integrate into a higher level social circle so as to realize the goal of recommending themselves or gaining some cooperative partners. Nowadays, circle marketing has become one of the main marketing strategies of social

networking. Since the circle can hunt loyal consumer groups, it can not only provide strong support for enterprises' brand communication and development, but also reduce marketing cost and give play to its promotion role. This survey has designed the item "appropriately using luxury goods contributes to the integration into some occasion or facilitates communication" to measure the influence that integration into the circle exerts on luxury goods purchasers.

Figure 4.23 is a bar chart concerning the difference in gender and age of consumers in favor of "integration into the circle". The chart shows, among the group of people with ages from 18 to 55, the ratio of respondents thinking that they were influenced by "integration into the circle" when purchasing luxury goods was 63% to 78%. Among them, only for the respondents with ages from 26 to 30 and from 31 to 35, the value of men consumers was slightly higher than that of women consumers, while for the respondents with other sections of ages, the situation was precisely on the contrary, meaning that the value of women consumers was generally higher than that of men consumers. For the group of respondents with ages from 46 to 55, gender difference of this indicator was the biggest, only 4%. In the group of core target clients, namely the group of people with ages from 18 to 35, the older they were, the more they were likely to integrate into the circle through purchasing luxury goods, while for group of people who were 36 years old or above, the situation was precisely on the contrary.

Generally speaking, for the respondents with every section of ages, except for the fact that the value of men consumers with ages from 26 to 35 in this indicator was slightly higher than that of women consumers, women consumers tended to "integrate into the circle" through purchasing

luxury goods compared with men consumers.

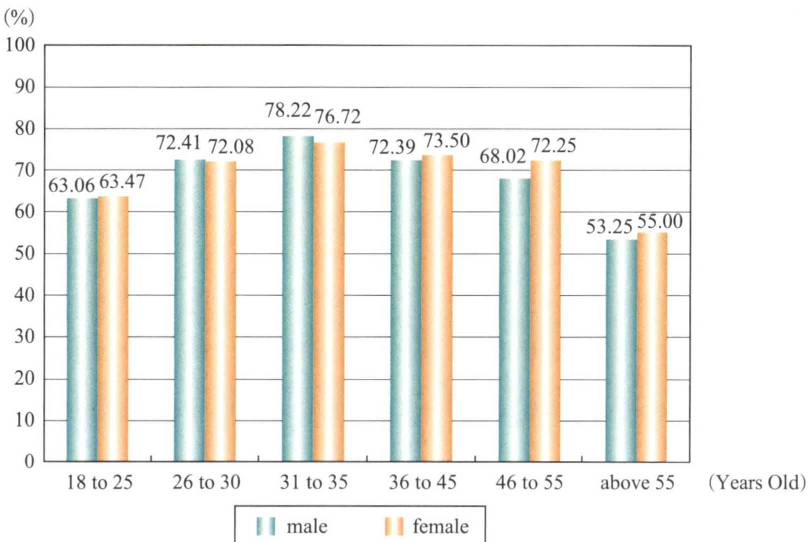

Figure 4.23 The Bar of Differences in Gender and Age of Consumers in Favor of Integration into the Circle

Does Chinese consumers' demands for "integration into the circle" vary from the difference in their occupations? The statistical result of dif ference in occupations of consumers in favor of "integration into the circle" was presented in Figure 4.24. The chart shows, the ratio of professionals choosing luxury goods as a tool to "integrate into the circle" was the highest, with the ratio amounting up to 78.05%. White-collars work in domestic firms and white-collars work in foreign firms also paid a lot of attention to "integration into the circle", with the ratio amounting up to more than 75%, which was higher than that of business owners and family members of business owners by about 15%. Thus it can be said that for most of middle class that played an important role in the society, the society of consumption was necessary and important since they pursued better life and wanted to integrate into a high-level social circle. In this context, the consumption of luxury goods served as a bridge in the process of rela-

tively lower class's integration into a relatively higher "circle".

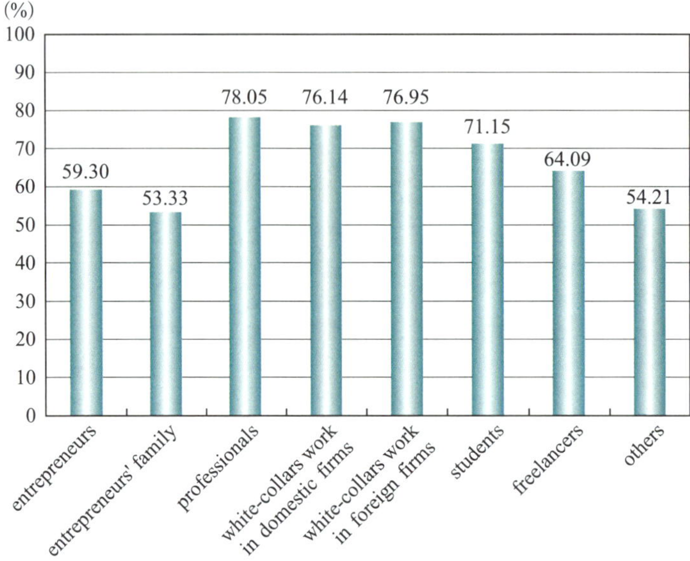

Figure 4.24 The Bar of Occupational Differences in Integration into the Circle

4.12 Preference for Classical Styles

Compared with fashionable styles or new arrivals of luxury goods, classical styles are the inheritance carrier of DNA of luxury goods and the time having elapsed brings classical styles glamour and value that is subsided by history and long-standing. As a symbolic product of luxury goods, classical styles have very high market recognition, are widely known and often have the same marketing effects with brand identity. This survey adopts the item "classical styles of luxury goods are more attracting for me compared with new arrivals" to measure the degree of Chinese consumers' preference for classical styles and new arrivals of luxury goods.

Figure 4.25 is a bar chart concerning the difference in gender and age of consumers in favor of "preference for classical styles". The chart shows, among the group of people with ages from 18 to 55, the ratio of respondents showing special preference for classical styles of luxury goods was 53% to 67%. Among them, only for the respondents with ages from 18 to 30, the value of men consumers was slightly higher than that of women consumers in this indicator, while for the respondents with other sections of ages, the situation was precisely on the contrary, meaning that the value of women consumers was generally higher than that of men consumers. For the group of respondents with ages from 46 to 55, gender difference of this indicator was the biggest, 6%. This means that women consumers in this group of people more liked classical styles of luxury goods compared with men consumers. For the group of respondents with ages from 26 to 30, gender difference of this indicator was little. In the group of core target clients, namely the group of people with ages from 18 to 35, the older they were, the more they were likely to show special preference for classical styles of luxury goods, while for group of people who were 36 years old or above, the tendency was precisely on the contrary.

Generally speaking, men consumers with ages from 18 to 30 showed special preference for classical styles of luxury goods compared with women consumers, while for respondents with other sections of ages, women consumers showed special preference for classical styles of luxury goods compared with men consumers.

Does Chinese consumers' demands for "preference for classical styles" vary from the difference in the condition of their family assets? The statistical result of difference in the condition of family assets of consumers showing special preference for classical styles of luxury goods was

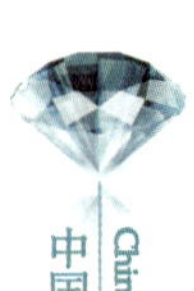

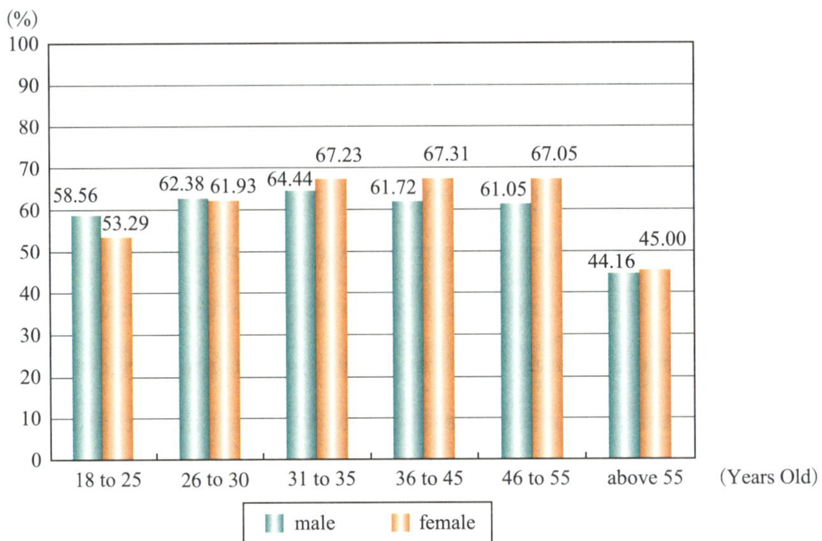

Figure 4.25 The Bar of Differences in Gender and Age of Consumers in Favor of Preference for Classic Style

presented in Figure 4.26. The straight line in the chart shows the variation tendency of degree of consumers' preference for luxury goods as their family assets increased. This tendency line reveals that the more family assets respondents had, the more they were likely to care about classical luxury goods. But research result was not completely the same with what the tendency line revealed. For respondents owning different family assets, their care about "preference for classical styles" generally present with an upward trend. Only for respondents owning more than 10 million Yuan family assets, their care about "preference for classical styles" generally presented with an downward trend, which in our mind was perhaps because of the fact that there was bigger space for consumers owning much more family assets to choose, so they were not likely to choose classical styles highly recognized by the public only, and instead they were likely to choose some styles of luxury goods which had limited quantity and highlight unique taste. The corresponding amount of family assets of respondents preferring classical styles the most ranged from 5 million to 10 million Yuan, with their ratio accounting for 68.38%, the highest. However, the group of people whose amount of family assets was less than one million showed the least preference for classical styles, which was lower than that of the former by about 13%. This chart also shows that on average, the value of the indicator "preference for classical styles" given by respondents whose amount of family assess was more than 10 million was over 63%. This information reveals that generally speaking, for consumers whose amount of family assess was more than 10 million Yuan, they showed special preference for classical luxury goods.

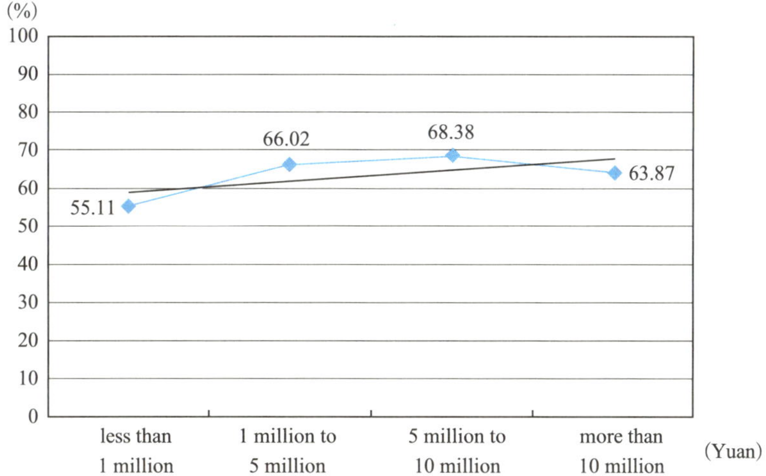

Figure 4.26 The Bar of Family Assets in Preference for Classical Styles

4.13 Brand Awareness

Brand awareness is a consumer' ability to know or recall a certain sort of products and a connection or impression of brands that make consumers remember them so deeply. The significance of brand awareness of

luxury goods lies in providing a justified reason for consumers' buying of high premium luxury goods through using brand reputation highly recognized by the public to bring consumers higher sense of brand value and good brand association. Consequently, consumers will feel dignity and glory. This survey adopts the following two items to measure the influence that brand awareness exerts on Chinese consumers' purchase of luxury goods. Item 1: I will firstly choose widely-known brands of luxury goods; Item 2: I will purchase luxury goods familiar to me.

Figure 4.27 is a bar chart concerning the difference in gender and age of consumers in favor of "brand awareness". The chart shows, among the group of people with ages from 18 to 55, the ratio of respondents considering brand awareness when purchasing luxury goods was 58% to 73%. Among them, except for the fact that for people who were more than 55 years old, the value of this indicator of men consumers was relatively higher than that of women consumers, for consumers with other sections of ages, the value of this indicator of women consumers was generally higher than that of men consumers. For the respondents who were more than 55 years old, gender difference of this indicator was the biggest, with the ration of men consumers paying more attention to brand awareness exceeding that of women consumers by about 5%. For the respondents with ages from 26 to 30, there was no obvious difference for this indicator. In the group of core target clients, namely the group of people with ages from 18 to 35, the older they were, the more they liked widely-known luxury goods, while for consumers who were 36 years old or above, the older they were, the less they liked widely-known luxury goods.

Generally speaking, among all the respondents, women consumers

with ages form 18 to 55 were easier to be influenced by brand awareness when purchasing luxury goods compared with men consumers, while for respondents who were more than 55 years old, men consumers paid more attention to brand awareness of luxury goods compared with women consumers.

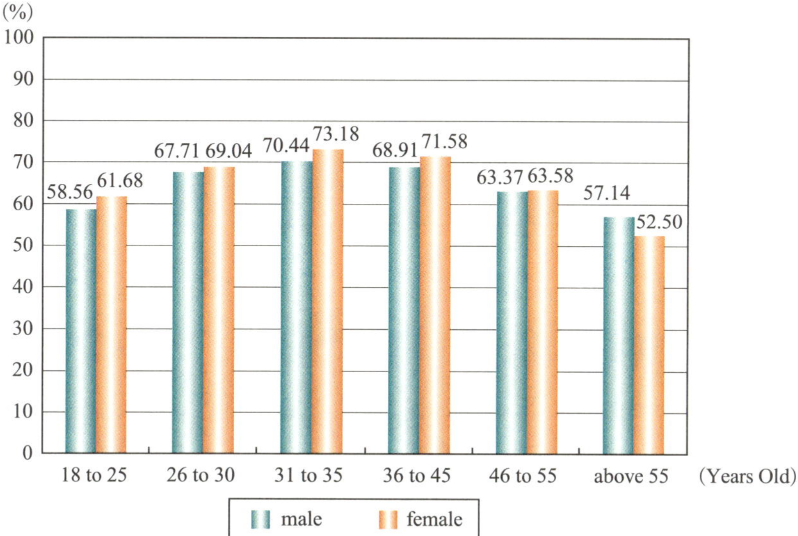

Figure 4.27 The Bar of Differences in Gender and Age of Consumers in Favor of Brand Awareness

Does Chinese consumers' demands for "brand awareness" of luxury goods vary from the difference in cities where they live in? As Chart 4.28 shows, the ratio of consumers from Shenzhen and Suzhou paying attention to brand awareness of luxury goods was more than 73% on average, and for residents from Guangzhou, Shanghai and Chengdu, their value in this indicator was more than 66% on average. In Beijing, 61.40% of consumers cared about "brand awareness".

After comparing the difference in cities where respondents in favor of "excellent quality" live in and the difference in cities where respondents paying attention to "brand awareness" live in, we have found that

for consumers from Shenzhen and Suzhou, they made distinct choices in these two indicators, which further reflected that besides first-tier cities, including Beijing, Shanghai and Guangzhou, consumers from other first-tier and second-tier cities, generally paid extensive attention to "brand awareness" and also showed that there was convergence effect in "brand awareness" between consumers from this sort of cities and consumers from Beijing, Shanghai and Guangzhou.

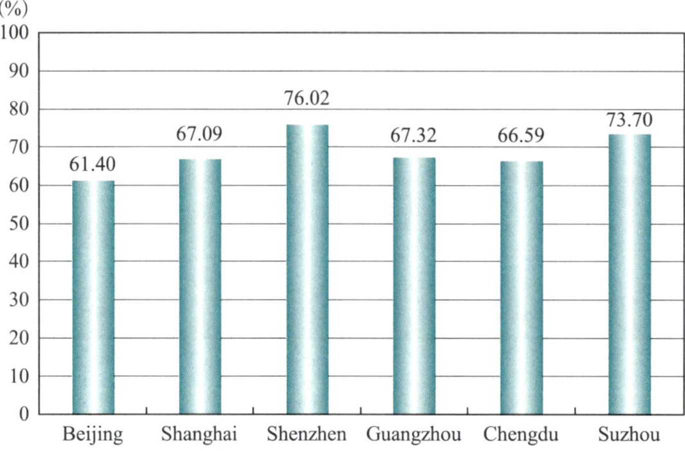

Figure 4.28 The Bar of City Differences in Brand Awareness

4.14 Price Sensitivity

Luxury goods are about premium price tag, with high price constitut ing one of its important characteristics. Prices distinguish luxury goods from normal goods and are the gap between consumers with different purchasing powers. But, positioning strategies of luxury brands define differentiated positions for different goods under one brand, with an aim to gain more profits by covering a broader market with such strategies. The result in the market mainly reflects in the price differences. This survey contains

four items to measure how the price strategies of luxury goods affect the purchasing behavior of Chinese consumers. Item one: I will make a perfect choice among quality, price and budget when purchasing luxury goods; Item 2: I will be attracted by discount information of luxury goods (overseas purchasing, duty-free, promotion activities); Item 3: I will patiently select luxury goods with relatively fair prices; Item 4: I will feel unease about the high prices of luxury goods after the purchase.

Figure 4.29 is the bar chart that shows the differences in gender and age of consumers in favor of price sensitivity. According to the figure, 61% to 67% of the people aged from 18 to 55 were very concerned with prices; among them, male consumers aged from 18 to 25 and over 55 gave more attention to prices than their female counterparts, with the rest of the age groups being the opposite. For this indicator, a big difference existed among the groups aged from 18 to 25 and from 46 to 55; in the first group age group, male consumers showed higher price sensitivity than female, with a difference of 9%, while female consumers led their male counterparts with 9% in the second age group. The difference in this indicator for the 26 to 30 age groups was around 4%, being the smallest.

On the whole, for respondents of all age groups, male had higher price sensitivity than female in the youngest and oldest age groups, that is, 18 to 25 age groups and over 55 age groups. While female had higher price sensitivity than male among the rest of the age groups, that is, 26 to 45 age groups.

Does price sensitivity of Chinese luxury goods consumers vary with differences in personal annual income? Figure 4.30 demonstrates the results of the price sensitivity for different annual incomes. The straight line in the figure shows that the "changes of consumers', price sensitivity as

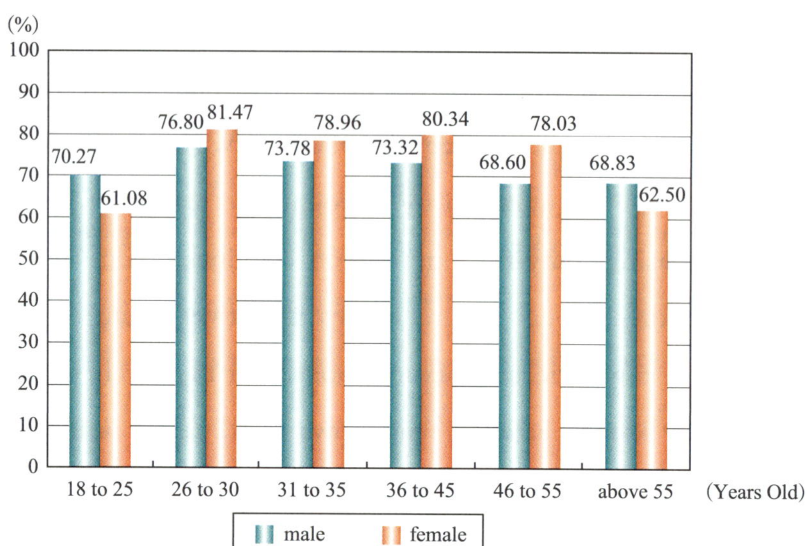

Figure 4.29 The Bar of Differences in Gender and Age of Consumers in Favor of Price Sensitivity

personal annual income increases". The trend line reveals that the higher the respondents' annual income, the lower their price sensitivity regarding luxury goods. To be specific, respondents with an annual income from 120 thousand to 10 million Yuan all showed high price sensitivity towards luxury goods, with more than 70% of them being highly concerned with it. The peak of price sensitivity occured in the 5million to 10 million Yuan groups, amounting to 80.22%. For wealthy people with over 10 million Yuan annual income, 57.45% of them were sensitive with prices, with only over 40% not being too concerned. This shows that prices of luxury goods were a big concern even for wealthy people since fairness was the basic principle of commodities trading, luxury goods being no exception. The greater exposure of wealthy groups to different prices of goods of a same brand affected their perceptions about fairness in trade as a result of regional price discrimination policy, and thus the purchase of luxury goods in the fairest market that they felt, such as outbound tourism shopping or overseas online shopping.

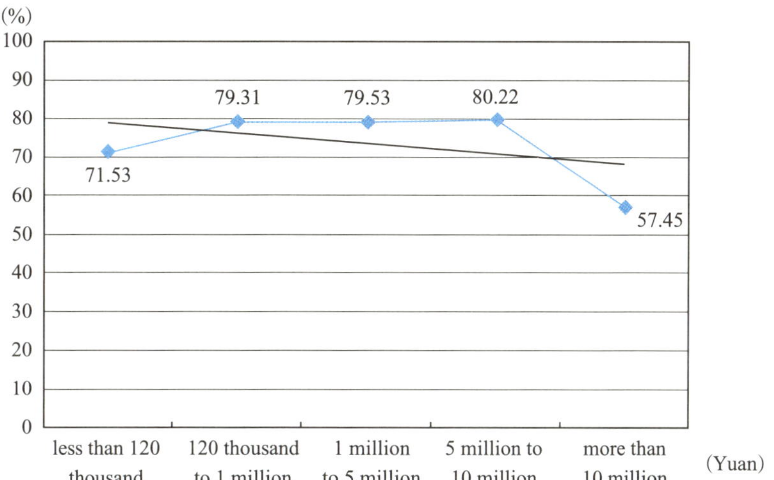

Figure 4.30 The Bar of Personal Annual Income in Price Sensitivity

4.15 Country-of-origin of Brands

Country-of-origin of brands refers to countries or regions that are linked to one product by consumers, regardless of where the product is produced. When consumers are very familiar with the brands of one country or region, they will abstract a country's or region's image from the characteristics of products under certain brand, and form a general perception of the products produced by that country or region. Such fixed impression of the country, once formed through a long time, will affect consumers' purchase behavior in the long run. Luxury goods consumers tend to include brands originating countries into brands' value. Due to historic reasons, China has missed a slew of prime opportunities to foster high-end brands, resulting in the abundance of foreign luxury brands in its high-end brands product markets and the reliance of Chinese consumers' on originating countries of luxury brands. To investigate how information of origi-

nating countries of luxury brands affects Chinese consumers' purchase behavior, this survey designed the item "the originating countries of luxury brands that I care".

Figure 4.31 is the bar chart that shows the differences in *country-of-origin of luxury brands* in terms of gender and age. According to the figure, 52% to 71% of the people aged from 18 to 55 cared about originating countries when buying luxury goods. Among them, 26-45 and over 55 year old male consumers demonstrated a higher number than their female counterparts, while 18-25 and 46-55 age groups exhibit an opposite trend. For this indicator, a big difference existed in the 46-55 age groups, with over 16% of female consumers being more concerned with *country-of-origin of luxury brands* than their male counterparts; the smallest difference between male and female was found in the 31-35 age groups. Among the 18-35 age groups, the core target customer group, the older the luxury goods consumers were, the more concerned they were with *country-of-origin of luxury brands*, with fluctuations existing for people aged over 36.

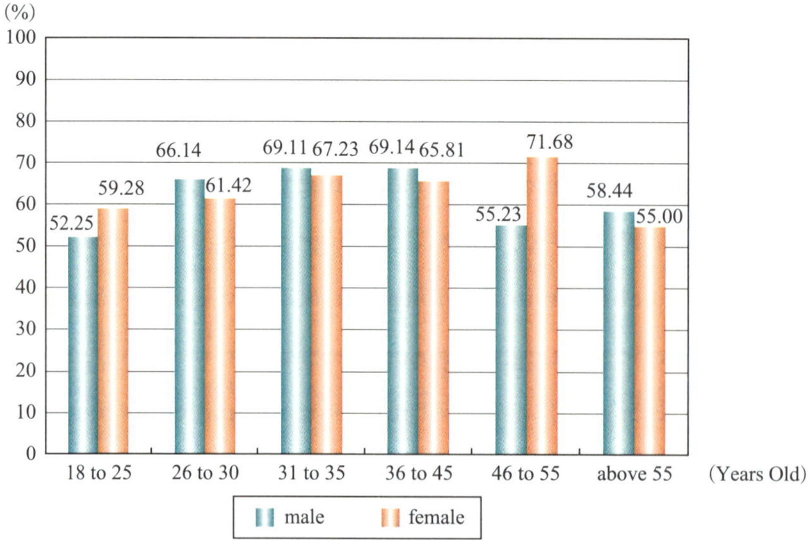

Figure 4.31 The Bar of Differences in Gender and Age of Consumers in Favor of Country-of-origin of Brand

On the whole, female consumers aged from 18 to 25 and from 46 to 55 showed a greater proportion than their male counterparts in terms of originating countries of luxury brands, while for the rest of age groups, male consumers demonstrating a greater percentage but with a relatively small difference than female consumers.

The aforesaid analysis of results reveals that *information of country-of-origin of luxury brands* has a great bearing on Chinese consumers' purchase behavior, which drove the research team to future analyze the impact of image of specific countries. Figure 4.32 shows the results of the *country-of-origin of luxury brands* regarding different countries. According to the figure, Chinese consumers' preference to originating countries of luxury goods was as follows: Italy (67.56%), the U.S.A (66.26%), France (66.05%), Switzerland (64.78%), Japan (63.50%), Germany (63.13%), the U.K (61.78%) and Spain (56.41%). This was different from the rank in the 2014 report, in which the top three were France, Italy and Switzerland. The 2015 results showed that the U.S.A has surpassed France, presenting itself as emerging originating countries of luxury brands. Such phenomenon closely related to the vigorous development of emerging light luxury brands in the U.S.A, and gives expression to changes in the purchase behavior of Chinese consumers' regarding luxury goods. Consumers were gradually changing their rigid impression about traditional luxury brands from Europe, and giving light luxury brands featuring cost-effectiveness, fashion and dynamism from other developed countries, such as those from North America a try, while maintaining their preferences to classic luxuries. This mirrored a transition in the purchase behavior of Chinese consumers regarding luxury goods towards mature and rational. Besides, Chinese consumers' preference to originating countries of luxury goods was sequenced as follows apart from the top three: Switzerland, Japan, Germany, the U.K and Spain. However, preferences for those five countries were not greatly varied, with all being about 60%. The corresponding indicators in 2014 were sequenced as the U.S.A States, the U.K, Germany, Japan and Spain, yet a large difference existed in the five countries regarding "*preference for countries*". The average number was about 20%, but the difference between the highest, 28.5% and the lowest, 7.1% reached 21.4%. The phenomenon of changes in the "*preference to countries*" demonstrated that information asymmetry has been greatly improved in this network era where brand information become more transparent and abundant, and that knowledge about luxury brands become more available to consumers. This allowed various luxury brands to secure more opportunities to get close to consumers. Product brands which better cater to consumers' new way of life have secured unprecedented market space by riding new consumption waves of diversification and individuation. This oweed to their efforts to conform to con-

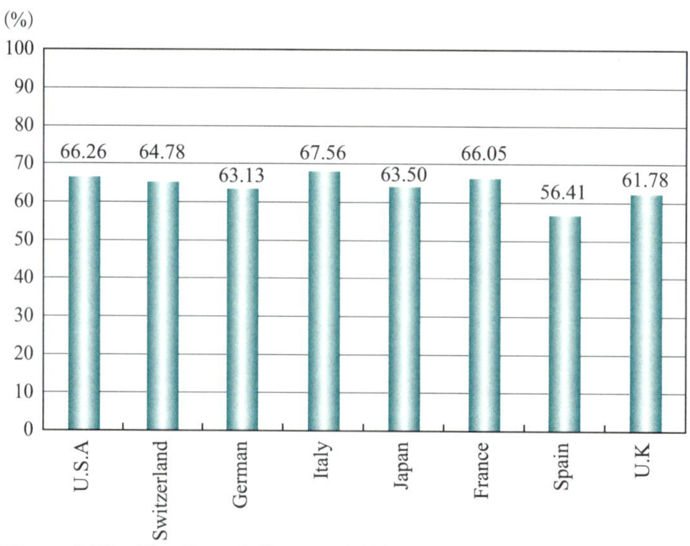

Figure 4.32 The Bar of Country Differences in Country-of-origin

sumers' idea of keeping abreast of the times and the trend in demands for diversified and customized products.

4.16 Summary of Generality and Particularity in the Characteristics of Chinese Consumers' Purchase Decision Regarding Luxury Goods

To sum up, fifteen factors affecting Chinese consumers' purchase decision regarding luxury goods and the differences in terms of gender and age have the following characteristics. The following summary is based on the demographic variables and differences in the country-of-origin of luxury brands. Among them, demographic variables include: gender, age, occupation, education background, personal annual income, family assets and residential cities.

4.16.1 Differences in terms of gender and age

(1) Age differences in male consumers' purchase decision regarding luxury goods.

For the core target customer groups of luxury goods, that is, respondents aged from 18 to 35, several factors presented the following characteristics: as age grew, the size of targeted group increased, involving 13 affecting factors: emotional outlets, self worth, scarcity limits, self-gift giving, good life, excellent quality, shopping situation, social relations, being diligent and ingenuous, integrating to circles, preference for classics, brand awareness and country-of-origin, except for opinion leadership and price sensitivity.

For the senior-age target customer groups of luxury goods, that is, respondents aged form 36 to 45, the aforesaid 13 factors, showed the reverse trend, except for country-of-origin. That trend went beyond to cover the non-targeted customer groups which age over 46.

(2) Age differences in female consumers' purchase decision regarding luxury goods.

For the core target customer groups of luxury goods, that is, respon dents aged from 18 to 35, ten factors present the following characteristics: as age grew, the size of targeted group increased. The ten factors are: emotional outlets, self-gift giving, good life, shopping situation, social relations, being diligent and ingenuous, integrating to circles, preference for classics, brand awareness and country-of-origin.

For the senior-age target customer groups of luxury goods, that is, respondents aged over 36, six factors (emotional outlets, excellent quality, shopping situation, integrating to circles, preferences for classics and brand awareness) showed the reverse trend. The changing trend of the remaining nine factors was fluctuating.

An analysis of the characteristics of female consumers' purchase decision regarding luxury goods revealed that such fifteen affecting factors were showing different population effect in female targeted customer groups at different age and male counterparts. In addition, the aforesaid analysis demonstrating the samples was of representative feature relating to age, but also such fifteen factors reflected the purchase characteristics of Chinese luxuries consumption main force.

(3) Gender differences in the characteristics of customers' purchase decision regarding luxury goods.

For the core target customer groups of luxury goods, that is, respon-

dents aged from 18 to 35, as age increases, factors that influenced consumers' purchase behavior showed the following three prominent changes in gender differences in terms of population effect. Firstly, more female consumers needed "self-gift giving" than their male counterparts. Secondly, as age grew, the differences in the size of male and female groups who purchased luxury goods out of "scarcity limits", "the good life", "excellent quality", "being diligent and ingenuous ", "opinion leadership" and "country-of-origin" were narrowing. Thirdly, the differences in the size of male and female groups who purchased luxury goods out of "emotional outlets", "self worth", "preferences for classics", "brand awareness", "price sensitivity", "shopping situation", "social relations", and others were fluctuating. Such fluctuating trend went beyond to cover the non-targeted customer groups aging over 46.

Compared with male consumers, more female consumers tended to be affected by most of the aforesaid 15 factors when purchasing luxury goods. However, "social relations" and "country-of-origin" attraced more attention from male consumers. Since 2014, global luxury goods market has shown the weakening purchase trend from male consumers, which could be explained from this research. In fact, in China' society, male attached more importance to their social role, represented by their acceptance as individuals in "social relations". That naturally gave luxury goods a symbolic role to play. Yet, along with the changes in China's political and economic landscape, the previous dominant characteristics of symbol needed to be "internalized" or "connoted", which presented a new task for enterprises in luxury business for designing brand development strategy. Moreover, "country-of-origin" symbolized the identity of luxury brands, which mattered more to Chinese male consumers than females. This ran

counter to the expansionary production of non-country of origins of brands to cut cost by some international luxury brands manufactures, which may partly explain the decreased purchase from male consumers.

4.16.2 Occupational differences in consumers' purchase decision regarding luxury goods

Consumers' occupational backgrounds have a bearing on their purchase decision regarding luxury goods. We have examined the following eight factors: shopping situation, the good life, getting to circles, social relations, emotional outlets, opinion leaderships, self worth and self-gift giving. We have found that white-collars are more affected by these eight factors in making purchase decisions, especially for white-collars in foreign companies. Such results gave expression to the complicated and diverse consumption motives of white-collars regarding luxury goods. Their high working pressure, high living cost of their city of residences, and their high educational level and open mind resulted that they needed to purchase luxury goods for the fulfillment of good life and self-value expression. In addition, the white-collars and professionals normally belonged to the middle class, which payed attention to the symbolic value of luxury goods. This could be seen from their eager to "get to circles", maintain "social relations", and enjoy "good life" through luxury goods. As social elites, entrepreneurs were less concerned about the "shopping situation" when purchasing luxury goods. They were also less likely to purchase luxury goods as a way of "emotional outlets". Such phenomena were may be linked with their rich and high-class spare time life, or with their more emotional outlets. Freelancer groups had a higher acceptance of "getting into circles", but paid less attention to "opinion leaderships".

This might result from their free and casual work, which made them dire of a higher-level class to expand their social network. Yet their free environment of long standing also made them less susceptible to be influenced by the surrounding people and things. The characteristics of purchase decisions of students and entrepreneurs' family members were also not so pronounced, which may relate to their relatively weak social independence and strong pragmatism.

4.16.3 Differences in personal annual income and family asset in the characteristics of Chinese consumers' purchase decision regarding luxury goods

The results of motives of "scarcity limits", "price sensitivity", "preferences for classics" in terms of annual personal income and family assets showed that groups with over 10 million Yuan income were generally concerned with the feature of "scarcity limits", while groups with less than 120 thousand Yuan paid less attention to this feature. At large, respondents of all income brackets showed higher price sensitivity, even for wealthy groups with over 10 million Yuan annual income. Almost sixty percent of such wealthy groups were price sensitive. Because fairness was the basic principle of commodities trading, with luxury goods being no exception. Regional price discrimination would naturally strike fair trading principle of consumers, who would naturally opt for market they felt the most fair to purchase luxury goods, such as outbound tourism shopping or overseas online shopping. For all respondents of all income brackets, "preferences for classics" constituted the generality, which served as the basis for the continued boom of luxury brands.

4.16.4 Differences in cities in the characteristics of Chinese consumers' purchase decision regarding luxury goods

Consumers' concern with "superb quality and brand awareness" from different cities was mainly reflected in the phenomenon that consumers in such cities as Suzhou, Shenzhen and Chengdu showed more interest than those in Beijing, Shanghai, Guangzhou. This illustrated that the consumption idea of Chinese consumers was more prosaically rational and mature regarding luxury goods, and cared more about superb quality and brand value of luxury goods. It was especially worthy of noted that such phenomenon only existed in such first-tier cities as Beijing, Shanghai and Guangzhou.

4.16.5 Differences in the education background in the characteristics of Chinese consumers' purchase decision regarding luxury goods

This research reveals that in China, most of the prominent intellectuals tended to be *diligent and ingenuous*, which constituted the component of traditional Confucius culture value system. Such value outlook not only served as the daily code of conduct for Chinese prominent intellectuals, but also guided their consumption behavior regarding luxury goods. In this vein, *being diligent and ingenuous* was a deep-seated analysis of purchasing behavior with Chinese characteristics regarding luxury goods.

4.16.6 Differences in the country-of-origin in the characteristics of Chinese consumers' purchase decision regarding luxury goods

In 2015, the U.S.A surpassed France to become the second favorite country of origin for Chinese consumers for the first time, only second to Italy. This shows that Chinese consumers not only pre ferred traditional countries of origin, but also willing to accept light luxury brand from North America, a reflection of Chinese consumers behaviors towards mature and rational regarding luxury goods.

Chapter 5 Analysis on Chinese Luxury Consumer Groups

In this chapter, the subtle influence of the traditional cultural values on the behaviors of Chinese luxury consumers will be explored. The consumption behavior characteristics will be found out by dividing consumer groups based on consumption values.

5.1 The Influence of Chinese Traditional Cultural Values

According to the analysis result of this investigation data, similar to 2014, the luxury consumption motivation of Chinese consumers was still very contradictory in 2015. It is shown that Chinese luxury consumers belong to a group between the groupism with repression of personality and the individualism with display of personality. They were featured with the vanity explicit motivation of grandiose flaunt as well as the demand motivation of simple low-key and utility functions. They did not belong to any extreme groups but showed certain tendency temporarily under the background of different time, occasions and demands, which reflected the

characteristics of versatility, dissociation and complexity in Chinese luxury consumption behavior. These characteristics brought great difficulty in profoundly understanding Chinese luxury consumption behavior.

According to related literature review, the cultural value is featured with time stability and behavior orientation. Therefore the profound understanding of consumers' cultural values can help to realize the regularity of Chinese consumers' consumption behavior. The cultural value system of modern Chinese is deeply influenced by the traditional cultural values which drives from Confucianism, Taoism and Buddhism. Confucianism, Confucianism, Buddhism and Taoism are integrated in Chinese religion whose cultural deposit is "harmony" consistently.

The basis of Confucianism is benevolence. It is advocated in Confucianism that people shall be adapted to the society and follow the feudal ethics, class division, birthright, status and relationship between different people as well as pecking order and pay attention to behavior norms as well as rank order. Golden mean is advocated in Confucianism as well, which is featured with low profile, diligence and thriftiness, kindness and politeness. The core value is summarized as "three principles and five virtues", namely the principles that "ruler guides subject, husband guides wife" and the virtues of "benevolence, justice, manners, wisdom and reputation". It is considered in Confucianism that "during the use of manners, harmony is the most important and it is the essence for governing ancient monarchs". If the manners are used among persons, families, societies and countries, people can enjoy pleasant feelings, harmonious families, orderly societies as well as the safe and harmonious world.

The basis of Taoism is Tao. It is advocated in Taoism that people shall be adapted to the nature and return to the nature. It is also advocated

that people shall live in harmony with nature by natural inaction (Wuwei) without desire, duplicitous mind and action to return to one's original nature. It believes in governance by doing nothing that goes against nature, namely, no violation of the natural law and no desire for everything. "Tao" is closely related to "morality" and the communication with Tao shall be obtained by request with morality: taking morality as the basis, behavior with morality, stopping the bad and advocating the good, being good as the water, being filial to parents, respecting the old and caring for the young, giving medicine to people for free to treat illness, taking pity on poor and disabled people, taking pleasure in helping people, supporting education, being modest and prudent, saving money to help others, loving nature, protecting the environment, living by oneself with hard work, earning the own living, being indifferent to fame and wealth and standing aloof from worldly success. In order to build a harmonious world, people shall treat others with due respect.

The basis of Buddhism is impermanence. It is advocated in Buddhism that people shall be adapted to principle and subsidiary causes. It also advocated that people shall "treasure the destiny and follow the destiny as well as causal circle". Buddhism believes that people may be attached to other things and people as long as they are alive, so people shall treasure the destiny as well as people and things around. It also believes that the destiny controls everything. In Buddhism, it is believed that external harmony and peace is determined by the inner peace and stability because the interaction between the inner unpeaceful thought and the external unpeaceful things will aggravate the situation. Therefore, the pure thought is advocated in Buddhism by pursuing "harmonious coexistence, kind words, common goals, equality of legal system, common views and

economic balance". The relevance between the "inner thought" and "external existence" which indicates that "the external existence is determined by people's thought" comes from the "origin theory" of Buddhism.

Although there are different emphases in Confucianism, Taoism and Buddhism, they are accepted and developed through constant evolution, complementation and integration. The integration and conflict of the three theories controls and influences the spiritual life of Chinese nation. Keeping the temperament is advocated in Confucianism, while cultivation of the temperament is advocated in Taoism and actual display of the temperament is advocated in Buddhism. It is known that "Confucianism controls the country, while Taoism controls people and Buddhism controls the temperament", namely, "Confucianism shows the way to deal with the common customs, while Taoism shows the way to neglect the common customs and Buddhism shows the way to get rid of the constraint of the common customs".

In order to further explore the influence of Chinese traditional cultural values on Chinese consumers' behavior, the new item used to measure Chinese traditional values is supplemented on the basis of the survey questionnaire in 2014. The analysis result of the data is shown in Table 5.1. 3238 of the 3347 respondents (accounting for 96.74%)were obviously shown to be influenced by Chinese traditional cultural values. In this research, the traditional values of Confucianism, Taoism and Buddhism were taken as the basic variables and the clustering methodology was adopted to classify people. Four different traditional culture oriented crowds were obtained: Confucianism and Taoism oriented type, Confucianism and Buddhism oriented type, Buddhism and Taoism oriented type as well as non-tradition oriented type.

Table 5.1 Group Organization Based on Traditional Culture Value

	Type 1	Type 2	Type 3	Type 4
Buddhist culture	3.56	4.42	4.26	1.82
Confucian culture	4.16	4.12	2.84	1.81
Taoist culture	4.18	3.08	4.34	1.84
Number (person)	2166	632	440	109
proportion (%)	64.71	18.88	13.15	3.26

5.2 Classification and Characteristics of Chinese Traditional Cultural Values Oriented Luxury Consumers

Type 1: Confucianism and Taoism oriented type. It is the largest group with 2166 people, accounting for 64.71%. In this type, both the score of Confucianism cultural values orientation and Taoism cultural values orientation were more than 4, so it was called "Confucianism and Taoism oriented group". Confucianism culture and Taoism culture originate from China and keep domination for a long time in Chinese society. The influence of Confucianism and Taoism on Chinese consumers' behavior is ingrained because of the characteristics of inclusiveness, internality and openness. The universal influence of Confucianism and Taoism culture is further proved by this investigation result. Consumers demonstrated their social status through luxury consumption or created and maintained the social network conductive to personal development through conspicuous consumption. The values motivation behind these behaviors is the concept of hierarchy in Confucianism (such as the accordance between behavior and status) and the concept of enjoyment in Taoism (such as "pursuit of the quality of life" and "respect of nature"). With respect to

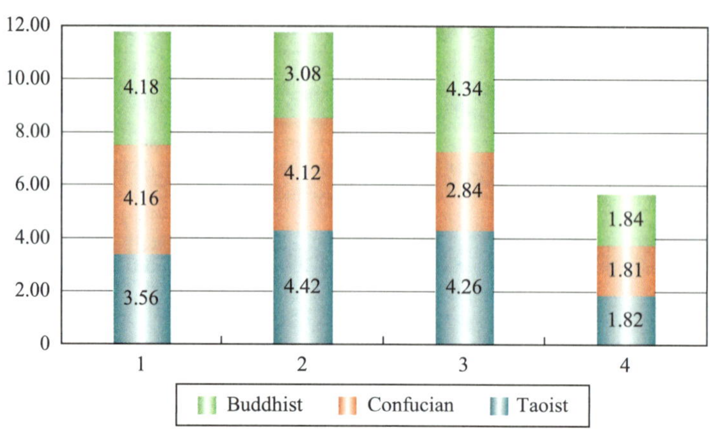

Figure 5.1 The Proportion Distribution of Three Culture in Four Group

Confucianism culture orientation, "the social significance of consumption" is to express and transmit certain information through individual consumption behavior, such as consumers' status, identity, personality, taste, temperament and identification. The measuring items in the questionnaires include: the symbol of success, shame culture, matching of behavior and character and the like. As for Taoism culture orientation, "the psychic gratification of consumption" is to gain the mental feeling of "good mood, sense of beauty, atmosphere, fine style and sentiment". The measuring items in the questionnaires include: paying attention to shopping environment, high price and high quality, smoothing mood and the like. Therefore, Confucianism and Taoism cultures have the subtle influence on the guiding role of Chinese luxury consumption view.

Type 2: Confucianism and Buddhism oriented type. It is the second largest group with 632 people, accounting for 18.88%. In this type, both the score of Confucianism cultural values orientation as well as Buddhism cultural values orientation were more than 4, and the score of the latter one was a little higher, so it is called "Confucianism were Buddhism oriented group". Fate and predestined relationship are emphasized in Bud-

dhism cultural values, and the item in the questionnaire is: believing in predestined relationship. Obviously, the diverse individual values of Chinese consumers were shown in Type 2, because they took Confucianism culture as the standard of behavior in social life, while on the spiritual level, they took Buddhism culture as the standard of behavior. The individual consumption behavior is featured with the sociality of pursuit of luxury consumption as well as the practicability of pursuit of functional products.

Type 3: Buddhism and Taoism oriented type. It is the third largest group with 440 people, accounting for 13.15%. In this type, both the score of Buddhism cultural values orientation as well as Taoism cultural values orientation were more than 4, and the score of the latter one was a little higher, so it is called "Buddhism and Taoism oriented group". Similarly to Type 2, the diverse individual values of Chinese consumers were shown in Type 3 as well, and they took Taoism culture as the standard of behavior in social life, while on the spiritual level, they took Buddhism culture as the standard of behavior. The individual consumption behavior was featured with self-enjoyment of pursuit of luxury consumption as well as practicability of pursuit of functional products.

Type 4: non-tradition oriented type. It is the fourth largest group with 109 people, accounting for 3.26%. Although there was a smaller number of people in this type, they were quite representative. They were newly arisen human influenced by western cultural values, paying less and less attention to traditional cultural values. However, it was necessary to conduct further research on this group of people.

It can be seen from the analysis above that the behavior of Chinese luxury consumers is featured with the potential market accumulation under the orientation of cultural values. According to the consumer behavior theory, the deepest and original influence factor of consumers' purchasing behavior is the drive of cultural values. In this research, the preliminary market segmentation of Chinese luxury consumers' cultural values is conducted and it is obvious that the further research of consumption behavior for each market segment will be very important.

Chapter 6 The Development of Luxury Market under New Normal

Our research group deeply studies the "new trend", "new features" and "new problems" in the field of luxury goods today together with other experts and scholars in this field. Therefore, we design focus group interviews and in-depth interviews for qualitative research. The theme of focus group interview is "Envision the development of luxury market in the new normal"; the theme of in-depth interviews is "the relationship between luxury industry and Internet technology". Both interviews cover the developments of different goods in luxury field, the overall development of luxury market, and the application of technology in luxury industry. The interview results provide insights of professional managers and scholars in this field. The following is the qualitative research report centering on this theme.

6.1 Focus Group Interview

6.1.1 Designing of Focus Group Interview

Based on the requirements on focus group interview in market research method, we organized this focus group. The research group invited a senior expert of academic study in luxury field as host. The group discussion lasted for 1.5 hours. The group members were all experts from luxury industry or academic field, or researchers in luxury goods, and sharply knew and understood luxury goods' development.

Table 6.1 The Organization of Focus Group

Male	Professional manager A in jewelry industry
	Professional manager B in polo company
	Business director C of Fashion Media
Female	Doctor of luxury management D
	Researchers E and F in the field of luxury goods

The focus group interview brought the research group brand-new and rich first-hand materials, which revealed the development of luxury market in today's "New Normal". Every expert and scholar discussed the various problems faced by the current luxury industry, put forward suggestions for solutions and made prospects for future luxury market's development.

6.1.2 Details of Focus Group Interview

The focus group interview was hosted by the expert from the Luxury Goods Research Center in University of International Business and Eco-

nomics (UIBE). Six guests did brainstorming on seven questions centering on the theme "the development of luxury market in the New Normal", contributed their penetrating judgments. The interview report is below.

Question 1: There is one opinion: For luxury brands, it seems that China is no longer the market satisfying their expectations. What do you think about China's luxury brands in the current "New Normal"?

A: From jewelry's point of view, though currently the jewelry sale volume has dropped, it is a good phenomenon. Because tax and profit rate are increasing, the transactions are greatly increasing in number. The increase of the mass's purchases prospects that the jewelry industry will grow better and better in the future.

B: From horse industry's point of view, China's horse industry started quite late, and there were only 5 horse clubs national wide in 1996. After nearly 20 years' development, there are over 600 clubs now in the country, and over 120 horse clubs in Beijing. For the time being, the demand for horses is increasing, the segmentation of horse sports is more specific, and the value of horses is being more reflected. Every year China's exported horse number and the participants in horse sports are increasing; the market prospect is very good.

C: In the past ten years, China went through a very good period. Though it is in its "adjustment stage", luxury goods are faced by various new challenges. However, thanks to China's huge population bonus, China is still one of the most important luxury markets.

D: It was very easy to make money before in China's luxury market; the growth was very fast; now after adjustment, it will develop better after several years' adjusting stage. Historically, the global luxury market was still in its low downturn in early 21st century, while after several years' ad-

justment, the market realized 8% or even double-digit growth in 2005. So adjustment is a good thing, and the future luxury market will develop more actively.

E: Today the global economy has enter into an adjustment stage, and luxury goods is no exception. It is very common to see drop in sales and the decrease of new stores. As long as the market actively adjust and face challenges head-on, the bright future will come soon.

F: As the economy develops fast, China's per-capita income is also rising; the group who are able and willing to buy luxury goods is expanding. Though China's luxury market is experiencing temporary downturn now due to the turn of market surrounding, brand pricing and other factors, China's consumption crowds and consumption characteristics change suffice to show that China market still has huge potential, and after reasonable adjustment, China's luxury market will have a good future.

Conclusion: In 2014, when mainland China's luxury market fell for the first time, the market showed concern universally and thought luxury goods has enter into harsh winter. The luxury brands used to stand high above began to lower prices and offer discount for the hope to increase sales. However, the result was not so satisfying. China's luxury market enter into a new stage: weakening growth and constant adjustment. Actually, this change in market agreed with the "New Normal" arising in China's current macro-economy. Based on every guest's opinion, they all hold optimistic attitude toward the luxury brands' development in China market in "New Normal". Specific to industry, though the sales volume in jewelry industry dropped the order quantity is increasing, which shows that more consumers begin to buy jewelry. As people's living standard is rising, more and more people began to participate in equestrianism and other

horse sports. The "civilianization" of horse sports signifies not the decline of this industry but its future prosperity. Our qualitative research shows that this two luxury industries have the same change characteristics: the participant group is growing. This phenomenon also agrees with the outstanding feature in China's luxury market development,i.e. luxury goods consumers are no longer limited to the super-rich, common white-collars are also able to buy luxury goods. Common crowds are seeking high-quality life and luxury brands have become a sign and image of quality life among Chinese consumers.

If we look back into the past, the law of any economy form or industry's development has the feature of weaved ups and downs. Speed is not everything, nor is figure. Only in improvement in quality and the adjustment in direction and system can advance luxury goods' sound development. All in all, China's luxury market's development is not so ideal for the time being, it is only a transition and adjustment stage and China's luxury market will enter into a more healthy development stage later.

Question 2: If we say luxury goods cannot be sold in China, some people would disagree, because they think it an adjustment of luxury brands and the bright future will come after this. How do you think about this?

A: In Beijing, due to jewelry industry's specialty, some might be missing in the statistics of its market performance. In fact, many Wechat shops and E-business sell jewelries and do transaction privately. As for jewelry industry's development, the present sale is good.

B: The sale of luxury goods encountered setbacks mainly because of price. Their prices are much higher than those in Europe or the United States. This is a kind of plunder, which causes they not be sold out in

China. Therefore, luxury brand suppliers have to adjust prices if they want to continue their development in China, which is a core question.

C: The conglomeration of luxury brands is a global phenomenon, so it does not mean that Chinese consumers don not buy, but they do not buy in China if luxury goods do not sell well in China. Luxury brands have entered into a global adjustment stage; though in China, the sales dropped in stores and consumers will respond to luxury brands' appeal and continue to buy as long as luxury brands hold their appeal as before.

D: Adjustment is a good thing. Many enterprises are passively faced by adjustment and changes in China market, especially changes in con-sumer market. If luxury brands can respond actively to market changes, it is still very easy to make money in luxury goods industry.

E: Adjustment itself is painful, but new development chances are al-so born from adjustment. The recent entry luxury goods and Internet E-business both brought new implications to luxury brands. The future is bright, and the road is tortuous.

F: Actually any consumers are inclined to buy experience products. As present, most consumers don not buy luxury goods mainly because of prices. As long as famous brands keep their brand features and adjust their pricing strategies and combine online and store sales, it is sure that consumers will come back soon.

Conclusion: Judging from the earning reports of several luxury brands, "bleak season" has already been the mainstream in this industry, and many companies simultaneously blame it on the serious decline in China market. Germany luxury brand Hugo Boss and British fashion group Burberry's earnings show that the drop in China market is the main reason for bad corporate performance. On the face of it, it indeed does

not sell well in China's luxury market. However, though market investigation and interviewee discussions, we find that there is much deeper information behind this. Firstly, we find that the products that do not sell well are men's wear, and wristwatches, whose sales both dropped by over 10% in 2014. We think that it is a short term phenomena in luxury goods market. In the long term, the market will return to nationality, where the majority of middle class will grow into the main luxury goods consumption power. Secondly, different from traditional luxury brands, many emerging brands develop very fast and new shops are increasing with satisfying sales. In addition, the jewelry industry mentioned by interviewees also mentioned good growth. Facing China market in "New Normal", luxury brands have to make changes in market strategies and tactics.

The research result shows that Chinese consumers' demand for luxury goods is always increasing, and due to price, quality, late new editions and other issues, consumers changed their buying place, from mainland to overseas. Now Chinese consumers are one of the largest luxury goods buying groups worldwide. Facing the huge market demand, it is necessary for luxury brands to actively adjust their positioning strategies in China market to attract Chinese consumers back to mainland. Only this can bring China's luxury market back to good times.

Question 3: In fact, since 2014, luxury goods has went through near ly two years in China market, what adjustments do you think that luxury companies have made deserve our attention?

B: Price is the fundamental one. Adjusting prices let consumers feel they are not plundered any more. Luxury brands should try to lower prices and earn more by selling more.

C: The change of marketing. It includes opening E-business on social

media,corporate website and co-operating with local Chinese E-business platform to access more Chinese consumers. It is also worthwhile to do trans-boundary business.

D: Price adjustment is only one aspect. The really effective adjust ment should be on product design and new product line. Facing the pref erence change of young target consumer group, luxury brands suppliers should develop new product lines, which can truly solve the underlying problem, but it is very hard to do so.

E: Lower price. After Chanel lowered it price, Dior, Cartier, Versace and so on began to lower price.

F: The promotion of new products and the development of E-business channel. Recently, women's wear, shoes and hand bags become luxury goods growth's light spots. Coach and other brands promoted other hand bags for women's occupational use and other products to drive sales. In addition, the opening-up of E-business channel is also a great measure.

Conclusion: In the aforementioned questions, we talk about the present development of luxury industry. Undoubtedly, the luxury industry encountered downturn at present, and major luxury brands all took measures to salvage the bleak situation. Based on our investigation and interviewees' speeches, we find that luxury brand suppliers manly have done the following adjustments:

First: price. Price is the quite important factor in marketing. Price's influence on consumers is most direct. This year there grew a price-lowering wind of internationally luxury brands in China market. They hope to stimulate mainland's consumer market using the advantage of price. From an economic point of view, market demand will normally changes opposite to price change: if price goes up, demand decreases; if price goes down, demand increases. There is some economic principle behind for luxury brands to lower price to tantalize consumers. However, luxury goods are special, and under some circumstances high price will also be the symbol of high quality and be chased by consumers.We think luxury brands' price lowering strategy in China really can attract those consumers sensitive to price and increase sales. But what makes us happier is that internationally luxury brands' price bias on China market is improving. Second: product. Facing Chinese consumers' strong purchasing power, luxury brands are attaching more importance to China market and promote products catering for Chinese consumers' preference. Many luxury brands will also add China market to new products release country. Third: channel. As Internet technology is becoming mature, many luxury brands are shifting their eyesight to online sales. In fact, the key of retailing is consumer. Wherever there is consumer, there should be channel. Today's consumers are used to Internet life, especially the young generation; online shopping has already been a part of their daily life. The joining of e-business is a supplement for traditional channel and also a part of future all-inclusive channel construction. Nevertheless, luxury goods companies' adjustments are not limited to price, products, and channel, many other aspects are also in adjustment. The adjustment is a long, constant and normalized process.

Question 4: So far, the first market is becoming saturated, where do you think luxury goods stores will open next?

A: It is not only a question of where, but also one of how. Taking jewelry industry as an example, about 59% to 60% of consumption in this industry is done in large and medium comprehensive shopping malls, about 32% in professional jewelry market. There are dozens of exclusive

stores in Beijing area, if new stores are opened in suburb area or third and fourth tier cities, there will be more jewelry markets.

B: Stores should be opened where people are able to consume. Luxury brands suppliers should be concerned on target group. The reason for Land Rover's sponsorship for polo is that there are its target consumers and it can accurately fond its target group. Therefore, new stores should be opened where there is precise target consumer group.

C: Since the first tier cities have saturated, the first and a half tier cities may witness more new stores. However, new store number is only one aspect; there might be trans-boundary co-operation of luxury brands, e. g. Armani residence in Chengdu.

D: Open online stores. In Internet era, online shops are greatly increasing. Burberry's T-mall shop is a very good example. It is also a very good method in attracting young consumers in digital era.

E: It is an "Internet +" era. In the past, we found products, while now products find us. It is very nature to open shops online, which will not only lower luxury brands suppliers' operation cost, but also offer consumers more product choices.

F: The chance to open new stores in second tier cities in slim. Judging from the data of past several years, traditional luxury brands did not expand successfully in second tier cities. They should utilize e-business platform to expand channel.

Conclusion: Since the first tier cities' economy is highly developed with large wealth accumulation, thus become the top destination when luxury brands entered into China. After 30 years' development, now the market in firsttier cities is nearly saturated. As China's urbanization accelerates and other areas' (except large cities) wealth is growing, the demand

for luxury goods consumption in many second and third tier cities is created. At present, luxury brands have shops in Hangzhou, Wenzhou, Qingdao, Dalian and other southeastern and northeastern cities. Western China except Chengdu, Xi'an, Changsha, Urumchi, will also become emerging places of luxury goods companies. Therefore, we say the second and thirdtier cities will be luxury brands suppliers' choice for new shops. But this does not mean that they will duplicate their method in first tier cities. They should adjust measures to local conditions, such as brands collection mode which develops well now. Some members in our group also have reservations, so further studies need to be done.

In our qualitative research, many participants talked of money, which agreed with the aforementioned channel adjustment; Internet has become the new platform for luxury brands to open new shops. It is believed that more and more luxury goods suppliers will try right e-business, and consumers will also benefit from this. Trans-boundary co-operation enriches luxury goods store forms, deepens consumers' recognition of luxury brands imperceptibly, and obtains good consumption experience. Whether the luxury shops are online or offline, or of what kind of form, fundamentally they have to be opened where there is consumption ability.

Question 5: At present, some Chinese consumers' interest in common luxury brands are dropping, does this mean new market chance for luxury group's second and third tier products or entry luxury brands?

C: As the time goes by, consumers will have diversified demand for brand; not only entry luxury brands but also many Chinese local emerging premium brands will have good market chance.

D: Entry luxury goods sell well in the United States. The earnings of several American entry luxury clothing giants are outstanding. There are

two reasons for this: one is that these bands have weak foundation thus develops well; the other is that consumers are becoming younger. Many young people in their 20s start their luxury goods consumption from entry luxury brands. Many luxury brands' loyal consumers will begin to buy entry luxury brands because of their more cost-effective. This is chance, but also causes many problems, for example, young people's consumption behavior is not stable, changes very much and is easy to be influenced by reference group. How to deal with young group's change is a very large challenge.

E: Consumers choose entry luxury brands mostly because of their diverse design. Compared with traditional brands, entry brands offer more flexible and diversified product design and categories. Judging from the data, the new shop numbers of entry luxury goods is much more than traditional luxury shop's. This is a new market chance.

F: Traditional luxury brands' styles are quite traditional and have obvious logo and other marks, which does not agree with young and middle-aged people's demand, who are today's main consumption power. For the young generation who seek fashion and novelty, emerging brands, fashionable and individualistic, indeed have advantages, and their market chance cannot be neglected.

Conclusion: The design of entry luxury brands is more fashionable and novel, the price is generally lower than traditional luxury brands, so they follow today's consumption trend of younger consumers, provide young consumers more diversified choice and satisfy their psychology of seeking novelty and loving individuality; meanwhile they provide brand new choice for traditional luxury brands' consumers. Entry luxury brands' high cost-effectiveness attracts some buyers' attention; therefore, entry lux-

ury brands including some independent designers' brands have great potential in the future, which also brings great shock to traditional luxury brands. They need to appropriately adjust to meet this challenge. But on the other hand, since entry luxury brands' consumers are younger and do not have mature consumption choice with limited taste, their brand preference is easy to change; therefore, how to cultivate loyal consumers, retain more consumers and expand market share is vitally important for them. They should adopt corresponding measures to deal with this possible change.

Question 6: What are the reasons for Chinese consumers to buy luxury goods oversea? How can they be recalled back to consume in mainland?

A: Price. Luxury brands suppliers can co-operate with Chinese businesses. The same products are produced in China mainland and do not need to be sold somewhere else, so the cost will be lower. Actually, now many luxury brands trust Chinese corporates to produce in China and reduce cost with the guarantee of quality, therefore, it is possible to rationalize price.

B: Price is the key. Luxury brands must stay calm in front of China market, and admit its importance. Before people are relatively blind when they bought luxury goods, while now Chinese consumers are becoming more mature and rational, so the price must be fair, otherwise their sales in China will necessarily drop.

C: Besides price difference, there is life style change of China's middle rich class or rich people. Nowadays, Chinese people are less constrained by visa. People love travelling abroad so it very common to buy luxury goods on the way. Therefore, how to call back consumers to con-

sume in mainland is quite difficult and needs further consideration.

D: The fundamental reason is that luxury brands do not pay enough attention to China market, which cause price discrimination, product discrimination and slow product upgrading. Many people choose to buy oversea because overseas products upgrade timely and have complete category. So if they want to recall Chinese consumers, they should attach enough importance to Chinese consumers.

E: The product quality is also a very big reason. Many luxury goods in China, especially from online shopping or purchasing agent, are not sure to be authentic, while the price in exclusive stores is too high. If they want to recall Chinese consumers to buy locally, luxury brands suppliers must undertake deeper management to its sales channel and crack down fake and inferior products.

F: The emerging of overseas traveling, to some extent, drives abroad consumption of luxury goods. But this is also basically caused by the large price difference of similar or same products between home and abroad.

Conclusion: Chinese consumers forsake adjacent exclusive stores and spare no effort to buy luxury goods abroad, the core reason for which is price. Suppliers' luxury goods price discrimination strategy and China's high tax on luxury goods drive their price in China market high, which makes Chinese consumers to go all the way to pursuit more reasonable price and further cause Chinese consumers to buy them in large quantity outside of China. In addition, as Chinese consumers' living standard is universally improved, especially middle class people are growing in large scale, travelling abroad which used to be very expensive and strange to most people has become a very convenient choice, therefore, a majority of

luxury goods consumers choose to buy them whiling travelling. The concern on product quality and the large number of fake goods abounds in the whole consumer market, and the authentic goods sold on counters lack complete after-sales maintenance service but the price is not competitive, which are all important factors leading Chinese consumers to purchase overseas. If luxury brands suppliers hope to recall Chinese consumers to China market, they should firstly adjust their pricing and make just pricing strategies, thus letting Chinese consumers not feel too unfair price discrimination when they see the price in China market. Moreover, they should improve their product quality and after-sales service and form a complete service mechanism, making Chinese consumers to enjoy quality goods and service at home.

Question 7: Please use one sentence to state the future development trend of international luxury brands.

A: It is still growing.

B: Advance with the times and know China market.

C: Challenge co-exists with chance.

D: The market needs to be segmented.

E: The development is inevitable.

F: Though tortuous, the road is bright.

Conclusion: Though for the present stage, there is awkward situation of stagnation in China's luxury goods consumer market, especially in 2014, it experienced negative growth for the first time. But the focus group interview's result shows that luxury goods market is in its temporary adjustment stage. The present slow development is a stabilizer for the immature Chinese luxury goods market. It stabilizes the market which used to be crazy in the past several years. It makes market's real situation and

the existing problem behind the quick market growth clear, and lets the market to adjust with a target. It is a chance for entry luxury brands and local independent designer brands. We believe that after this stage's continuous adjustment, the future is bright.

6.1.3 Results of Focus Group Interview

In the past several years, China's luxury goods market grew fast then slowed down. In 2014, it even witnessed negative growth for the first time. Under the "New Normal", for many luxury brands chance and challenge co-exist in luxury goods market's development. On one hand, the global economy development slows down and slows the development of luxury goods industry' s development, traditional big brands open less new shops and they offer discount and continue to lower price; they are not so successful as before. On the other hand, some problems existing in China's luxury goods consumer market are also exposed, such as luxury brands' lack of enough attention to consumers' consumption experience, high prices, and incomplete after-sales service, which are problem needing to be urgently solved and also the precondition to expand China's luxury goods market.

Generally speaking, chance and challenge co-exist in luxury goods market under "New Normal". Accompanying the consumption habit's change of China's mainstream consumer group, entry luxury will become a new breakthrough for luxury goods industry's development, and become a strong growth point in luxury goods market. As Internet play a more important role in corporate operation and market events, luxury goods industry will fully utilize Internet's advantage to seek for new growth point, and integrate online and offline resources to adapt to modern luxury goods

consumers' new life style and consumption habit. Adjusting the pricing strategy and product strategy in China market are also the urgent problems that need suppliers' special consideration. The foundation of these is the right understanding of target consumers' demand.

The adjustment stage facing by luxury brands suppliers is not absolutely negative phenomenon. It reminds them to healthily and wisely view China's luxury goods market, follow the laws of economics and market, and operate China market based on the understanding of consumers' demand and in sustainable development's point of view and face Chinese luxury goods consumers. In this sense, there is always good time for luxury goods industry.

6.2 In-depth Expert Interviews

6.2.1 In-depth Expert Interviews Design and Content

Interview background: Before 2012, China's luxury goods consumption grew at the speed of double digit, but later due to the influence of international economic environment, whether in China market or in global market, luxury goods sales shrink year by year. Facing the severe business environment, many luxury giants begin to seek for new business mode. The founder of Richemont Anton Rupert used to reach out the olive branch to its old rivals LVMH and Kering, hoping to build up a globalized luxury brands e-business platform to tackle future challenge. Whether the ideal that three luxury giants joint hands to open e-business can be realized, the luxury goods industry will shake hand with Internet, and the

luxury goods retailing will develop in the direction of "retailing + IT" in the future.

Interview objective: As China's economy enters into"New Normal", China's luxury goods market inevitably encounters downturn. Under the new background, luxury brands come to Internet one by one and use new technology to tackle market's change. The research group's objective of using in-depth interview is to study the influence of Internet on luxury goods industry and its future development trend of luxury goods market.

Interview time: September, 2015

Interview city: Beijing

Interview questions:

(1) What is the influence of Internet technology on luxury goods industry?

(2) What is luxury goods industry's development trend in the future?

Expert I: ex -director of one luxury brand who has 10 years' working experience in luxury industry.

Opinion of the expert:

Firstly, I want to share how I entered into luxury goods industry. After my graduation from university, I worked as a HR in a fund company. At that time, Ernest & Young released a report, which showed that China's luxury goods market would reach No.2 worldwide in 2012. After some research, I decided to resign and join in this industry. I started from a salesperson, and followed the 10-year development of China's luxury goods market and in 2012, it really reached No. 2. As the saying goes, the ducks firstly know that the river's water is getting warm. As for the downturn in the industry, as a frontline luxury retailing manager, I have already felt this, which was also a chance for me to change my job to In-

ternet industry. After 2013, it seemed to be the start of China luxury goods industry's harsh winter.

In the past 10 years, China's luxury goods store's salespersons did not need to smile to sell goods. But after 2013, even they smiled during the whole service' it was still very hard for them to sell. Frankly speaking, in the past 10 years, the management of China's luxury goods was extensive type. Whether on service detail or on shopping experience, we did not take much energy, but in the future the fine management of luxury goods will be an inevitable trend. The fine management cannot be realized only by manpower. Internet technology, e-business technology or information integration technology will drive luxury goods' segmentation technology. On the other hand, with the turning of market environment, China's luxury goods consumption shifted from gift consumption to private individual consumption, and emphasized consumers' experience, i.e. the principle of user first in Internet thinking. Against the two large backgrounds, using mobile terminal and mobile Internet technology to realize intelligent management on retailing business is a supplementation to the existing retailing system. Frankly speaking, luxury goods industry is not the one standing ahead and embracing new technology. Rather it emphasizes the inheritance over one hundred years and artisan craftsmanship. For new technology, it, to some extent, passively accepts. But during the past half to one year, its acceptance of new technology was quite quick. For example, the fire tier brand Chanel, which is co-operating with us, is accepting and using voice and other technology. Though luxury brands are trying to do e-business and O2O, they do not put much energy and resource. They use Internet technology more on marketing and shop management. Luxury brands use internet technology to conduct standardized, measurable, and formal man-

agement on stores, use mobile internet technology to be quick and effective in information delivery. Frontline managers use internet technology to manage whenever and wherever possible to comprehensively improve management efficiency. The internet technology and mobile client terminal will be more applied to luxury goods market's management in the future. These edge-cutting technologies will greatly improve luxury brands' market management efficiency, save management cost and innovate management mode, thus advancing the market's development. We have good reason to believe that China's future luxury goods market has large development space.

Expert II: Chairman of an investment management company in Beijing. The company has established the further operating relationship with Gucci, Prada, Nike, Adidas, Li Ning, Toread and other hundreds of well-known brands at home and abroad. It also realized the friendly cooperation with more than ten domestic well-known online retailers such as Tmall, Vip.com, JD.com, Secoo and the like.

Opinions of the expert:

At first I want to share my experience of getting in touch with luxuries in 2010, which was a little early. At that time, there were several luxury boutiques in bad operation in Beijing and I found out the reason was that the management team was not good enough through analysis. They mainly purchased luxuries through luxury buyers as well as overseas luxury boutiques and the inventory problem could not be solved. At the same time, we were doing online sales of sport brands and had been formed a large scale, so some luxury brands owners asked us to do online sales for them. We were the first to open luxury exclusive shops on JD.com and the second on Tmall. The net sales amount of one month on Tmall was

more than 300000 Yuan,so we found that it was profitable to sell luxuries online and we had been conducted online sales of luxuries since then. We witnessed the change of luxury sales from easy and incompact sales to data based sales. We conducted precision marketing by aiming at the consumers to seek and analyze online luxury consumers so as to find out their consumption habit. We paid more attention to data analysis than product operation and mainly aimed at online consumers by sending messages to them timely. Although the price of luxury brands was very high, there were mass stock as well, which gave opportunities to online retailers to sell luxuries. We sold out-of-season commodities at first when we aimed at those inventories. These out-of-season commodities could be sold well because the style of luxury brands such as Gucci and LV changed a little every year and mainland consumers paid more attention to logos. Now, many luxury brands begin to release commodities with distinct characteristics and more and more people prefer consumption paying no attention to logos according to the data.

We must sell luxuries according to the regulations of luxury companies, including discounts and areas for setting up stores. Many luxury companies begin to conduct online sales but the online sales now are very disappointing. There are two reasons why the number of people who purchase luxuries abroad has increased a lot: the overseas price advantage and the pursuit of quality. On the whole, the opportunity for online development of luxuries is to develop customized products and limited products for 20% people. The online business platform we are operating now is the one that people can purchase overseas "luxuries" even Australia lobsters through purchase in advance and advance sale on it. The registered overseas luxury stores and overseas buyers can provide services for online

consumers. Therefore, in the future, we can conduct precision marketing in use of internet technology and database technology to search and analyze online luxury consumers as well as their consumption habit. Online sales may be the highlight of luxury sales in the future.

6.2.2 In-depth Expert Interview Conclusion

After more than one decade's fast development, China's luxury goods market experienced slow growth and shrinking scale in the past one to two year and entered into adjustment stage. In its adjustment stage, it is facing chances and challenges. The largest chance is the combination of luxury goods industry and internet technology, which uses internet technology to sell online and offline, comprehensively improves consumers' shopping experience, do more specific marketing and service and increase brand management efficiency. Meanwhile, the largest challenge is how to better use internet technology to create more value for luxury goods industry. In the long run, chances are more than challenges. If luxury goods industry can seize the chances brought by the market revolution driven by internet technology, its market will probably achieve remarkable development.

6.3 Qualitative Research's Conclusion

This research group's qualitative research always centers on "luxury goods market's development in New Normal" and "the relationship between luxury goods industry and internet technology" two themes. The focus group and in-depth interview provide us important opinions and experts' views to understand and study China's luxury goods market's development. At the same time, we find that the judgments of some brand managers, experts and scholars from luxury goods' frontlines support the main conclusion of the monographic study on China's luxury goods market, and also reflect the basic performance, New Features and new trends of it. The macro-economic environment and application of internet technology in New Normal are the two important macro-environmental factors influencing the development of China's luxury goods market.

Chapter 7 Future Expectation of Chinese Luxury Brand Market

In the early 1980s, international luxury brands entered Chinese market. Generally speaking, the first 30 years in China was the test period for international luxury brands, while 2009-2012 was the period of prosperous development for luxury brands. However, the situation was reversed from 2014 and the negative growth happened for the first time in the luxury brand market in mainland China. Old and large luxury brands owners slowed the speed of opening stories and expansion and closed some stores in China to reduce the total stores. They also adjusted and discounted prices on a large scale frequently. At the same time, the internet had been influencing the traditional business mode of luxury brands in China. All these changes are caused by current national macro-economic adjustment. Meanwhile, Chinese luxury consumers' luxury purchase for years, study of luxury brands as well as product knowledge, experience accumulation, rational consuming behavior and mature consumption values also contribute to these changes. Under the "New Normal" situation, Chinese luxury market is full of opportunities and challenges.

In the transition period of luxury goods market in China, the team of "Chinese consumer behavior research on luxury goods" of the University

of International Business and Economics continued to pay fieldtrips to the first and secondtier cities for studying on the changes in this period. The team strove to explain the Chinese consumer behavior on luxury goods in terms of motivations and the values of China's traditional culture, and figured out the features of such consumers together with the research results obtained at the former stage. The research will show the whole status and the trend of the market.

7.1 The China's Luxury Goods Market is still at the Phase of Adjustment

On the basis of the 2015 annual Chinese consumer behavior research on luxury goods and 2014 Chinese consumer behavior report on luxury goods, national macroeconomic data of 2014 and 2015, reports prepared by internationally recognized consulting companies, official data of luxury brands and reliable news and information, it was to be sure that China's luxury goods market was still at the phase of adjustment. Undoubtedly, the international luxury goods went very well in 2002 to 2012 with the rapid growth of China's economy. Exciting performance can be seen in aspects of the quantity of shops and sales volume of the same brand, and China's worldwide market share. Under the impact of financial crisis in 2008, the growth rate of China's economy slowed gradually, as put a pressure on the growth of luxury goods market. In 2013, the growth grate of such goods in mainland China was 2%. Even 1% negative growth occurred in 2014. But China is still the biggest buyer of luxury goods around the world. In our opinion, the market in China started to be stable

and mature since 2013. And the sluggish growth rate occurred in 2013 was the inevitable situation in the development process from an infant to a mature market. Since 2014 to today, the market in China has been in the transition period taking the adjustment as a priority. The continuous period will remain in a long time. After the period, however, the market here would enter into a new stage where it begins to recovery and grow properly.

The expansion modes the luxury brands took in China show that long-term oriented development strategies are come into being to obtain the stability, targeting consumers, novelty and huge growth. In 2013, most top luxury goods brands were cautious about opening more shops and attached more importance on refurbishment or update. They did not open numbers of shops blindly and rapidly as they did in the past. The number of new shops in 2014 was dramatically lower than 2013. But it's not the case for the decorating budgets. This totally shows sense and calmness, which present their consistent orientation to high-end stores. Actually, rapid market growth rate is against the advantage of luxury goods-the quality. It's no doubt that the "scarcity" and "delicate" are the special features the luxury brands should maintain. Opposite to the behavior of traditional top international brands, many new luxury brands like Coach from America accelerated their expansion speed in China. It highlights the contrast in this phase that light luxury brands maintain great momentum of growth. In fact, it reflects a China's new feature of social stratification including the rise of middle class, new pattern of consumption both in cities and countries due to the urbanization, and that the people born in the 1970s to 1900s are the main force of consumer markets. The light luxury goods are parts of the affluent class's daily consumption as well as display

personalities of young generation. The harmony between the intrinsic features of such goods and the market structure of China assures the goods a sustainable development space.

In 2015, many luxury goods in China reduced their prices in large scale, especially the Chanel and Gucci in Hong Kong. For a long time, the strategies of price discrimination the top international luxury brands took in China have been reproached widely, forcing many Chinese consumers purchasing such goods at abroad instead of home. Together with the thriving overseas tourism, the situation of going shopping at abroad has been increasing. In the case, price reduction is the only option left to win back the lost consumer. The research, however, shows that the actual situation is not the one as they wished. It proves that it is not an effective strategy. If they want to win back the consumer, they should focus on product conceptions and be well aware that the good time for earning money easy has gone permanently. Chinese consumers start to hold mature concepts in the luxury goods consumption. But many problems facing the China's market, it needs to be improved through durable adjustment.

The "New Normal" of China's economy is characterized by "mid and high speed, and new engine". Scientific and technical innovation is the new engine. While the luxury goods market is going through the decline with its growth rate slowing, the China's economy is going through adjustment. According to objective economy and market laws, it's inevitable that the luxury goods market will undergo adjustment. The luxury goods market will benefit from the scientific and technical innovation in the "New Normal" of China's economy. Combing the luxury goods industry with the internet technology is a creative and promising way to improve the industry. The way may be the new growth pole of luxury brands after the adjustment.

7.2 The Operation Valuing Classical and Innovation will Assure the Luxury Goods Market Sustainable Growth

The classical styles of luxury goods are typically popular among consumers for their unique design and superior functions. The research shows that the China's luxury goods market has a three tiered market structure: 62.89% was conservative, 8.75% was pioneer and 28.35% was hesitate. The ratio was roughly 6:1:3. On the basis of the data of 2014 and 2015, the ratio did not change. Special attention should be paid by theorists and business circle to the situation.

With the Chinese consumer behavior on luxury goods being mature, the market witnesses evident changes. In clothing industry, for example, the exclusively tailored clothes are popular for its design styles equivalent to that of the internationally leading brands and its unique features. The clothes really belong to the "individual". With the increasing of Chinese's living standard and pursuit of personality, the exclusively tailored life styles will be commonly seen. We estimated that the exclusive tailor market will be thriving, and the tailor market for minority consumers will maintain stable as well as the scale tailor market may recovery in medium and long term in China's luxury goods market.

7.3 The Omni-channel Mode of Luxury Goods Industry is Improving

The main channels consist of the boutique, outlet store, procurement for friends, domestic online shopping, overseas online shopping, outbound tourism shopping, etc. A 2015 research on this subject shows that the boutique, enjoying high reputation, was the most preferred choice of shopping. However, with the maturity of outbound tourism and the lower prices of luxury goods at abroad, the overseas shopping is increasing inevitably, putting pressure on the boutiques in China. Besides, with the Internet booming, the e-commerce tends to plan an increasingly vital role in international businesses. The luxury goods industry is no exception. In fact, emerging business modes like the O2O, which combines the offline businesses with Internet, can be seen in the traditional luxury goods retail business. Some big and vanguard luxury brands have tried the e-commerce. The omni-channel mode is emerging in and valued by the luxury goods retail business.

The omni-channel retail is a new channel with higher structure, which evolves from single-channel and multichannel to the cross channel. The omni-channel retail meets consumers' demands for channels at different stages of purchasing and modern life style. It will deliver more comprehensive consumption experience. Depending on the increasingly developed Internet technology, especially the mobile Internet technology, the omni-channel retail allows consumers to purchase for various kinds of goods at anywhere in their fractional time. This is beyond the traditional

retail channel's capabilities. Only by taking effective countermeasures, integrating their boutiques, shops in large shopping center, computer shops, online stores at social networks, mobile stores, etc., can the luxury brands satisfy the consumer' demands. The omni-channel mode in China is at its infant period. Facing the opportunity as well as challenge, the luxury brands should pay attention to it and take measures at early stage.

7.4 The Personalized Consumption is Emerging in the Rational Consumers of Luxury Goods

It was prospected in the 2014 Chinese consumer behavior report that the rational consumption of luxury goods would become evidently. According to the observation on features and tendency of luxury goods consumer behaviors in the past year, we realize the prospection is quite right. And we find that personalized consumption is emerging under such circumstances.

It can be seen from the change and development of global luxury markets that the development of luxury market changes from irrational growth to rational recovery, which features obviously conspicuous consumption in the earlier stage and coexistence of conspicuous consumption as well as rational consumption later. In the early stage when luxuries entered into Chinese market, many Chinese people bought luxuries to cater to others but ignored self-demand, taking no account of the matching between luxury style and their temperament. However, it can be seen from this investigation that when Chinese consumers buy luxuries now, they care a lot whether the luxury style matches their temperament, which re-

flects that Chinese luxury consumers' consuming behavior is becoming more mature. 70% of the respondents said that they had a self-disciplined luxury consumption behavior. In fact, with the income improvement of Chinese middle class, the disposable income increases, which enables them to buy luxuries. What's more, because of the open and rich social life, consumers can know more about various luxury brands, study brand knowledge, understand brand culture and distinguish brand values, which promotes the idealization and maturity of luxury consumption behavior. This is an obvious change of luxury brand awareness for Chinese luxury consumers, which indicates that they are changing from simply consumption of imitation and showing off to personalized and self-identified consumption.

The generations after 80s and 90s take a great proportion of Chinese luxury consumers and they become the main consumers after graduation. The two generations are similarly because they are high-profile, self-centered and pay more attention to the quality of life and details than their elder generation. The new rich stratum with good education is young, fashionable and more individual than the rich people of the last generation. According to the investigation, the target luxury consumers are people aged 18 to 35 and they pay more and more attention to "self-worth" with the increase of age. People pursue individuality, so the individual luxury consumption is more and more obvious. The luxury consumption gradually returns to the range with the limit of purchasing power and the consuming behavior is gradually established on the basis of brand culture identity.

Besides, it is important to know that Chinese luxury consumption behavior is featured with potential market cluster under the orientation of cultural values. In this investigation, four consumer groups are concluded

based on cultural values, including Confucianism and Taoism oriented type, Confucianism and Buddhism oriented type, Buddhism and Taoism oriented type as well as non-tradition oriented type. There were more than half of the people belong to Confucianism and Taoism oriented type. This conclusion proved that Chinese traditional cultural values, especially the Confucianism and Taoism had a great influence on Chinese consumers. Collectivism in Confucianism made Chinese luxury consumers who paid attention to "circles, social relationship and social hierarchy" achieved their pursuit of social status as well as quality of life. Therefore, through the judgment for the driving effect of cultural values based on consumers' behaviors, not only the motivation for consumers' personality characteristics can be explained, but the consumers' behaviors in the future can be analyzed and predicted. This is obviously the most fundamental driving factor which distinguishes Chinese luxury consumers' behaviors from that of western luxury consumers.

After years of rapid development, China has become the real luxury consumption power. People who became rich first had no rational and mature consumption value during early luxury consumption period, so the phenomena of price comparison as well as showing off logos appeared. The new rich are willing to know luxury brands via multiple channels; compare different stores during purchase and buy luxuries with high quality that suits themselves. With the improvement of life quality year after year, price is no longer the primary consideration to select luxuries. Therefore, people will not purchase luxuries because of the high price for showing off or blindly pursue the luxuries in lowest price but take product experience and service as the most important thing.

In short, "new consumption" is the feature of Chinese consumption

market under the situation of "New Normal", indicating that the large-scale, homogeneous and popular consumption is transformed to consumption with diversity, difference and high quality, which enables people to enter the new stage of high quality and specialty. It is clearly pointed out by the country that five out of six major categories, namely service consumption, information consumption, green consumption, fashion consumption and quality consumption are in positive correlation with luxury consumption. Combined with the new economic development policy as well as the research result of this issue, it can be judged that the integral development of the luxury market in the future is the general trend because it is supported by national development strategies and Chinese market environment. The development of luxury consumption market driven by the technological innovation will be the future developmental direction. However, it is necessary for the luxury market to go through a transitional development during the period of adjustment, because it conforms to the general rule and logic of market development. Especially, luxury consumption is not the same as extravagance and waste because the quality and cultural connotation are more important for the consumers during luxury consumption. Luxury consumption reflects the pursuit of better life. The luxury brand price discrimination happened in Chinese market in the past need to be adjusted and the luxury brands owners need to consider the consistency and balance between Chinese market strategy and global market strategy. Under the "New Normal" situation of Chinese economy, the luxury brands owners should seek for the sustainable development on the premise of adapting to Chinese market environment as well as the consumer demand characteristics of Chinese luxury consumers.